영어 원서로 읽는 고전

Collected Stories of O. Henry

영어 원서로 읽는 고전 Collected Stories of O. Henry

펴낸곳: 북스트릿
원작: 윌리엄 시드니 포터 William Sydney Porter
편집 및 주석: 신찬범
북커버 및 내지 디자인: 북스트릿
E-mail: invino70@gmail.com
Homepage: https://bookstreetpress.modoo.at
Blog: blog.naver.com/invino70
Fax: 0504-405-6711
초판 2021년 4월 7일

© 2021 북스트릿 BookStreet
북스트릿의 허락없는 이 책의 일부 또는 전부의 무단 복제, 전재, 발췌를 금합니다

ISBN: 979-11-90536-16-5

영어 원서로 읽는 고전

Collected Stories of O. Henry

William Sydney Porter

북스트릿
BookStreet

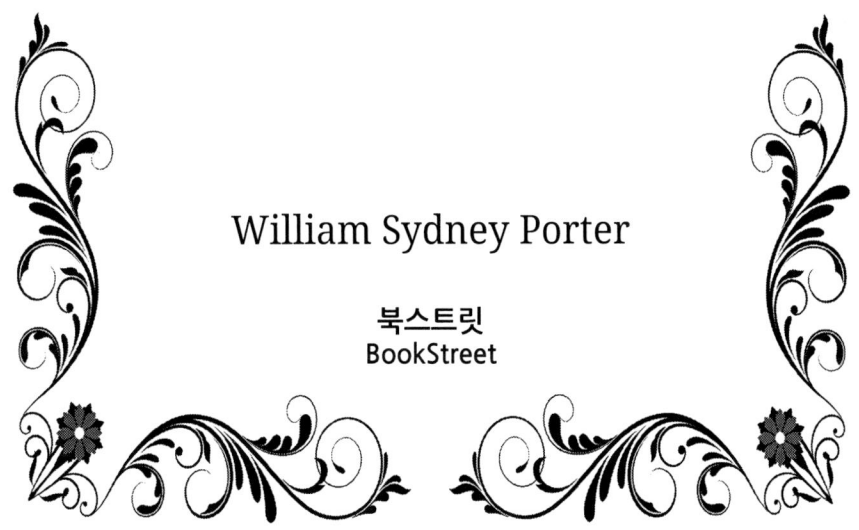

머리말

    이 책은 영문 고전을 깊이 있게 이해하고 감상하기 위해 기획되었습니다.

    영어 원서를 읽는 데에 있어서 가장 큰 어려움 중 하나는 생소한 단어와 구 등을 매번 영어사전에서 찾아봐야 하는 번거로움입니다. 이러한 이유로 영어 원서의 독해가 쉽지 않은 것으로 인식되고 있으며, 특히 영어가 모국어가 아닌 분이나 영어를 공부하시는 분에게 어려움이 있습니다.

    이 책은 이러한 어려움을 고려하여 영어 원서를 읽는 도중에 빈번하게 영어사전을 찾아봐야 하는 번거로움을 대폭 줄였으며, 영어사전을 될 수 있는 대로 적게 참조하면서 더 수월하게 영어 원서를 읽을 수 있게 했습니다.

    이 책에는 영문 고전의 원본 텍스트가 수록되어 있습니다. 문장 해석에 중요한 숙어, 구동사, 그 외 어려운 단어와 구 들을 선택하고 강조했습니다. 이들 단어와 구를 각 페이지 왼쪽에 단락별로 정의하고 설명했습니다. 각 단어의 발음기호를 기재하여, 어휘력을 높이는 데 도움이 되게 했습니다.

    이 책이 독자분이 영문 고전을 읽는 데 의미 있는 도움이 되기를 바랍니다.

신찬범

Collected Stories of O. Henry

The Gift of the Magi ·· 11

A Retrieved Reformation ·································· 21

The Last Leaf ·· 35

After Twenty Years ·· 46

The Love-philtre of Ikey Schoenstein ················ 53

Between Rounds ··· 62

The Cop and the Anthem ·································· 73

The Skylight Room ·· 85

The Handbook of Hymen ··································· 96

Jeff Peters as a Personal Magnet ····················· 116

Shearing the Wolf ··· 128

A Service of Love ·· 139

The Green Door ·· 149

PHŒBE	162
The Pendulum	191
The Ransom of Red Chief	200
The Duplicity of Hargraves	219
One Dollar's Worth	242
While the Auto Waits	255
Squaring the Circle	265
The Princess and the Puma	273
A Cosmopolite in a Café	284
Witches' Loaves	294
Hearts and Hands	301
Mammon and the Archer	306

Collected Stories of O. Henry

The Gift of the Magi

bulldoze [búldòuz] v.
우격다짐하다, 억지를 부리다
imputation [ìmpjutéiʃən] n.
비난, 비방, 오명
parsimony [pá:rsəmòuni] n.
인색; 극도의 절약

One dollar and eighty-seven cents. That was all. And sixty cents of it was in pennies. Pennies saved one and two at a time by **bulldozing** the grocer and the vegetable man and the butcher until one's cheeks burned with the silent **imputation** of **parsimony** that such close dealing implied. Three times Della counted it. One dollar and eighty-seven cents. And the next day would be Christmas.

flop [flɑp / flɔp] v.
펄썩 앉다
instigate [ínstəgèit] v.
부추기다, 선동하다
reflection [riflékʃ-ən] n.
성찰, 생각, 사상
sniffle [sníf-əl] n.
훌쩍이며 욺

There was clearly nothing to do but **flop** down on the shabby little couch and howl. So Della did it. Which **instigates** the moral **reflection** that life is made up of sobs, **sniffles**, and smiles, with sniffles predominating.

While the mistress of the home is gradually

furnished [fə́:rniʃt] adj.
가구가 있는
flat [flæt] n.
플랫식 주택
(각층에 1가구가 살게 만든 아파트)
mendicancy [méndikənsi] n.
거지 생활, 구걸, 동냥
vestibule [véstəbjù:l] n.
현관, 현관의 객실
coax [kouks] v.
설득하다, 어르다, 구슬르다
appertain [æ̀pərtéin] v.
귀속하다, 관계하다
unassuming [ʌ̀nəsjú:miŋ] adj.
젠체하지 않는, 겸손한

attend [əténd] v.
보살피다, 돌보다

subsiding from the first stage to the second, take a look at the home. A **furnished flat** at $8 per week. It did not exactly beggar description, but it certainly had that word on the lookout for the **mendicancy** squad.

In the **vestibule** below was a letter-box into which no letter would go, and an electric button from which no mortal finger could **coax** a ring. Also **appertaining** thereunto was a card bearing the name "Mr. James Dillingham Young."

The "Dillingham" had been flung to the breeze during a former period of prosperity when its possessor was being paid $30 per week. Now, when the income was shrunk to $20, the letters of "Dillingham" looked blurred, as though they were thinking seriously of contracting to a modest and **unassuming** D. But whenever Mr. James Dillingham Young came home and reached his flat above he was called "Jim" and greatly hugged by Mrs. James Dillingham Young, already introduced to you as Della. Which is all very good.

Della finished her cry and **attended** to her cheeks with the powder rag. She stood by the window and looked out dully at a grey cat walking a grey fence in a grey backyard. Tomorrow would be Christmas Day, and she had only $1.87 with which to buy Jim a present. She had been saving every penny she could for months, with this result. Twenty dollars a week doesn't go far. Expenses had been greater than she had calculated. They always are. Only $1.87 to buy a present for Jim. Her Jim. Many a happy hour she had spent planning for something nice for him. Something fine and rare and **sterling**—something just a little bit near to being worthy of the honour of being owned by Jim.

There was a **pier-glass** between the windows of the room. Perhaps you have seen a pier-glass in an $8 flat. A very thin and very agile person may, by observing his reflection in a rapid sequence of longitudinal strips, obtain a fairly accurate conception of his looks. Della, being slender, had mastered the art.

Suddenly she whirled from the window and stood before the glass. Her eyes were shining brilliantly, but her face had lost its colour within twenty seconds. Rapidly she pulled down her hair and let it fall to its full length.

Now, there were two possessions of the James Dillingham Youngs in which they both took a **mighty** pride. One was Jim's gold watch that had been his father's and his grandfather's. The other was Della's hair. **Had the Queen of Sheba lived** in the flat across the **airshaft**, Della would have let her hair hang out the window some day to dry just to **depreciate** Her

---

sterling [stə́ːrliŋ] adj.
가치 있는, 신뢰할 만한

pier glass:
(창과 창 사이 벽에 거는) 체경

mighty [máiti] adj.
대단한, 굉장한
Had the Queen of Sheba lived:
If the Queen of Sheba lived
air shaft:
환기통
depreciate [dipríːʃièit] v.
가치를 떨어뜨리다

cascade [kæskéid] n.
(작은) 폭포
falter [fɔ́:ltər] v.
비틀거리다, 주저하다

collect [kəlékt] v.
(생각을) 정리하다, (마음을) 가다듬다
pant [pænt] v.
숨을 거칠게 내쉬다, 헐떡이다

On went her old brown jacket; on went her old brown hat. With a whirl of skirts and with the brilliant sparkle still in her eyes, she fluttered out the door and down the stairs to the street.

Majesty's jewels and gifts. Had King Solomon been the janitor, with all his treasures piled up in the basement, Jim would have pulled out his watch every time he passed, just to see him pluck at his beard from envy.

So now Della's beautiful hair fell about her rippling and shining like a **cascade** of brown waters. It reached below her knee and made itself almost a garment for her. And then she did it up again nervously and quickly. Once she **faltered** for a minute and stood still while a tear or two splashed on the worn red carpet.

On went her old brown jacket; on went her old brown hat. With a whirl of skirts and with the brilliant sparkle still in her eyes, she fluttered out the door and down the stairs to the street.

Where she stopped the sign read: "Mme. Sofronie. Hair Goods of All Kinds." One flight up Della ran, and **collected** herself, **panting**. Madame, large, too white, chilly, hardly looked the "Sofronie."

"Will you buy my hair?" asked Della.

"I buy hair," said Madame. "Take yer hat off and let's have a sight at the looks of it."

Down rippled the brown cascade.

"Twenty dollars," said Madame, lifting the mass with a practised hand.

"Give it to me quick," said Della.

metaphor [métəfɔ̀ːr, -fər] n.
은유
ransack [rǽnsæk] v.
샅샅이 찾다
turn inside out:
(철저히) 찾다, 뒤지다
fob chain:
시계의 가는 쇠줄
chaste [tʃeist] adj.
정숙한, 고상한
meretricious [mèrətríʃəs] adj.
저속한, 겉치레의
on the sly:
살그머니, 남 모르게
on account of:
~ 때문에

give way:
물러서다, 양보하다
ravage [rǽvidʒ] n.
파괴, 황폐
tremendous [triméndəs] adj.
굉장한, 대단한
mammoth [mǽməθ] adj.
거대한

Oh, and the next two hours tripped by on rosy wings. Forget the hashed **metaphor**. She was **ransacking** the stores for Jim's present.

She found it at last. It surely had been made for Jim and no one else. There was no other like it in any of the stores, and she had **turned** all of them **inside out**. It was a platinum **fob chain** simple and **chaste** in design, properly proclaiming its value by substance alone and not by **meretricious** ornamentation—as all good things should do. It was even worthy of The Watch. As soon as she saw it she knew that it must be Jim's. It was like him. Quietness and value—the description applied to both. Twenty-one dollars they took from her for it, and she hurried home with the 87 cents. With that chain on his watch Jim might be properly anxious about the time in any company. Grand as the watch was, he sometimes looked at it **on the sly on account of** the old leather strap that he used in place of a chain.

When Della reached home her intoxication **gave way** a little to prudence and reason. She got out her curling irons and lighted the gas and went to work repairing the **ravages** made by generosity added to love. Which is always a **tremendous** task, dear friends—a **mammoth** task.

Within forty minutes her head was covered

truant [trúːənt] adj.
게으름피우는, 무단 결석하는

Coney Island:
코니아일랜드; 뉴욕 브룩클린의 휴양지

immovable [imúːvəbəl] adj.
움직이지 않는, 부동의
setter [sétəːr] n.
세터 (사냥감을 발견하면 곧 서서 그 소재를 알리도록 훈련된 사냥개)
quail [kweil] n.
메추라기

with tiny, close-lying curls that made her look wonderfully like a **truant** schoolboy. She looked at her reflection in the mirror long, carefully, and critically.

"If Jim doesn't kill me," she said to herself, "before he takes a second look at me, he'll say I look like a **Coney Island** chorus girl. But what could I do—oh! what could I do with a dollar and eighty-seven cents?"

At 7 o'clock the coffee was made and the frying-pan was on the back of the stove hot and ready to cook the chops.

Jim was never late. Della doubled the fob chain in her hand and sat on the corner of the table near the door that he always entered. Then she heard his step on the stair away down on the first flight, and she turned white for just a moment. She had a habit for saying little silent prayers about the simplest everyday things, and now she whispered: "Please God, make him think I am still pretty."

The door opened and Jim stepped in and closed it. He looked thin and very serious. Poor fellow, he was only twenty-two—and to be burdened with a family! He needed a new overcoat and he was without gloves.

Jim stopped inside the door, as **immovable** as a **setter** at the scent of **quail**. His eyes were fixed upon Della, and there was an expression in them that she could not read, and it terrified her. It was not anger, nor surprise, nor disapproval, nor horror, nor any of the sentiments that she had been prepared for. He simply stared at her fixedly with that peculiar expression on his face.

Della wriggled off the table and went for him.

"Jim, darling," she cried, "don't look at me that way. I had my hair cut off and sold it because I couldn't have lived through Christmas without giving you a present. It'll grow out again—you won't mind, will you? I just had to do it. My hair grows awfully fast. Say 'Merry Christmas!' Jim, and let's be happy. You don't know what a nice—what a beautiful, nice gift I've got for you."

"You've cut off your hair?" asked Jim, **laboriously**, as if he had not arrived at that **patent** fact yet even after the hardest mental labor.

"Cut it off and sold it," said Della. "Don't you like me just as well, anyhow? I'm me without my hair, ain't I?"

Jim looked about the room curiously.

"You say your hair is gone?" he said, with an air almost of **idiocy**.

"You needn't look for it," said Della. "It's sold, I tell you—sold and gone, too. It's Christmas Eve, boy. Be good to me, for it went for you. Maybe the hairs of my head were numbered,"

chop [tʃɑp / tʃɔp] n.
두껍게 베어 낸 고깃점

trance [træns, trɑ:ns] n.
열중, 망연 자실
discreet [diskrí:t] adj.
지각있는, 신중한
inconsequential [inkɑ̀nsik-wénʃəl / -kɔ̀n-] adj.
불합리한, 중요하지 않은
wit [wit] n.
재치 있는 사람, 재사
magi [méidʒai] n.
(동방의) 박사들
(마태복음 2:1-12 참조)
assertion [əsə́:rʃən] n.
주장, 단언

unwrap [ʌnrǽp] v.
포장을 풀다

necessitate [nisésətèit] v.
필요로 하다

she went on with sudden serious sweetness, "but nobody could ever count my love for you. Shall I put the **chops** on, Jim?"

Out of his **trance** Jim seemed quickly to wake. He enfolded his Della. For ten seconds let us regard with **discreet** scrutiny some **inconsequential** object in the other direction. Eight dollars a week or a million a year—what is the difference? A mathematician or a **wit** would give you the wrong answer. The **magi** brought valuable gifts, but that was not among them. This dark **assertion** will be illuminated later on.

Jim drew a package from his overcoat pocket and threw it upon the table.

"Don't make any mistake, Dell," he said, "about me. I don't think there's anything in the way of a haircut or a shave or a shampoo that could make me like my girl any less. But if you'll **unwrap** that package you may see why you had me going a while at first."

White fingers and nimble tore at the string and paper. And then an ecstatic scream of joy; and then, alas! a quick feminine change to hysterical tears and wails, **necessitating** the immediate employment of all the comforting powers of the lord of the flat.

For there lay The Combs—the set of combs, side and back, that Della had worshipped for long in a Broadway window. Beautiful combs, pure tortoise shell, with jewelled rims—just the shade to wear in the beautiful vanished hair. They were expensive combs, she knew, and her heart had simply **craved** and **yearned** over them without the least hope of possession. And now, they were hers, but the **tresses** that should have adorned the coveted adornments were gone.

But she hugged them to her bosom, and at length she was able to look up with dim eyes and a smile and say: "My hair grows so fast, Jim!"

And then Della leaped up like a little singed cat and cried, "Oh, oh!"

Jim had not yet seen his beautiful present. She held it out to him eagerly upon her open palm. The dull precious metal seemed to flash with a reflection of her bright and **ardent** spirit.

"Isn't it a **dandy**, Jim? I hunted all over town to find it. You'll have to look at the time a hundred times a day now. Give me your watch. I want to see how it looks on it."

Instead of obeying, Jim tumbled down on the couch and put his hands under the back of his head and smiled.

"Dell," said he, "let's put our Christmas presents away and keep 'em a while. They're too nice to use just at present. I sold the watch to get the money to buy your combs. And now

---

crave [kreiv] v.
간절히 원하다, 열망하다
yearn [jəːrn] v.
갈망하다
tress [tres] n.
머리 타래

ardent:[άːrdənt] adj.
열렬한, 정열적인

dandy [dǽndi] n.
훌륭한 물건, 일품

manger [méindʒə:r] n.
여물통, 구유
lamely [leimli] adv.
불완전하게, 힘없이
relate [riléit] v.
이야기하다, 말하다

suppose you put the chops on."

The magi, as you know, were wise men—wonderfully wise men—who brought gifts to the Babe in the **manger**. They invented the art of giving Christmas presents. Being wise, their gifts were no doubt wise ones, possibly bearing the privilege of exchange in case of duplication. And here I have **lamely related** to you the uneventful chronicle of two foolish children in a flat who most unwisely sacrificed for each other the greatest treasures of their house. But in a last word to the wise of these days let it be said that of all who give gifts these two were the wisest. Of all who give and receive gifts, such as they are wisest. Everywhere they are wisest. They are the magi.

But in a last word to the wise of these days let it be said that of all who give gifts these two were the wisest. Of all who give and receive gifts, such as they are wisest. Everywhere they are wisest. They are the magi.

A Retrieved Reformation

assiduously [əsídʒuəsli] adv.
열심히, 부지런히
warden [wɔ́:rdn] n.
교도소장
pardon [páːrdn] n.
특사, 사면
governor [ɡʌ́vərnər] n.
주지사
sentence [séntəns] n.
판결, 선고
stir [stəːr] n.
(속어) 교도소

A guard came to the prison shoe-shop, where Jimmy Valentine was **assiduously** stitching uppers, and escorted him to the front office. There the **warden** handed Jimmy his **pardon**, which had been signed that morning by the **governor**. Jimmy took it in a tired kind of way. He had served nearly ten months of a four-year **sentence**. He had expected to stay only about three months, at the longest. When a man with as many friends on the outside as Jimmy Valentine had is received in the "**stir**" it is hardly worth while to cut his hair.

"Now, Valentine," said the warden, "you'll

brace up:
힘이나 인내심을 내다
make a man of someone:
성숙하고 책임있는 사람이 되다
at heart:
마음속은, 진심은, 사실은
crack [kræk] v.
(금고 등을) 부수다, 털다
safe [seif] n.
금고
alibi [ǽləbài] n.
현장 부재(증명), 알리바이
compromise [kámprəmàiz / kɔ́m-] v.
(신용, 명성 등을) 위태롭게 하다, 손상하다
high-toned [háitóund] adj.
고상한, 고결한, 뛰어난
have it in for a person:
앙심을 품다, 트집을 잡다

go out in the morning. **Brace up**, and **make a man of yourself**. You're not a bad fellow **at heart**. Stop **cracking safes**, and live straight."

"Me?" said Jimmy, in surprise. "Why, I never cracked a safe in my life."

"Oh, no," laughed the warden. "Of course not. Let's see, now. How was it you happened to get sent up on that Springfield job? Was it because you wouldn't prove an **alibi** for fear of **compromising** somebody in extremely **high-toned** society? Or was it simply a case of a mean old jury that **had it in for you**? It's always one or the other with you innocent victims."

"Me?" said Jimmy, still blankly virtuous. "Why, warden, I never was in Springfield in my life!"

"Take him back, Cronin!" smiled the warden, "and fix him up with outgoing clothes. Unlock him at seven in the morning, and let him come to the bull-pen. Better think over my advice, Valentine."

At a quarter past seven on the next morning Jimmy stood in the warden's outer office. He had on a suit of the villainously fitting, ready-made clothes and a pair of the stiff, squeaky shoes that the state furnishes to its discharged compulsory guests.

The clerk handed him a railroad ticket and the five-dollar bill with which the law expected

A Retrieved Reformation

him to **rehabilitate** himself into good citizenship and prosperity. The warden gave him a cigar, and shook hands. Valentine, 9762, was chronicled on the books, "Pardoned by Governor," and Mr. James Valentine walked out into the sunshine.

Disregarding the song of the birds, the waving green trees, and the smell of the flowers, Jimmy headed straight for a restaurant. There he tasted the first sweet joys of liberty in the shape of a broiled chicken and a bottle of white wine—followed by a cigar a grade better than the one the warden had given him. From there he proceeded leisurely to the **depot**. He tossed a quarter into the hat of a blind man sitting by the door, and boarded his train. Three hours set him down in a little town near the state line. He went to the café of one Mike Dolan and shook hands with Mike, who was alone behind the bar.

"Sorry we couldn't make it sooner, Jimmy, me boy," said Mike. "But we had that protest from Springfield to **buck** against, and the governor nearly **balked**. Feeling all right?"

"Fine," said Jimmy. "Got my key?"

He got his key and went upstairs, unlocking the door of a room at the rear. Everything was just as he had left it. There on the floor was still Ben Price's collar-button that had been

---

rehabilitate [rìːhəbílətèit] v.
원상태로 되돌리다, 회복시키다

disregard [dìsrigáːrd] v.
무시하다, 등한시하다
depot [díːpou / dépou] n.
역, 정거장

buck [bʌk] v.
저항하다, 반대하다
balk [bɔːk] v.
좌절시키다, 방해하다

eminent [émənənt] adj.
저명한, 유명한, 신분이 높은

torn from that **eminent** detective's shirt-band when they had overpowered Jimmy to arrest him.

Pulling out from the wall a folding-bed, Jimmy slid back a panel in the wall and dragged out a dust-covered suit-case. He opened this and gazed fondly at the finest set of burglar's tools in the East. It was a complete set, made of specially tempered steel, the latest designs in drills, punches, braces and bits, jimmies, clamps, and augers, with two or three novelties, invented by Jimmy himself, in which he took pride. Over nine hundred dollars they had cost him to have made at ——, a place where they make such things for the profession.

tasteful [téistfəl] adj.
멋있는, 품위 있는, 우아한

In half an hour Jimmy went downstairs and through the café. He was now dressed in **tasteful** and well-fitting clothes, and carried his dusted and cleaned suitcase in his hand.

genially [dʒí:njəli] adv.
온화하게, 다정하게

"Got anything on?" asked Mike Dolan, **genially.**

"Me?" said Jimmy, in a puzzled tone. "I don't understand. I'm representing the New York Amalgamated Short Snap Biscuit Cracker and Frazzled Wheat Company."

on/upon the spot:
그 자리에서, 즉석에서
release [rilí:s] n.
석방, 해방

This statement delighted Mike to such an extent that Jimmy had to take a seltzer-and-milk **on the spot.** He never touched "hard" drinks.

A week after the **release** of Valentine, 9762,

clue [klu:] n.
실마리, 단서
author [ɔ́:θər] n.
창조자, 장본인
to the tune of:
~의 값으로, ~이라는 액수의
crater [kréitər] n.
분화구
eruption [irʌ́pʃən] n.
(화산의) 폭발, 분출

autograph [ɔ́:təgræf / -grὰ:f] n.
자필, 서명
resume [rizú:m / -zjú:m] v.
다시 시작하다, 계속하다
tumbler [tʌ́mblər] n.
텀블러; 자물쇠 안의 회전하는 쇠붙이
do one's bit:
의무를 다하다, 본분을 다하다 (자신의 행위에 책임을 지다)
clemency [klémənsi] n.
관대, 자비
foolishness [fú:liʃnis] n.
어리석음, 지각없음

there was a neat job of safeburglary done in Richmond, Indiana, with no **clue** to the **author**. A scant eight hundred dollars was all that was secured. Two weeks after that a patented, improved, burglar-proof safe in Logansport was opened like a cheese **to the tune of** fifteen hundred dollars, currency; securities and silver untouched. That began to interest the rogue-catchers. Then an old-fashioned banksafe in Jefferson City became active and threw out of its **crater** an **eruption** of bank-notes amounting to five thousand dollars. The losses were now high enough to bring the matter up into Ben Price's class of work. By comparing notes, a remarkable similarity in the methods of the burglaries was noticed. Ben Price investigated the scenes of the robberies, and was heard to remark:

"That's Dandy Jim Valentine's **autograph**. He's **resumed** business. Look at that combination knob—jerked out as easy as pulling up a radish in wet weather. He's got the only clamps that can do it. And look how clean those **tumblers** were punched out! Jimmy never has to drill but one hole. Yes, I guess I want Mr. Valentine. He'll **do his bit** next time without any short-time or **clemency foolishness**."

Ben Price knew Jimmy's habits. He had

getaway [gétəwèi] n.
도망, 도주
confederate [kənfédərit] n.
공범, 공모자
dodger [dádʒər / dó-] n.
몸을 피하는 사람, 책임을 회피하는 사람
retribution [rètrəbjúːʃ-ən] n.
징벌, 응보
elusive [ilúːsiv] adj.
잘 잡히지 않는
cracksman [kræksmən] n.
도둑, 금고털이

scarce [skɛəːrs] adj.
드문, 희귀한

collar [kálər / kólər] v.
붙들어 세우고 이야기하다
by and by:
이윽고, 곧

learned them while working up the Springfield case. Long jumps, quick **get-aways**, no **confederates**, and a taste for good society—these ways had helped Mr. Valentine to become noted as a successful **dodger** of **retribution**. It was given out that Ben Price had taken up the trail of the **elusive cracksman**, and other people with burglar-proof safes felt more at ease.

One afternoon Jimmy Valentine and his suit-case climbed out of the mail-hack in Elmore, a little town five miles off the railroad down in the black-jack country of Arkansas. Jimmy, looking like an athletic young senior just home from college, went down the board side-walk toward the hotel.

A young lady crossed the street, passed him at the corner and entered a door over which was the sign, "The Elmore Bank." Jimmy Valentine looked into her eyes, forgot what he was, and became another man. She lowered her eyes and coloured slightly. Young men of Jimmy's style and looks were **scarce** in Elmore.

Jimmy **collared** a boy that was loafing on the steps of the bank as if he were one of the stockholders, and began to ask him questions about the town, feeding him dimes at intervals. **By and by** the young lady came out, looking royally unconscious of the young man with the suit-case, and went her way.

A Retrieved Reformation

"Isn't that young lady Polly Simpson?" asked Jimmy, with **specious guile**.

"Naw," said the boy. "She's Annabel Adams. Her pa owns this bank. What'd you come to Elmore for? Is that a gold watch-chain? I'm going to get a bulldog. Got any more dimes?"

Jimmy went to the Planters' Hotel, registered as Ralph D. Spencer, and engaged a room. He leaned on the desk and declared his platform to the clerk. He said he had come to Elmore to look for a location to go into business. How was the shoe business, now, in the town? He had thought of the shoe business. Was there an opening?

The clerk was impressed by the clothes and manner of Jimmy. He, himself, was something of a pattern of fashion to the thinly gilded youth of Elmore, but he now perceived his **shortcomings**. While trying to **figure out** Jimmy's manner of tying his **four-in-hand** he **cordially** gave information.

Yes, there ought to be a good opening in the shoe **line**. There wasn't an exclusive shoe-store in the place. The dry-goods and general stores handled them. Business in all lines was fairly good. Hoped Mr. Spencer would decide to locate in Elmore. He would find it a pleasant town to live in, and the people very **sociable**.

Mr. Spencer thought he would stop over in

---

specious [spíːʃəs] adj.
허울 좋은, 남의 눈을 속이는
guile [gail] n.
교활, 간계, 기만

Jimmy Valentine looked into her eyes, forgot what he was, and became another man.

shortcoming [ʃɔ́ːrtkʌ̀miŋ] n.
결점, 단점
figure out:
알다, 이해하다
four-in-hand [fɔ́ːrinhæ̀nd] n.
(보통으로 매는) 넥타이
cordially [kɔ́ːrdʒəli / -diəli] adv.
성심껏, 진심으로

line [lain] n.
직업, 사업, 장사
sociable [sóuʃəb-əl] adj.
사교적인, 사귀기 쉬운, 붙임성 있는

the town a few days and look over the situation. No, the clerk needn't call the boy. He would carry up his suit-case, himself; it was rather heavy.

Mr. Ralph Spencer, the **phœnix** that arose from Jimmy Valentine's ashes—ashes left by the flame of a sudden and **alterative** attack of love—remained in Elmore, and prospered. He opened a shoe-store and secured a good run of trade.

Socially he was also a success, and made many friends. And he accomplished the wish of his heart. He met Miss Annabel Adams, and became more and more captivated by her charms.

At the end of a year the situation of Mr. Ralph Spencer was this: he had won the respect of the community, his shoe-store was flourishing, and he and Annabel were engaged to be married in two weeks. Mr. Adams, the typical, plodding, country banker, approved of Spencer. Annabel's pride in him almost equalled her affection. He was as much at home in the family of Mr. Adams and that of Annabel's married sister as if he were already a member.

One day Jimmy sat down in his room and wrote this letter, which he mailed to the safe address of one of his old friends in St. Louis:

---

phoenix [fíːniks] n. 피닉스, (이집트 신화의) 불사조 (500년 또는 600년에 한번씩 스스로 타 죽고, 그 재 속에서 다시 태어난다는 영조(靈鳥))
alterative [ɔ́ːltərèitiv, -tərətiv] adj. 변화를 일으키는

Mr. Ralph Spencer, the phœnix that arose from Jimmy Valentine's ashes— ashes left by the flame of a sudden and alterative attack of love—remained in Elmore, and prospered.

wind up:
정리하다, 끝맺다
score [skɔːr] n.
빚, 부채, 원한
crooked [krúkid] adj.
비뚤어진, 부정직한

Dear Old Pal:

I want you to be at Sullivan's place, in Little Rock, next Wednesday night, at nine o'clock. I want you to **wind up** some little matters for me. And, also, I want to make you a present of my kit of tools. I know you'll be glad to get them—you couldn't duplicate the lot for a thousand dollars. Say, Billy, I've quit the old business—a year ago. I've got a nice store. I'm making an honest living, and I'm going to marry the finest girl on earth two weeks from now. It's the only life, Billy—the straight one. I wouldn't touch a dollar of another man's money now for a million. After I get married I'm going to sell out and go West, where there won't be so much danger of having old **scores** brought up against me. I tell you, Billy, she's an angel. She believes in me; and I wouldn't do another **crooked** thing for the whole world. Be sure to be at Sully's, for I must see you. I'll bring along the tools with me.

Your old friend,
Jimmy

unobtrusively [ʌ̀nəbtrúːsivli] adv. 남의 눈에 띄지 않게, 살며시
buggy [bʌ́gi] n.
말 한 필이 끄는 경마차

On the Monday night after Jimmy wrote this letter, Ben Price jogged **unobtrusively** into Elmore in a livery **buggy**. He lounged about town in his quiet way until he found out what he wanted to know. From the drug-store across the street from Spencer's shoe-store he got a good look at Ralph D. Spencer.

"Going to marry the banker's daughter are you, Jimmy?" said Ben to himself, softly. "Well, I don't know!"

The next morning Jimmy took breakfast at the Adamses. He was going to Little Rock that day to order his wedding-suit and buy something nice for Annabel. That would be the first time he had left town since he came to Elmore. It had been more than a year now since those last professional "jobs," and he thought he could safely venture out.

After breakfast quite a family party went downtown together—Mr. Adams, Annabel, Jimmy, and Annabel's married sister with her two little girls, aged five and nine. They came by the hotel where Jimmy still boarded, and he ran up to his room and brought along his suitcase. Then they went on to the bank. There stood Jimmy's horse and buggy and Dolph Gibson, who was going to drive him over to the railroad station.

All went inside the high, carved oak railings into the banking-room—Jimmy included, for Mr. Adams's future son-in-law was welcome anywhere. The clerks were pleased to be greeted by the good-looking, agreeable young man who was going to marry Miss Annabel. Jimmy set his suitcase down. Annabel, whose heart was bubbling with happiness and lively youth, put on Jimmy's hat, and picked up the suitcase. "Wouldn't I make a nice **drummer**?" said Annabel. "My! Ralph, how heavy it is? Feels like it was full of gold bricks."

"Lot of nickel-plated shoe-horns in there," said Jimmy, coolly, "that I'm going to return. Thought I'd save express charges by taking them up. I'm getting awfully **economical**."

The Elmore Bank had just put in a new safe and **vault**. Mr. Adams was very proud of it, and insisted on an inspection by every one. The vault was a small one, but it had a new patented door. It fastened with three solid steel bolts thrown simultaneously with a single handle, and had a time-lock. Mr. Adams **beamingly** explained its workings to Mr. Spencer, who showed a **courteous** but not too intelligent interest. The two children, May and Agatha, were delighted by the shining metal and funny clock and knobs.

While they were thus engaged Ben Price **sauntered** in and leaned on his elbow, looking casually inside between the railings. He told the **teller** that he didn't want anything; he was just waiting for a man he knew.

Suddenly there was a scream or two from the women, and a **commotion**. Unperceived

knob [nɑb / nɔb] n.
노브, (돌리는) 스위치 또는 다이얼
combination [kɑ̀mbənéiʃən / kɔ̀m-] n.
(자물쇠 등을 열기 위해) 맞추는 숫자나 문자의 조합
tug [tʌg] v.
세게 잡아당기다
groan [groun] v.
고통, 노여움, 절망 등의 소리를 내다
faint [feint] adj.
어렴풋한, 희미한, 약한
panic [pǽnik] n.
공황, 공포, 겁먹음

stand [stænd] v.
견디다, 버티어 내다

frantic [frǽntik] adj.
정신없는, 미칠 것 같은
anguish [ǽŋgwiʃ] n.
(심신의) 고통, 괴로움, 번민

by the elders, May, the nine-year-old girl, in a spirit of play, had shut Agatha in the vault. She had then shot the bolts and turned the **knob** of the **combination** as she had seen Mr. Adams do.

The old banker sprang to the handle and **tugged** at it for a moment. "The door can't be opened," he **groaned**. "The clock hasn't been wound nor the combination set."

Agatha's mother screamed again, hysterically.

"Hush!" said Mr. Adams, raising his trembling hand. "All be quiet for a moment. Agatha!" he called as loudly as he could. "Listen to me." During the following silence they could just hear the **faint** sound of the child wildly shrieking in the dark vault in a **panic** of terror.

"My precious darling!" wailed the mother. "She will die of fright! Open the door! Oh, break it open! Can't you men do something?"

"There isn't a man nearer than Little Rock who can open that door," said Mr. Adams, in a shaky voice. "My God! Spencer, what shall we do? That child—she can't **stand** it long in there. There isn't enough air, and, besides, she'll go into convulsions from fright."

Agatha's mother, **frantic** now, beat the door of the vault with her hands. Somebody wildly suggested dynamite. Annabel turned to Jimmy, her large eyes full of **anguish**, but not

A Retrieved Reformation 33

yet **despairing**. To a woman nothing seems quite impossible to the powers of the man she worships.

"Can't you do something, Ralph—*try*, won't you?"

He looked at her with a queer, soft smile on his lips and in his keen eyes.

"Annabel," he said, "give me that rose you are wearing, will you?"

Hardly believing that she heard him **aright**, she unpinned the bud from the bosom of her dress, and placed it in his hand. Jimmy stuffed it into his vest-pocket, threw off his coat and pulled up his shirt-sleeves. With that act Ralph D. Spencer **passed away** and Jimmy Valentine **took his place**.

"Get away from the door, all of you," he commanded, shortly.

He set his suitcase on the table, and opened it out flat. From that time on he seemed to be **unconscious** of the presence of any one else. He laid out the shining, queer **implements** swiftly and orderly, whistling softly to himself as he always did when at work. In a deep silence and immovable, the others watched him as if under a **spell**.

In a minute Jimmy's pet drill was biting smoothly into the steel door. In ten minutes—breaking his own burglarious record—he threw

---

despairing [dispéəriŋ] adj.
절망적인, 자포자기의

aright [əráit] adv.
올바르게, 틀림없이
pass away:
없어지다, 사라지다
take one's place:
(원래의 또는 제대로 된) 자리를 차지하다

unconscious [ʌnkánʃəs / -kɔ́n-] adj. 의식하지 못하는, 알아채지 못하는
implement [ímpləmənt] n.
도구, 기구
spell [spel] n.
주문, 마법

back the bolts and opened the door.

Agatha, almost collapsed, but safe, was gathered into her mother's arms.

Jimmy Valentine put on his coat, and walked outside the railings towards the front door. As he went he thought he heard a far-away voice that he once knew call "Ralph!" But he never hesitated.

At the door a big man **stood** somewhat **in his way**.

"Hello, Ben!" said Jimmy, still with his strange smile. "Got around at last, have you? Well, let's go. I don't know that it makes much difference, now."

And then Ben Price acted rather strangely.

"Guess you're mistaken, Mr. Spencer," he said. "Don't **believe** I **recognize** you. Your buggy's waiting for you, ain't it?"

And Ben Price turned and strolled down the street.

The Last Leaf

In a little district west of Washington Square the streets have run crazy and broken themselves into small strips called "places." These "places" make strange angles and curves. One street crosses itself a time or two. An artist once discovered a valuable possibility in this street. Suppose a collector with a bill for paints, paper and canvas should, in traversing this route, suddenly meet himself coming back, without a cent having been paid on account!

So, to **quaint** old **Greenwich Village** the art people soon came **prowling**, **hunting** for north windows and eighteenth-century gables and Dutch attics and low rents. Then they **imported** some pewter mugs and a chafing dish or two

---

quaint [kweint] adj.
예스러운, 고아한
Greenwich Village:
그리니치 빌리지; 뉴욕 맨해튼의 예술가, 학생 중심의 지역
prowl [praul] v.
헤매다, 서성이다
hunt [hʌnt] v.
찾아 헤매다
import [impɔ́:rt] v.
가져오다, 들여오다, 수입하다

studio [stjú:diòu] n.
(예술가의) 작업장, 아틀리에
table d'hôte [tá:b-əldóut, tǽb-]
n. (호텔 등의) 공동식탁
congenial [kəndʒí:njəl] adj.
마음에 맞는

pneumonia [njumóunjə, -niə]
n. 폐렴
ravager [rǽvidʒər] n.
파괴자, 약탈자
smite [smait] v.
때리다
by the score:
다수로, 대규모로
maze [meiz] n.
미로, 미궁
chivalric [ʃivǽlrik / ʃívəl-] adj.
기사도의, 기사적인
mite [mait] n.
작은 것, 작은 아이
zephyr [zéfə:r] n.
미풍, 산들바람
duffer [dʌ́fər] n.
(속어) 행상인

from Sixth avenue, and became a "colony."

At the top of a squatty, three-story brick Sue and Johnsy had their **studio**. "Johnsy" was familiar for Joanna. One was from Maine; the other from California. They had met at the ***table d'hote*** of an Eighth street "Delmonico's," and found their tastes in art, chicory salad and bishop sleeves so **congenial** that the joint studio resulted.

That was in May. In November a cold, unseen stranger, whom the doctors called **Pneumonia**, stalked about the colony, touching one here and there with his icy fingers. Over on the east side this **ravager** strode boldly, **smiting** his victims **by scores**, but his feet trod slowly through the **maze** of the narrow and moss-grown "places."

Mr. Pneumonia was not what you would call a **chivalric** old gentleman. A **mite** of a little woman with blood thinned by California **zephyrs** was hardly fair game for the red-fisted, short-breathed old **duffer**. But Johnsy he smote; and she lay, scarcely moving, on her painted iron bedstead, looking through the small Dutch window-panes at the blank side of the next brick house.

One morning the busy doctor invited Sue into the hallway with a shaggy, gray eyebrow.

"She has one chance in—let us say, ten," he said, as he shook down the mercury in his clinical thermometer. "And that chance is for her to want to live. This way people have of lining-up on the side of the **undertaker** makes the entire **pharmacopeia** look silly. Your little lady has made up her mind that she's not going to get well. Has she anything on her mind?"

"She—she wanted to paint the Bay of Naples some day," said Sue.

"Paint?—**bosh**! Has she anything on her mind worth thinking about twice—a man, for instance?"

"A man?" said Sue, with a **jew's-harp twang** in her voice. "Is a man worth—but, no, doctor; there is nothing of the kind."

"Well, it is the weakness, then," said the doctor. "I will do all that science, so far as it may filter through my efforts, can accomplish. But whenever my patient begins to count the carriages in her funeral procession I **subtract** 50 per cent. from the **curative** power of medicines. If you will get her to ask one question about the new winter styles in cloak sleeves I will promise you a one-in-five chance for her, instead of one in ten."

After the doctor had gone Sue went into the workroom and cried a Japanese napkin to a pulp. Then she swaggered into Johnsy's room with her drawing board, whistling **ragtime**.

Johnsy lay, scarcely making a ripple under

the bedclothes, with her face toward the window. Sue stopped whistling, thinking she was asleep.

She arranged her board and began a **pen-and-ink** drawing to illustrate a magazine story. Young artists must **pave their way to** Art by drawing pictures for magazine stories that young authors write to pave their way to Literature.

As Sue was sketching a pair of elegant horse-show riding trousers and a monocle on the figure of the hero, an Idaho cowboy, she heard a low sound, several times repeated. She went quickly to the bedside.

Johnsy's eyes were open wide. She was looking out the window and counting — counting backward.

"Twelve," she said, and a little later "eleven;" and then "ten," and "nine;" and then "eight" and "seven," almost together.

Sue looked **solicitously** out the window. What was there to count? There was only a bare, **dreary** yard to be seen, and the blank side of the brick house twenty feet away. An old, old **ivy vine**, **gnarled** and decayed at the roots, climbed half way up the brick wall. The cold breath of autumn had stricken its leaves from the vine until its skeleton branches clung, almost bare, to the crumbling bricks.

"What is it, dear?" asked Sue.

"Six," said Johnsy, in almost a whisper. "They're falling faster now. Three days ago there were almost a hundred. It made my head ache to count them. But now it's easy. There goes another one. There are only five left now."

"Five what, dear? Tell your Sudie."

"Leaves. On the ivy vine. When the last one falls I must go, too. I've known that for three days. Didn't the doctor tell you?"

"Oh, I never heard of such nonsense," complained Sue, with magnificent scorn. "What **have** old ivy leaves **to do with** your getting well? And you used to love that vine so, you naughty girl. Don't be a **goosey**. Why, the doctor told me this morning that your chances for getting well real soon were—let's see exactly what he said—he said the chances were ten to one! Why, that's almost as good a chance as we have in New York when we ride on the street cars or walk past a new building. Try to take some **broth** now, and let Sudie go back to her drawing, so she can sell the editor man with it, and buy port wine for her sick child, and pork chops for her greedy self."

"You needn't get any more wine," said Johnsy, keeping her eyes fixed out the window. "There goes another. No, I don't want any broth. That leaves just four. I want to see the last one fall

---

have to do with something: 관련이 있다
goosey [gúːsi] adj. 거위 같은, 어리석은
broth [brɔ(ː)θ, brɑθ] n. 묽은 수프

hand in:
건네다, 제출하다

before it gets dark. Then I'll go, too."

"Johnsy, dear," said Sue, bending over her, "will you promise me to keep your eyes closed, and not look out the window until I am done working? I must **hand** those drawings **in** by to-morrow. I need the light, or I would draw the shade down."

"Couldn't you draw in the other room?" asked Johnsy, coldly.

"I'd rather be here by you," said Sue. "Besides I don't want you to keep looking at those silly ivy leaves."

"Tell me as soon as you have finished," said Johnsy, closing her eyes, and lying white and still as a fallen statue, "because I want to see the last one fall. I'm tired of waiting. I'm tired of thinking. I want to turn loose my hold on everything, and go sailing down, down, just like one of those poor, tired leaves."

"Try to sleep," said Sue. "I must call Behrman up to be my model for the old hermit miner. I'll not be gone a minute. Don't try to move 'til I come back."

Old Behrman was a painter who lived on the ground floor beneath them. He was past sixty and had a Michael Angelo's Moses beard curling down from the head of a satyr along the body of an imp. Behrman was a failure in art. Forty years he had wielded the brush without getting near enough to touch the hem of his Mistress's robe. He had been always about to paint a **masterpiece**, but had never yet begun it. For several years he had painted nothing except **now and then** a **daub** in the line of commerce or advertising. He earned a little by serving as a model to those young artists in the colony who could not pay the price of a professional. He drank gin to excess, and still talked of his coming masterpiece. For the rest he was a fierce little old man, who **scoffed** terribly at softness in any one, and who regarded himself as especial mastiff-in-waiting to protect the two young artists in the studio above.

Sue found Behrman smelling strongly of juniper berries in his dimly lighted den below. In one corner was a blank **canvas** on an **easel** that had been waiting there for twenty-five years to receive the first line of the masterpiece. She told him of Johnsy's fancy, and how she feared she would, indeed, light and **fragile** as a leaf herself, float away when her slight hold upon the world grew weaker.

Old Behrman, with his red eyes plainly streaming, shouted his contempt and derision for such idiotic imaginings.

"**Vass**!" he cried. "Is dere people in de world **mit der** foolishness to die because leafs dey drop off from a **confounded** vine? I haf not

---

masterpiece [mǽstə:rpìːs, mǽːs-] n.
걸작, 명작
now and then:
때때로, 이따금
daub [dɔːb] n.
서투른 그림
scoff [skɔːf, skɑf] v.
비웃다, 조롱하다

canvas [kǽnvəs] n.
캔버스, 화포
easel [íːzəl] n.
화가(畫架), 이즐
fragile [frǽdʒəl / -dʒail] adj.
허약한, 깨지기 쉬운, 섬세한

Vass:
독일어로 what
cf. (German) was
mit:
독일어로 with
der:
독일어로 the
confounded [kənfáundid, kɑn- / kɔn-] adj.
말도 안 되는, 터무니 없는

morbid [mɔ́:rbid] adj.
병적인, 병적으로 과민한
horrid [hɔ́:rid, hár-] adj.
지독한, 얄미운, 몹시 싫은
flibbertigibbet [flíbər-tidʒìbit] n.
경박한 사람

heard of such a thing. No, I will not bose as a model for your fool hermit-dunderhead. Vy do you allow dot silly pusiness to come in der brain of her? Ach, dot poor leetle Miss Yohnsy."

"She is very ill and weak," said Sue, "and the fever has left her mind **morbid** and full of strange fancies. Very well, Mr. Behrman, if you do not care to pose for me, you needn't. But I think you are a **horrid** old — old **flibbertigibbet**."

"You are just like a woman!" yelled Behrman. "Who said I will not bose? Go on. I come mit you. For half an hour I haf peen trying to say dot I am ready to bose. Gott! dis is not any blace in which one so goot as Miss Yohnsy shall lie sick. Some day I vill baint a masterpiece, and ve shall all go away. Gott! yes."

Johnsy was sleeping when they went upstairs. Sue pulled the shade down to the window-sill, and motioned Behrman into the other room. In there they peered out the window fearfully at the ivy vine. Then they looked at each other for a moment without speaking. A persistent, cold rain was falling, mingled with snow. Behrman, in his old blue shirt, took his seat as the hermit miner on an upturned kettle for a rock.

When Sue awoke from an hour's sleep the next morning she found Johnsy with dull, wide-open eyes staring at the drawn green shade.

"Put it up; I want to see," she ordered, in a whisper.

Wearily Sue obeyed.

But, **lo**! After the beating rain and **fierce gusts** of wind that had endured through the **livelong** night, there yet stood out against the brick wall one ivy leaf. It was the last on the vine. Still dark green near its stem, but with its serrated edges tinted with the yellow of dissolution and decay, it hung **bravely** from a branch some twenty feet above the ground.

"It is the last one," said Johnsy. "I thought it would surely fall during the night. I heard the wind. It will fall to-day, and I shall die at the same time."

"Dear, dear!" said Sue, leaning her worn face down to the pillow, "think of me, if you won't think of yourself. What would I do?"

But Johnsy did not answer. The lonesomest thing in all the world is a soul when it is making ready to go on its mysterious, far journey. The fancy seemed to possess her more strongly as one by one the ties that bound her to friendship and to earth were loosed.

The day wore away, and even through the twilight they could see the lone ivy leaf clinging to its stem against the wall. And then, with the coming of the night the north wind was again loosed, while the rain still beat against

---

lo [lou] int.
(고어) 보라 (Lo and behold)
fierce [fiərs] adj.
사나운, 모진, 맹렬한
gust [gʌst] n.
돌풍, 질풍
livelong [lívlɔ̀:ŋ / -lɔ̀ŋ] adj.
온[꼬박], 내내
bravely [bréivli] adv.
용감하게, 훌륭하게

But, lo! After the beating rain and fierce gusts of wind that had endured through the livelong night, there yet stood out against the brick wall one ivy leaf.

the windows and pattered down from the low Dutch eaves.

When it was light enough Johnsy, the merciless, commanded that the shade be raised.

The ivy leaf was still there.

Johnsy lay for a long time looking at it. And then she called to Sue, who was stirring her chicken broth over the gas stove.

"I've been a bad girl, Sudie," said Johnsy. "Something has made that last leaf stay there to show me how wicked I was. It is a sin to want to die. You may bring me a little broth now, and some milk with a little port in it, and—no; bring me a hand-mirror first, and then pack some pillows about me, and I will sit up and watch you cook."

An hour later she said:

"Sudie, some day I hope to paint the Bay of Naples."

The doctor came in the afternoon, and Sue had an excuse to go into the hallway as he left.

"**Even** chances," said the doctor, taking Sue's thin, shaking hand in his. "With good nursing you'll win. And now I must see another **case** I have downstairs. Behrman, his name is—some kind of an artist, I believe. Pneumonia, too. He is an old, weak man, and the **attack** is **acute**. There is no hope for him; but he goes to the hospital to-day to be made more comfortable."

---

even [í:vən] adj.
대등한, 호각의, 반반의
case [keis] n.
병, 부상; 환자
attack [ətǽk] n.
발병, 발작
acute [əkjúːt] adj.
(병이) 급성의, 심각한

nutrition [nju:tríʃ-ən] n.
영양, 음식물

The next day the doctor said to Sue: "She's out of danger. You've won. **Nutrition** and care now—that's all."

And that afternoon Sue came to the bed where Johnsy lay, contentedly knitting a very blue and very useless woolen shoulder scarf, and put one arm around her, pillows and all.

"I have something to tell you, white mouse," she said. "Mr. Behrman died of pneumonia today in the hospital. He was ill only two days. The janitor found him on the morning of the first day in his room downstairs helpless with pain. His shoes and clothing were wet through and icy cold. They couldn't imagine where he had been on such a dreadful night. And then they found a lantern, still lighted, and a ladder that had been dragged from its place, and some scattered brushes, and a palette with green and yellow colors mixed on it, and—look out the window, dear, at the last ivy leaf on the wall. Didn't you wonder why it never fluttered or moved when the wind blew? Ah, darling, it's Behrman's masterpiece—he painted it there the night that the last leaf fell."

After Twenty Years

on the beat:
순찰 중에
depeople [diːpíːpl] v.
인구를 감소시키다

twirl [twəːrl] v.
빙빙 돌리다, 휘두르다
intricate [íntrəkit] adj.
뒤엉킨, 복잡한
stalwart [stɔ́ːlwəːrt] adj.
건장한, 튼튼한
swagger [swǽgər] v.
뽐내는 태도 또는 걸음
vicinity [visínəti] n.
근처, 부근

The policeman **on the beat** moved up the avenue impressively. The impressiveness was habitual and not for show, for spectators were few. The time was barely 10 o'clock at night, but chilly gusts of wind with a taste of rain in them had well nigh **depeopled** the streets.

Trying doors as he went, **twirling** his club with many **intricate** and artful movements, turning now and then to cast his watchful eye adown the pacific thoroughfare, the officer, with his **stalwart** form and slight **swagger**, made a fine picture of a guardian of the peace. The **vicinity** was one that kept early hours. Now and then you might see the lights of a cigar store or of an all-night lunch counter; but the majority of the doors belonged to business places that had long since been closed.

When about midway of a certain block the policeman suddenly slowed his walk. In the doorway of a darkened hardware store a man leaned, with an unlighted cigar in his mouth. As the policeman walked up to him the man spoke up quickly.

"It's all right, officer," he said, **reassuringly**. "I'm just waiting for a friend. It's an **appointment** made twenty years ago. Sounds a little funny to you, doesn't it? Well, I'll explain if you'd like to make certain it's all straight. About that long ago there used to be a restaurant where this store stands—'Big Joe' Brady's restaurant."

"Until five years ago," said the policeman. "It was torn down then."

The man in the doorway struck a match and lit his cigar. The light showed a pale, square-jawed face with keen eyes, and a little white scar near his right eyebrow. His **scarfpin** was a large diamond, oddly set.

"Twenty years ago to-night," said the man, "I dined here at 'Big Joe' Brady's with Jimmy Wells, my best **chum**, and the finest **chap** in the world. He and I were raised here in New York, just like two brothers, together. I was

---

reassuringly [rìːəʃúˑəriŋ] adv.
마음 놓이게, 기운 차리게
appointment [əpɔ́intmənt] n.
약속

scarfpin [skάːrfpìn] n.
넥타이 핀

chum [tʃʌm] n.
친구
chap [tʃæp] n.
사내, 아이, 친구

> The man in the doorway struck a match and lit his cigar. The light showed a pale, square-jawed face with keen eyes, and a little white scar near his right eyebrow.

> correspond [kɔ̀:rəspánd, kár-/ kɔ̀rəspɔ́nd] v.
> 편지 왕래하다, 통신하다
> proposition [prɑ̀pəzíʃən / prɔ̀p-] n.
> 상대해야 할 사람 혹은 문제
> stanch [stɑːntʃ, stɔːntʃ] adj.
> 충실한, 견실한, 신뢰할 수 있는
> turn up:
> (사람이) 나타나다, 모습을 보이다

eighteen and Jimmy was twenty. The next morning I was to start for the West to make my fortune. You couldn't have dragged Jimmy out of New York; he thought it was the only place on earth. Well, we agreed that night that we would meet here again exactly twenty years from that date and time, no matter what our conditions might be or from what distance we might have to come. We figured that in twenty years each of us ought to have our destiny worked out and our fortunes made, whatever they were going to be."

"It sounds pretty interesting," said the policeman. "Rather a long time between meets, though, it seems to me. Haven't you heard from your friend since you left?"

"Well, yes, for a time we **corresponded**," said the other. "But after a year or two we lost track of each other. You see, the West is a pretty big **proposition**, and I kept hustling around over it pretty lively. But I know Jimmy will meet me here if he's alive, for he always was the truest, **stanchest** old chap in the world. He'll never forget. I came a thousand miles to stand in this door to-night, and it's worth it if my old partner **turns up**."

The waiting man pulled out a handsome watch, the lids of it set with small diamonds.

"Three minutes to ten," he announced. "It

was exactly ten o'clock when we parted here at the restaurant door."

"Did pretty well out West, didn't you?" asked the policeman.

"You bet! I hope Jimmy has done half as well. He was a kind of **plodder**, though, good fellow as he was. I've had to compete with some of the sharpest wits going to get my **pile**. A man gets in a groove in New York. It takes the West to put a razor-edge on him."

The policeman twirled his club and took a step or two.

"I'll **be on my way**. Hope your friend comes around all right. Going to **call time on** him **sharp**?"

"I should say not!" said the other. "I'll give him half an hour at least. If Jimmy is alive on earth he'll be here by that time. So long, officer."

"Good-night, sir," said the policeman, passing on along his beat, trying doors as he went.

There was now a fine, cold **drizzle** falling, and the wind had risen from its uncertain puffs into a steady blow. The few foot passengers **astir** in that **quarter** hurried dismally and silently along with coat collars turned high and pocketed hands. And in the door of the hardware store the man who had come a thousand miles to fill an appointment, uncertain

---

plodder [plɑdər / plɔdər] n.
터벅터벅 걷는 사람, 꾸준히 노력하는 사람
pile [pail] n.
큰돈, 재산

be on one's way:
떠나는, 길을 나서는
call time on:
끝내다, 마감하다
sharp [ʃɑːrp] adv.
꼭, 정각에

drizzle [drízl] n.
이슬비, 보슬비, 가랑비
astir [əstə́ːr] adj.
움직이는, 활동하는
quarter [kwɔ́ːrtər] n.
(도시의) 구역, 지구, 거리

almost to absurdity, with the friend of his youth, smoked his cigar and waited.

About twenty minutes he waited, and then a tall man in a long overcoat, with collar turned up to his ears, hurried across from the opposite side of the street. He went directly to the waiting man.

"Is that you, Bob?" he asked, doubtfully.

"Is that you, Jimmy Wells?" cried the man in the door.

"Bless my heart!" exclaimed the new arrival, grasping both the other's hands with his own. "It's Bob, sure as fate. I was certain I'd find you here if you were still in existence. Well, well, well!—twenty years is a long time. The old restaurant's gone, Bob; I wish it had lasted, so we could have had another dinner there. How has the West treated you, old man?"

"**Bully**; it has given me everything I asked it for. You've changed lots, Jimmy. I never thought you were so tall by two or three inches."

"Oh, I grew a bit after I was twenty."

"Doing well in New York, Jimmy?"

"**Moderately**. I have a position in one of the city departments. Come on, Bob; we'll go around to a place I know of, and have a good long talk about old times."

The two men started up the street, arm in arm. The man from the West, his **egotism**

---

bully [búli] adj.
훌륭한, 멋진, 근사한

moderately [mǽd-əritli / mɔ́d-] adv. 적당하게, 알맞게

egotism [í:goutìzəm, égou-] n.
자부, 자만심

outline [áutlàin] v.
요점을 말하다, 약술하다

glare [glɛər] n.
번쩍이는 빛, 눈부신 빛
gaze [geiz] v.
가만히 보다, 응시하다

Roman [róumən] n.
매부리코; a Roman nose
pug [pʌg] n.
사자코; pug nose
under arrest:
체포된, 구금된

on time:
정각에, 제시간에

enlarged by success, was beginning to **outline** the history of his career. The other, submerged in his overcoat, listened with interest.

At the corner stood a drug store, brilliant with electric lights. When they came into this **glare** each of them turned simultaneously to **gaze** upon the other's face.

The man from the West stopped suddenly and released his arm.

"You're not Jimmy Wells," he snapped. "Twenty years is a long time, but not long enough to change a man's nose from a **Roman** to a **pug**."

"It sometimes changes a good man into a bad one," said the tall man. "You've been **under arrest** for ten minutes, 'Silky' Bob. Chicago thinks you may have dropped over our way and wires us she wants to have a chat with you. Going quietly, are you? That's sensible. Now, before we go on to the station here's a note I was asked to hand to you. You may read it here at the window. It's from Patrolman Wells."

The man from the West unfolded the little piece of paper handed him. His hand was steady when he began to read, but it trembled a little by the time he had finished. The note was rather short.

Bob: I was at the appointed place **on time**. When you struck the match to light your cigar

plain-clothes man [plein-klouðzmən, -mæn] n.
사복 형사

I saw it was the face of the man wanted in Chicago. Somehow I couldn't do it myself, so I went around and got a **plain clothes man** to do the job.

JIMMY.

His hand was steady when he began to read, but it trembled a little by the time he had finished.

The Love-philtre of Ikey Schoenstein

bric-a-brac [bríkəbræ̀k] n.
골동품, 고물, 장식품
painkiller [péinkìlər] n.
진통제

The Blue Light Drug Store is downtown, between the Bowery and First Avenue, where the distance between the two streets is the shortest. The Blue Light does not consider that pharmacy is a thing of **bric-a-brac**, scent and ice-cream soda. If you ask it for **pain-killer** it will not give you a bonbon.

macerate [mǽsərèit] v.
담가서 부드럽게 하다
percolate [pə́:rkəlèit] v.
거르다, 여과하다
laudanum [lɔ́:d-ənəm] n.
아편제
paregoric [pæ̀rəgɔ́:rik / -gɔ́r-] n.
진통제

The Blue Light scorns the labour-saving arts of modern pharmacy. It **macerates** its opium and **percolates** its own **laudanum** and **paregoric**. To this day pills are made behind its tall prescription desk—pills rolled out on its own pill-tile, divided with a spatula, rolled

covey [kávi] n.
한 무리, 일행
hilarious [hiléəriəs, hai-] adj.
유쾌한, 즐거운, 법석대는

glacé [glæséi] adj.
(French) 반드럽고 윤이 나는
occult [əkʌ́lt, ákʌlt / ɔkʌ́lt] adj.
신비로운, 비밀의, 초자연적인
venerate [vénərèit] v.
존경하다, 공경하다, 받들어 모시다
coniform [kóunəfɔ̀:rm] adj.
원뿔꼴의

room [ru:m, rum] v.
묵다, 하숙하다
square [skwɛə:r] n.
(사방이 길로 둘러싸인) 시가의 한 구획
circumlocution [sə̀:rkəmloukjú:ʃən] n.
에둘러 말하기
tincture [tíŋktʃə:r] v.
착색하다, 물들이다
menstruum [ménstruəm] n.
용매(溶媒), 용제(溶劑)

with the finger and thumb, dusted with calcined magnesia and delivered in little round pasteboard pill-boxes. The store is on a corner about which **coveys** of ragged-plumed, **hilarious** children play and become candidates for the cough drops and soothing syrups that wait for them inside.

Ikey Schoenstein was the night clerk of the Blue Light and the friend of his customers. Thus it is on the East Side, where the heart of pharmacy is not **glacé**. There, as it should be, the druggist is a counsellor, a confessor, an adviser, an able and willing missionary and mentor whose learning is respected, whose **occult** wisdom is **venerated** and whose medicine is often poured, untasted, into the gutter. Therefore Ikey's **coniform**, be-spectacled nose and narrow, knowledge-bowed figure was well known in the vicinity of the Blue Light, and his advice and notice were much desired.

Ikey **roomed** and breakfasted at Mrs. Riddle's two **squares** away. Mrs. Riddle had a daughter named Rosy. The **circumlocution** has been in vain—you must have guessed it—Ikey adored Rosy. She **tinctured** all his thoughts; she was the compound extract of all that was chemically pure and officinal—the dispensatory contained nothing equal to her. But Ikey was timid, and his hopes remained insoluble in the **menstruum**

weak-kneed [wíːkníːd] adj.
나약한, 결단력이 없는
purblind [pə́ːrblàind] adj.
반(半)소경의, 눈이 침침한

a fly in the ointment:
옥에 티; 일이나 상황을 망치는 사람 또는 사물
pat [pæt] adj.
적절한, 안성맞춤인
trope [troup] n.
비유적 표현; 은유, 과장
outfielder [áutfìːldər] n.
외야수
off the bat:
즉시, 주저하지 않고

indomitable [indámətəbəl / -dɔ́m-] adj.
꺾이지 않는, 굴복하지 않는
good-natured [gúdnéitʃərd] adj. (마음씨가) 착한, 온후한
mortar [mɔ́ːrtəːr] n.
막자 사발
countenance [káuntənəns] n.
얼굴 표정, 안색

of his backwardness and fears. Behind his counter he was a superior being, calmly conscious of special knowledge and worth; outside he was a **weak-kneed**, **purblind**, motorman-cursed rambler, with ill-fitting clothes stained with chemicals and smelling of socotrine aloes and valerianate of ammonia.

The **fly in Ikey's ointment** (thrice welcome, **pat trope**!) was Chunk McGowan.

Mr. McGowan was also striving to catch the bright smiles tossed about by Rosy. But he was no **outfielder** as Ikey was; he picked them **off the bat**. At the same time he was Ikey's friend and customer, and often dropped in at the Blue Light Drug Store to have a bruise painted with iodine or get a cut rubber-plastered after a pleasant evening spent along the Bowery.

One afternoon McGowan drifted in in his silent, easy way, and sat, comely, smooth-faced, hard, **indomitable**, **good-natured**, upon a stool.

"Ikey," said he, when his friend had fetched his **mortar** and sat opposite, grinding gum benzoin to a powder, "get busy with your ear. It's drugs for me if you've got the line I need."

Ikey scanned the **countenance** of Mr. McGowan for the usual evidences of conflict, but found none.

"Take your coat off," he ordered. "I guess already that you have been stuck in the ribs

dago [déigou] n. (속어·경멸적) 남부 유럽 사람 (이탈리아·스페인·포르투갈 태생)	
diagnosis [dàiəgnóusis] n. 진단, 식별	
pestle [péstl] n. 막자, 공이	
getaway [gétəwèi] n. 도망, 도주	
affirmative [əfə́:rmətiv] n. 긍정, 확언	
stand up: 바람맞히다	
ill at ease: 불편한, 초조한, 불안한	
demeanor [dimí:nər] n. 태도, 품행	
false start: 부정 출발, 실패한 시도	

with a knife. I have many times told you those **Dagoes** would do you up."

Mr. McGowan smiled. "Not them," he said. "Not any Dagoes. But you've located the **diagnosis** all right enough—it's under my coat, near the ribs. Say! Ikey—Rosy and me are goin' to run away and get married to-night."

Ikey's left forefinger was doubled over the edge of the mortar, holding it steady. He gave it a wild rap with the **pestle**, but felt it not. Meanwhile Mr. McGowan's smile faded to a look of perplexed gloom.

"That is," he continued, "if she keeps in the notion until the time comes. We've been layin' pipes for the **getaway** for two weeks. One day she says she will; the same evenin' she says nixy. We've agreed on to-night, and Rosy's stuck to the **affirmative** this time for two whole days. But it's five hours yet till the time, and I'm afraid she'll **stand** me **up** when it comes to the scratch."

"You said you wanted drugs," remarked Ikey.

Mr. McGowan looked **ill at ease** and harassed—a condition opposed to his usual line of **demeanour**. He made a patent-medicine almanac into a roll and fitted it with unprofitable carefulness about his finger.

"I wouldn't have this double handicap make a **false start** to-night for a million," he said.

The Love-philtre of Ikey Schoenstein   57

"I've got a little **flat** up in Harlem all ready, with chrysanthemums on the table and a kettle ready to boil. And I've engaged a **pulpit pounder** to be ready at his house for us at 9.30. It's got to **come off**. And if Rosy don't change her mind again!"—Mr. McGowan ceased, a **prey** to his doubts.

"I don't see then yet," said Ikey, shortly, "what makes it that you talk of drugs, or what I can be doing about it."

"Old man Riddle don't like me a little bit," went on the **uneasy suitor**, **bent** upon **marshalling** his arguments. "For a week he hasn't let Rosy step outside the door with me. If it wasn't for losin' a boarder they'd have **bounced** me long ago. I'm makin' $20 a week and she'll never regret **flyin' the coop** with Chunk McGowan."

"You will excuse me, Chunk," said Ikey. "I must make a **prescription** that is to be called for soon."

"Say," said McGowan, looking up suddenly, "say, Ikey, ain't there a drug of some kind—some kind of powders that'll make a girl like you better if you give 'em to her?"

Ikey's lip beneath his nose curled with the scorn of superior **enlightenment**; but before he could answer, McGowan continued:

"Tim Lacy told me he got some once from a **croaker** uptown and fed 'em to his girl in

---

flat [flæt] n.
플랫식 주택
(각층에 1가구가 살게 만든 아파트)
pulpit pounder:
(속어) 목사
come off:
성공하다, 잘 되어 가다
prey [prei] n.
희생자, 피해자

uneasy [ʌníːzi] adj.
불안한, 꺼림칙한, 걱정되는
suitor [súːtər] n.
구혼자
bent [bent] adj.
열중한, 전념한
marshall [mɑ́ːrʃ-əl] v.
정리하다, 열거하다
bounce [bauns] v.
내쫓다, 내던지다
fly the coop:
도망치다
prescription [priskrípʃən] n.
처방, 처방전

enlightenment [enláitnmənt] n.
계발, 계몽, 교화

croaker [kroukər] n.
(속어) 의사

ace-high [éisháí] adj.
인기 있는, 아주 멋진

Ikey's lip beneath his nose curled with the scorn of superior enlightenment

renege [riníg, -ní:g] v.
약속을 어기다, 취소하다
mule [mju:l] n.
노새

foolishness [fú:liʃnis] n.
어리석음, 지각없음
balk [bɔ:k] v.
주저하다, 뒷걸음치다

soda water. From the very first dose he was **ace-hig**h and everybody else looked like thirty cents to her. They was married in less than two weeks."

Strong and simple was Chunk McGowan. A better reader of men than Ikey was could have seen that his tough frame was strung upon fine wires. Like a good general who was about to invade the enemy's territory he was seeking to guard every point against possible failure.

"I thought," went on Chunk hopefully, "that if I had one of them powders to give Rosy when I see her at supper to-night it might brace her up and keep her from **reneging** on the proposition to skip. I guess she don't need a **mule** team to drag her away, but women are better at coaching than they are at running bases. If the stuff'll work just for a couple of hours it'll do the trick."

"When is this **foolishness** of running away to be happening?" asked Ikey.

"Nine o'clock," said Mr. McGowan. "Supper's at seven. At eight Rosy goes to bed with a headache. At nine old Parvenzano lets me through to his back yard, where there's a board off Riddle's fence, next door. I go under her window and help her down the fire-escape. We've got to make it early on the preacher's account. It's all dead easy if Rosy don't **balk** when the flag drops. Can you fix me one of them powders, Ikey?"

Ikey Schoenstein rubbed his nose slowly.

"Chunk," said he, "it is of drugs of that nature that **pharmaceutists** must have much carefulness. To you alone of my **acquaintance** would I **intrust** a powder like that. But for you I shall make it, and you shall see how it makes Rosy to think of you."

Ikey went behind the prescription desk. There he crushed to a powder two soluble tablets, each containing a quarter of a grain of **morphia**. To them he added a little sugar of milk to increase the bulk, and folded the mixture neatly in a white paper. Taken by an adult this powder would insure several hours of heavy **slumber** without danger to the sleeper. This he handed to Chunk McGowan, telling him to administer it in a liquid if possible, and received the **hearty** thanks of the backyard Lochinvar.

The subtlety of Ikey's action becomes apparent upon **recital** of his subsequent move. He sent a messenger for Mr. Riddle and **disclosed** the plans of Mr. McGowan for **eloping** with Rosy. Mr. Riddle was a stout man, brick-dusty of complexion and sudden in action.

"Much **obliged**," he said, briefly, to Ikey. "The lazy Irish **loafer**! My own room's just above

---

pharmaceutist [fɑ̀ːrməsúːtist] n. 조제자, 약사(藥師)
acquaintance [əkwéintəns] n. 아는 사람, 친분관계
intrust [intrʌ́st] v. 맡기다, 위임하다

morphia [mɔ́ːrfiə] n. 모르핀
slumber [slʌ́mbəːr] n. 잠, 수면
hearty [hɑ́ːrti] adj. 진심의, 따뜻한

recital [risáitl] n. 이야기, 기술
disclose [disklóuz] v. 폭로하다, 누설하다
elope [ilóup] v. (남녀가) 눈이 맞아 달아나다
obliged [əbláidʒd] adj. 감사한, 고마운
loafer [lóufər] n. 게으름쟁이, 떠돌이

bridal [bráidl] adj.
신부의, 결혼식의
chaise [ʃeiz] n.
2륜 경마차

clutch [klʌtʃ] n.
지배, 수중, 손아귀
Morpheus [mɔ́:rfiəs, -fju:s] n.
모르페우스(잠의 신 Hypnos 의 아들로, 꿈의 신); 잠, 수면
bloodthirsty [blʌ́dθə̀:rsti] adj.
피에 굶주린, 잔인한, 살기등등한
discomfiture [diskʌ́mfitʃər] n.
실패, 좌절, 패배

lo [lou] int.
(고어) 보라 (Lo and behold)

pull off:
잘 해내다
Elysium [ilíziəm, -ʒəm] n.
엘리시움 (영웅·선인이 사후에 가는 낙원); 이상향, 최상의 행복
on time:
정각에, 제시간에
under the wire:
간신히, 겨우, 빠듯하게
stammer [stǽmə:r] v.
더듬으며 말하다

Rosy's. I'll just go up there myself after supper and load the shot-gun and wait. If he comes in my back yard he'll go away in a ambulance instead of a **bridal chaise**."

With Rosy held in the **clutches** of **Morpheus** for a many-hours deep slumber, and the **bloodthirsty** parent waiting, armed and forewarned, Ikey felt that his rival was close, indeed, upon **discomfiture**.

All night in the Blue Light Drug Store he waited at his duties for chance news of the tragedy, but none came.

At eight o'clock in the morning the day clerk arrived and Ikey started hurriedly for Mrs. Riddle's to learn the outcome. And, **lo**! as he stepped out of the store who but Chunk McGowan sprang from a passing street car and grasped his hand—Chunk McGowan with a victor's smile and flushed with joy.

"**Pulled** it **off**," said Chunk with **Elysium** in his grin. "Rosy hit the fire-escape **on time** to a second, and we was **under the wire** at the Reverend's at 9.30 ¼. She's up at the flat—she cooked eggs this mornin' in a blue kimono—Lord! how lucky I am! You must pace up some day, Ikey, and feed with us. I've got a job down near the bridge, and that's where I'm heading for now."

"The—the—powder?" **stammered** Ikey.

on the square:
정직하게, 곧이곧대로
hocus-pocus [hóukəspóukəs] n.
속임수
thoroughbred [θə́:roubrèd] n.
출신이 좋은 사람, 기품 있는 사람
lamp [læmp] n.
(속어) 눈(eyes)
party [pá:rti] n.
(문제의) 사람, 인물
dump [dʌmp] v.
떨구다, 부리다

"Oh, that stuff you gave me!" said Chunk, broadening his grin; "well, it was this way. I sat down at the supper table last night at Riddle's, and I looked at Rosy, and I says to myself, 'Chunk, if you get the girl get her **on the square**—don't try any **hocus-pocus** with a **thoroughbred** like her.' And I keeps the paper you give me in my pocket. And then my **lamps** fall on another **party** present, who, I says to myself, is failin' in a proper affection toward his comin' son-in-law, so I watches my chance and **dumps** that powder in old man Riddle's coffee—see?"

..., and I looked at Rosy, and I says to myself, 'Chunk, if you get the girl get her on the square—don't try any hocus-pocus with a thoroughbred like her.' And I keeps the paper you give me in my pocket. And then my lamps fall on another party present, ...

Between Rounds

almanac [ɔ́:lmənæk] n.
달력, 역서
heydey [héidèi] n.
전성기
hay fever:
꽃가룻병, 고초열(꽃가루로 인한 알레르기성 염증)
pinochle [pí:nəkl, -nʌkl] n.
카드놀이의 일종

stoop [stu:p] n.
현관 입구의 계단, 포치

The May moon shone bright upon the private boarding-house of Mrs. Murphy. By reference to the **almanac** a large amount of territory will be discovered upon which its rays also fell. Spring was in its **heydey**, with **hay fever** soon to follow. The parks were green with new leaves and buyers for the Western and Southern trade. Flowers and summer-resort agents were blowing; the air and answers to Lawson were growing milder; hand-organs, fountains and **pinochle** were playing everywhere.

The windows of Mrs. Murphy's boarding-house were open. A group of boarders were seated on the high **stoop** upon round, flat mats like German pancakes.

Between Rounds 63

In one of the second-floor front windows Mrs. McCaskey awaited her husband. Supper was cooling on the table. Its heat went into Mrs. McCaskey.

At nine Mr. McCaskey came. He carried his coat on his arm and his pipe in his teeth; and he apologised for disturbing the boarders on the steps as he selected spots of stone between them on which to set his size 9, width Ds.

As he opened the door of his room he received a surprise. Instead of the usual stove-lid or potato-masher for him to **dodge**, came only words.

Mr. McCaskey **reckoned** that the **benign** May moon had softened the breast of his **spouse**.

"I heard ye," came the oral substitutes for kitchenware. "Ye can apollygise to **riff-raff** of the streets for settin' yer **unhandy** feet on the tails of their frocks, but ye'd walk on the neck of yer wife the length of a clothesline without so much as a 'Kiss me fut,' and I'm sure it's that long from rubberin' out the windy for ye and the **victuals** cold such as there's money to buy after drinkin' up yer wages at Gallegher's every Saturday evenin', and the gas man here twice to-day for his."

"Woman!" said Mr. McCaskey, **dashing** his coat and hat upon a chair, "the noise of ye is an insult to me appetite. When ye run down

---

dodge [dɑdʒ / dɔdʒ] v.
피하다, 비키다, 모면하다

reckon [rékən] v.
생각하다, 간주하다
benign [bináin] adj.
자비로운, 다정한, 온화한
spouse [spaus, spauz] n.
배우자, 남편, 아내
riffraff [rífræf] n.
하층민
unhandy [ʌnhǽndi] adj.
서투른, 거북한, 불편한
victual [vítl] n.
음식, 양식

dash [dæʃ] v.
내던지다, 부딪뜨리다

mortar [mɔ́:rtə:r] n.
모르타르, 회반죽
acrimony [ǽkrəmòuni] n.
표독스러움, 신랄함
dissent [disént] n.
이의, 의견 차이
see to (someone or something):
주의깊게 돌보다, 확실히 하다

barometer [bərámitər / -rɔ́m-] n.
기압계, 바로미터
foretell [fɔ:rtél] v.
예언하다, 예고하다
crockery [krákəri / krɔ́k-] n.
도자기, 토기

novice [návis / nɔ́v-] n.
신참자, 초심자
repartee [rèpɑ:rtí:] n.
재치 있는 즉답
entrée [á:ntrei] n.
앙트레; 메인 요리 또는 메인 요리 이전에 나오는 음식
retort [ritɔ́:rrt] v.
받아넘기다, 응수하다

politeness ye take the **mortar** from between the bricks of the foundations of society. 'Tis no more than exercisin' the **acrimony** of a gentleman when ye ask the **dissent** of ladies blockin' the way for steppin' between them. Will ye bring the pig's face of ye out of the windy and **see to** the food?"

Mrs. McCaskey arose heavily and went to the stove. There was something in her manner that warned Mr. McCaskey. When the corners of her mouth went down suddenly like a **barometer** it usually **foretold** a fall of **crockery** and tinware.

"Pig's face, is it?" said Mrs. McCaskey, and hurled a stewpan full of bacon and turnips at her lord.

Mr. McCaskey was no **novice** at **repartee**. He knew what should follow the **entrée**. On the table was a roast sirloin of pork, garnished with shamrocks. He **retorted** with this, and drew the appropriate return of a bread pudding in an earthen dish. A hunk of Swiss cheese accurately thrown by her husband struck Mrs. McCaskey below one eye. When she replied with a well-aimed coffee-pot full of a hot, black, semi-fragrant liquid the battle, according to courses, should have ended.

But Mr. McCaskey was no 50-cent *table d'hôter*. Let cheap Bohemians consider coffee

faux pas [fóupá:] n.
실수, 과실, 실책
finger bowl:
식탁에서 손가락을 씻는 그릇
matrimonial [mӕtrəmóuniəl]
adj. 결혼의, 부부의
adversary [ӕdvərsèri / -səri] n.
적, 상대
cordial [kɔ́:rdʒəl / -diəl] n.
기운나게 하는 것(음료, 음식 등)
gastronomical [gӕstrəná-mikəl] adj.
요리의, 미식의
duel [djú:əl] n.
결투
armistice [á:rməstis] n.
휴전, 정전

row [rau] n.
말다툼, 언쟁, 소동

betoken [bitóukən] v.
나타내다
dire [daiər] adj.
무서운, 비참한, 절박한
extremity [ikstréməti] n.
막다름, 궁지

the end, if they would. Let them make that *faux pas*. He was foxier still. **Finger-bowls** were not beyond the compass of his experience. They were not to be had in the Pension Murphy; but their equivalent was at hand. Triumphantly he sent the granite-ware wash basin at the head of his **matrimonial adversary**. Mrs. McCaskey dodged in time. She reached for a flatiron, with which, as a sort of **cordial**, she hoped to bring the **gastronomical duel** to a close. But a loud, wailing scream downstairs caused both her and Mr. McCaskey to pause in a sort of involuntary **armistice**.

On the sidewalk at the corner of the house Policeman Cleary was standing with one ear upturned, listening to the crash of household utensils.

"'Tis Jawn McCaskey and his missis at it again," meditated the policeman. "I wonder shall I go up and stop the **row**. I will not. Married folks they are; and few pleasures they have. 'T will not last long. Sure, they'll have to borrow more dishes to keep it up with."

And just then came the loud scream below stairs, **betokening** fear or **dire extremity**. "'Tis probably the cat," said Policeman Cleary, and walked hastily in the other direction.

The boarders on the steps were fluttered. Mr. Toomey, an insurance solicitor by birth and an investigator by profession, went inside to analyse the scream. He returned with the news that Mrs. Murphy's little boy, Mike, was lost. Following the messenger, out bounced Mrs. Murphy—two hundred pounds in tears and hysterics, clutching the air and howling to the sky for the loss of thirty pounds of freckles and mischief. **Bathos**, truly; but Mr. Toomey sat down at the side of Miss Purdy, millinery, and their hands came together in sympathy. The two old maids, Misses Walsh, who complained every day about the noise in the halls, inquired immediately if anybody had looked behind the clock.

Major Grigg, who sat by his fat wife on the top step, arose and buttoned his coat. "The little one lost?" he exclaimed. "I will **scour** the city." His wife never allowed him out after dark. But now she said: "Go, Ludovic!" in a baritone voice. "Whoever can look upon that mother's **grief** without springing to her **relief** has a heart of stone." "Give me some thirty or—sixty cents, my love," said the Major. "Lost children sometimes **stray** far. I may need **carfares**."

Old man Denny, hall room, fourth floor back, who sat on the lowest step, trying to read a paper by the street lamp, turned over a page to follow up the article about the carpenters'

Between Rounds   67

strike. Mrs. Murphy shrieked to the moon: "Oh, ar-r-Mike, f'r Gawd's sake, where is me little bit av a boy?"

"When'd ye see him last?" asked old man Denny, with one eye on the report of the Building Trades League.

"Oh," **wailed** Mrs. Murphy, "'twas yisterday, or maybe four hours ago! I dunno. But it's lost he is, me little boy Mike. He was playin' on the **sidewalk** only this mornin'—or was it Wednesday? I'm that busy with work, 'tis hard to keep up with dates. But I've looked the house over from top to **cellar**, and it's gone he is. Oh, for the love av Hiven——"

Silent, grim, **colossal**, the big city has ever stood against its **revilers**. They call it hard as iron; they say that no pulse of pity beats in its bosom; they compare its streets with lonely forests and deserts of **lava**. But beneath the hard crust of the lobster is found a **delectable** and **luscious** food. Perhaps a different **simile** would have been wiser. Still, nobody should **take offence**. We would call no one a lobster without good and sufficient claws.

No **calamity** so touches the common heart of humanity as does the straying of a little child. Their feet are so uncertain and feeble; the ways are so steep and strange.

Major Griggs hurried down to the corner,

---

wail [weil] n.
울부짖다, 통곡하다
sidewalk [sáidwɔ̀:k] n.
보도, 인도
cellar [sélər] n.
지하실, 저장실

colossal [kəlásəl / -lɔ́sl] adj.
막대한, 거대한
reviler [riváilər] n.
욕쟁이, 험담가
lava [láːvə, lǽvə] n.
용암, 화산암
delectable [diléktəbəl] adj.
즐거운, 기쁜, 유쾌한
luscious [lʌ́ʃəs] adj.
감미로운, 달콤한
simile [síməliː] n.
직유(直喩)
take offence:
화를 내다
calamity [kəlǽməti] n.
재난, 불행, 비운

servitor [sə́:rvətə:r] n.
점원, 종업원

They call it hard as iron; they say that no pulse of pity beats in its bosom; they compare its streets with lonely forests and deserts of lava. But beneath the hard crust of the lobster is found a delectable and luscious food.

dashing [dǽʃiŋ] adj.
기세 좋은, 팔팔한, 씩씩한
befall[bifɔ́:l] v.
발생하다, 일어나다

arbitration [à:rbitréiʃən] n.
중재, 조정
second wind:
(원기나 기력의) 회복
outcry [áutkrài] n.
절규, 외침

and up the avenue into Billy's place. "Gimme a rye-high," he said to the **servitor**. "Haven't seen a bow-legged, dirty-faced little devil of a six-year-old lost kid around here anywhere, have you?"

Mr. Toomey retained Miss Purdy's hand on the steps. "Think of that dear little babe," said Miss Purdy, "lost from his mother's side—perhaps already fallen beneath the iron hoofs of galloping steeds—oh, isn't it dreadful?"

"Ain't that right?" agreed Mr. Toomey, squeezing her hand. "Say I start out and help look for um!"

"Perhaps," said Miss Purdy, "you should. But, oh, Mr. Toomey, you are so **dashing**—so reckless—suppose in your enthusiasm some accident should **befall** you, then what—"

Old man Denny read on about the **arbitration** agreement, with one finger on the lines.

In the second floor front Mr. and Mrs. McCaskey came to the window to recover their **second wind**. Mr. McCaskey was scooping turnips out of his vest with a crooked forefinger, and his lady was wiping an eye that the salt of the roast pork had not benefited. They heard the **outcry** below, and thrust their heads out of the window.

"'Tis little Mike is lost," said Mrs. McCaskey, in a hushed voice, "the beautiful, little, trouble-making angel of a **gossoon**!"

"The bit of a boy mislaid?" said Mr. McCaskey, leaning out of the window. "Why, now, that's bad enough, entirely. The childer, they be different. If 't was a woman I'd be willin', for they leave peace behind 'em when they go."

Disregarding the **thrust**, Mrs. McCaskey caught her husband's arm.

"Jawn," she said, sentimentally, "Missis Murphy's little bye is lost. 'Tis a great city for losing little boys. Six years old he was. Jawn, 'tis the same age our little bye would have been if we had had one six years ago."

"We never did," said Mr. McCaskey, lingering with the fact.

"But if we had, Jawn, think what sorrow would be in our hearts this night, with our little Phelan run away and stolen in the city nowheres at all."

"Ye talk foolishness," said Mr. McCaskey. "'Tis Pat he would be named, after me old father in Cantrim."

"Ye lie!" said Mrs. McCaskey, without anger. "Me brother was worth tin dozen bog-trotting McCaskeys. After him would the bye be named." She leaned over the window-sill and looked down at the hurrying and bustle below.

"Jawn," said Mrs. McCaskey, softly, "I'm sorry I was **hasty** wid ye."

---

gossoon [gɑsúːn / gɔs-] n.
소년, 젊은이

disregard [dìsrigáːrd] v.
무시하다, 등한시하다

thrust [θrʌst] n.
혹평, 비난, 빈정대기

hasty [héisti] adj.
조급한, 경솔한, 성마른

"'Twas hasty puddin', as ye say," said her husband, "and hurry-up turnips and get-a-move-on-ye coffee. 'Twas what ye could call a quick lunch, all right, and tell no lie."

Mrs. McCaskey slipped her arm inside her husband's and took his rough hand in hers.

"Listen at the cryin' of poor Mrs. Murphy," she said. "'Tis an awful thing for a bit of a bye to be lost in this great big city. If 'twas our little Phelan, Jawn, I'd be breakin' me heart."

Awkwardly Mr. McCaskey withdrew his hand. But he laid it around the nearing shoulder of his wife.

"'Tis foolishness, of course," said he, roughly, "but I'd **be cut up** some meself if our little—Pat was kidnapped or anything. But there never was any childer for us. Sometimes I've been ugly and hard with ye, Judy. Forget it."

They leaned together, and looked down at the heart-drama being acted below.

Long they sat thus. People **surged** along the sidewalk, crowding, questioning, filling the air with rumours, and **inconsequent surmises**. Mrs. Murphy plowed back and forth in their midst, like a soft mountain down which plunged an audible cataract of tears. **Couriers** came and went.

Loud voices and a renewed **uproar** were raised in front of the boarding-house.

---

be cut up:
슬픔에 빠지다, 마음을 상하다

surge [səːrdʒ] v.
파동치다, 밀려오다
inconsequent [inkánsikwènt, -kwənt / -kɔ́nsikwənt] adj.
비논리적인, 일관성이 없는
surmise [sərmáiz] n.
추측, 짐작
courier [kúriər, kə́ːri-] n.
급사, 메신저
uproar [ʌ́prɔ̀ːr] n.
소란, 소동

Between Rounds 71

"What's up now, Judy?" asked Mr. McCaskey.

"'Tis Missis Murphy's voice," said Mrs. McCaskey, **harking**. "She says she's after finding little Mike asleep behind the roll of old linoleum under the bed in her room."

Mr. McCaskey laughed loudly.

"That's yer Phelan," he shouted, **sardonically**. "Divil a bit would a Pat have done that trick. If the bye we never had is strayed and stole, by the powers, call him Phelan, and see him hide out under the bed like a **mangy pup**."

Mrs. McCaskey arose heavily, and went toward the dish closet, with the corners of her mouth drawn down.

Policeman Cleary came back around the corner as the crowd **dispersed**. Surprised, he upturned an ear toward the McCaskey apartment, where the crash of irons and chinaware and the ring of hurled kitchen utensils seemed as loud as before. Policeman Cleary took out his **timepiece**.

"By the deported snakes!" he exclaimed, "Jawn McCaskey and his lady have been fightin' for an hour and a quarter by the watch. The missis could give him forty pounds weight. Strength to his arm."

Policeman Cleary strolled back around the corner.

Old man Denny folded his paper and hurried

---

hark [hɑ́ːrk] v.
귀 기울이다

sardonically [sɑːrdɑ́nikəli/
-dɔ́nikəli] adv.
빈정대듯이, 야유하듯이
mangy [méindʒi] adj.
누추한, 더러운
pup [pʌp] n.
강아지

disperse [dispə́ːrs] v.
흩어지다, 헤어지다
timepiece [táimpìːs] n.
시계

up the steps just as Mrs. Murphy was about to lock the door for the night.

The Cop and the Anthem

honk [hɔːŋk, hɑŋk, / hɔŋk] v.
(기러기가) 울다
at hand:
손이 닿는 곳에, 가까이에, 머지 않아

Jack Frost:
(의인화된) 서리, 혹한
denizen [dénəzən] n.
주민, 거주자
footman [fútmən] n.
종복(從僕), 하인, 마부

On his bench in Madison Square Soapy moved uneasily. When wild geese **honk** high of nights, and when women without sealskin coats grow kind to their husbands, and when Soapy moves uneasily on his bench in the park, you may know that winter is near **at hand**.

A dead leaf fell in Soapy's lap. That was **Jack Frost**'s card. Jack is kind to the regular **denizens** of Madison Square, and gives fair warning of his annual call. At the corners of four streets he hands his pasteboard to the North Wind, **footman** of the mansion of All

cognizant [kágnəzənt / kɔ́g-] adj.
인식하고 있는, 인식력 있는
rigor, rigour [rígə:r] n.
어려움, (한서(寒暑)의) 혹독함

soporific [sàpərífik, sòupə-] adj.
졸리게 하는, 최면의
Boreas [bɔ́:riəs] n.
보레아스, 북풍의 신; 북풍, 삭풍
bluecoat [blú:kòut] n.
청색 옷을 입은 사람; 경찰관

hegira [hidʒáirə, hédʒərə] n.
헤지라(Mecca에서 Medina로의 Mohammed의 도피; 622년), 도피, 이주
repulse [ripʌ́ls] v.
격퇴하다, 물리치다
loom [lu:m] v.
어렴풋이 보이다, 중대하게 느껴지다

Three months of assured board and bed and congenial company, safe from Boreas and bluecoats, seemed to Soapy the essence of things desirable.

Outdoors, so that the inhabitants thereof may make ready.

Soapy's mind became **cognizant** of the fact that the time had come for him to resolve himself into a singular Committee of Ways and Means to provide against the coming **rigour**. And therefore he moved uneasily on his bench.

The hibernatorial ambitions of Soapy were not of the highest. In them there were no considerations of Mediterranean cruises, of **soporific** Southern skies or drifting in the Vesuvian Bay. Three months on the Island was what his soul craved. Three months of assured board and bed and congenial company, safe from **Boreas** and **bluecoats**, seemed to Soapy the essence of things desirable.

For years the hospitable Blackwell's had been his winter quarters. Just as his more fortunate fellow New Yorkers had bought their tickets to Palm Beach and the Riviera each winter, so Soapy had made his humble arrangements for his annual **hegira** to the Island. And now the time was come. On the previous night three Sabbath newspapers, distributed beneath his coat, about his ankles and over his lap, had failed to **repulse** the cold as he slept on his bench near the spurting fountain in the ancient square. So the Island **loomed** big and timely in Soapy's mind. He scorned the provisions

The Cop and the Anthem 75

made in the name of charity for the city's dependents. In Soapy's opinion the Law was more **benign** than **Philanthropy**. There was an endless round of institutions, **municipal** and **eleemosynary**, on which he might set out and receive lodging and food accordant with the simple life. But to one of Soapy's proud spirit the gifts of charity are encumbered. If not in coin you must pay in humiliation of spirit for every benefit received at the hands of philanthropy. As Caesar had his Brutus, every bed of charity must have its toll of a bath, every loaf of bread its compensation of a private and personal **inquisition**. Wherefore it is better to be a guest of the law, which though conducted by rules, does not **meddle** unduly with a gentleman's private affairs.

Soapy, having decided to go to the Island, at once set about accomplishing his desire. There were many easy ways of doing this. The pleasantest was to dine luxuriously at some expensive restaurant; and then, after declaring **insolvency**, be handed over quietly and without **uproar** to a policeman. An **accommodating magistrate** would do the rest.

Soapy left his bench and strolled out of the square and across the level sea of asphalt, where Broadway and Fifth Avenue flow together. Up Broadway he turned, and halted at a

---

benign [bináin] adj.
자비로운, 다정한, 온화한
philanthropy [filǽnərəpi] n.
박애, 인자, 자선
municipal [mju:nísəp-əl] adj.
지방 자치체의, 시정의,
eleemosynary [èlimásənèri,
-máz / èlii:mɔ́sənəri] adj.
(은혜를) 베푸는, 자선의
inquisition [ìnkwəzíʃən] n.
조사, 심문, 심사
meddle [médl] v.
참견하다, 간섭하다

insolvency [insálvənsi / -sɔ́l-] n.
(빚의) 반제(返濟)불능, 채무
초과, 파산(상태)
uproar [ápró:r] n.
소란, 소동
accommodating [əkámədèitiŋ
/ əkɔ́m-] adj.
잘 돌보아주는, 친절한, 마음씨
가 좋은
magistrate [mǽdʒəstrèit,-trit] n.
법관, 판사

choice [tʃɔis] adj.
고르고 고른, 뛰어난
protoplasm [próutouplæ̀zəm] n.
원형질
four-in-hand [fɔ́:rinhæ̀nd] n.
(보통으로 매는) 넥타이
mallard [mǽlərd] n.
청둥오리
Chablis [ʃǽbli(:), ʃɑ:blí:] n.
샤블리(프랑스 Burgundy산의 백포도주)
Camembert [kǽməmbɛ̀ər(-)] n.
카망베르(프랑스산의 치즈)
demitasse [démitæ̀s, -tɑ̀:s] n.
작은 잔의 블랙커피 또는 에스프레소

decadent [dékədənt, dikéidənt] adj. 쇠퇴해가는, 타락으로 향하는
ignoble [ignóubəl] adj.
비천한, 열등한

glittering café, where are gathered together nightly the **choicest** products of the grape, the silkworm and the **protoplasm**.

Soapy had confidence in himself from the lowest button of his vest upward. He was shaven, and his coat was decent and his neat black, ready-tied **four-in-hand** had been presented to him by a lady missionary on Thanksgiving Day. If he could reach a table in the restaurant unsuspected success would be his. The portion of him that would show above the table would raise no doubt in the waiter's mind. A roasted **mallard** duck, thought Soapy, would be about the thing—with a bottle of **Chablis**, and then **Camembert**, a **demi-tasse** and a cigar. One dollar for the cigar would be enough. The total would not be so high as to call forth any supreme manifestation of revenge from the café management; and yet the meat would leave him filled and happy for the journey to his winter refuge.

But as Soapy set foot inside the restaurant door the head waiter's eye fell upon his frayed trousers and **decadent** shoes. Strong and ready hands turned him about and conveyed him in silence and haste to the sidewalk and averted the **ignoble** fate of the menaced mallard.

Soapy turned off Broadway. It seemed that his route to the coveted island was not to be

The Cop and the Anthem 77

epicurean [èpikjurí:ən] adj.
에피쿠로스의, 쾌락주의의, 식도락의
limbo [límbou] n.
구치소, 교도소
conspicuous [kənspíkjuəs] adj.
눈에 잘 띄는
cobblestone [kábəlstòun / kɔ́bəlstòun] n.
조약돌, 자갈
dash [dæʃ] v.
내던지다, 부딪뜨리다

figure out:
알다, 이해하다
sarcasm [sá:rkæz-əm] n.
빈정댐, 비꼼, 풍자

parley [pá:rli] v.
이야기를 나누다, 교섭하다
minion [mínjən] n.
(권력자의) 앞잡이, 부하
take to (one's) heels:
도망치다

cater [kéitər] v.
음식, 서비스 등을 제공하다, 요구에 응하다
napery [néipəri] n.
식탁용의 흰 천; 테이블보, 냅킨 등의 총칭

an **epicurean** one. Some other way of entering **limbo** must be thought of.

At a corner of Sixth Avenue electric lights and cunningly displayed wares behind plate-glass made a shop window **conspicuous**. Soapy took a **cobblestone** and **dashed** it through the glass. People came running around the corner, a policeman in the lead. Soapy stood still, with his hands in his pockets, and smiled at the sight of brass buttons.

"Where's the man that done that?" inquired the officer excitedly.

"Don't you **figure out** that I might have had something to do with it?" said Soapy, not without **sarcasm**, but friendly, as one greets good fortune.

The policeman's mind refused to accept Soapy even as a clue. Men who smash windows do not remain to **parley** with the law's **minions**. They **take to their heels**. The policeman saw a man half way down the block running to catch a car. With drawn club he joined in the pursuit. Soapy, with disgust in his heart, loafed along, twice unsuccessful.

On the opposite side of the street was a restaurant of no great pretensions. It **catered** to large appetites and modest purses. Its crockery and atmosphere were thick; its soup and **napery** thin. Into this place Soapy took his

telltale [téltèil] adj.
누설하는, 나타내는
flapjack [flǽpdʒæk] n.
핫케이크
betray [bitréi] v.
드러내다, 나타내다

youse [juːz, jəz] pron.
you (usually more than one person)

callous [kǽləs] adj.
무감각한, 냉담한
pitch [pitʃ] v.
던지다, 내던지다, 팽개치다
rosy [róuzi] adj.
장밋빛의, 유망한, 밝은

woo [wuː] v.
구애하다, 추구하다
fatuously [fǽtʃuəsli] adv.
멍청하게, 얼빠진 듯이
cinch [sintʃ] n.
확실한 일, 편한 일
guise [gaiz] n.
외관, 모습, 겉보기
sprightly [spráitli] adj.
기운찬, 쾌활한, 명랑한

accusive shoes and **telltale** trousers without challenge. At a table he sat and consumed beefsteak, **flapjacks**, doughnuts and pie. And then to the waiter he **betrayed** the fact that the minutest coin and himself were strangers.

"Now, get busy and call a cop," said Soapy. "And don't keep a gentleman waiting."

"No cop for **youse**," said the waiter, with a voice like butter cakes and an eye like the cherry in a Manhattan cocktail. "Hey, Con!"

Neatly upon his left ear on the **callous** pavement two waiters **pitched** Soapy. He arose, joint by joint, as a carpenter's rule opens, and beat the dust from his clothes. Arrest seemed but a **rosy** dream. The Island seemed very far away. A policeman who stood before a drug store two doors away laughed and walked down the street.

Five blocks Soapy travelled before his courage permitted him to **woo** capture again. This time the opportunity presented what he **fatuously** termed to himself a "**cinch**." A young woman of a modest and pleasing **guise** was standing before a show window gazing with **sprightly** interest at its display of shaving mugs and inkstands, and two yards from the window a large policeman of severe demeanour leaned against a water plug.

It was Soapy's design to assume the role of

The Cop and the Anthem 79

the despicable and execrated "**masher**." The refined and elegant appearance of his victim and the **contiguity** of the **conscientious** cop encouraged him to believe that he would soon feel the pleasant official clutch upon his arm that would insure his winter quarters on the right little, tight little isle.

Soapy straightened the lady missionary's ready-made tie, dragged his shrinking cuffs into the open, set his hat at a killing **cant** and **sidled** toward the young woman. He made eyes at her, was taken with sudden coughs and "hems," smiled, **smirked** and went **brazenly** through the **impudent** and **contemptible litany** of the "masher." With half an eye Soapy saw that the policeman was watching him fixedly. The young woman moved away a few steps, and again bestowed her absorbed attention upon the shaving mugs. Soapy followed, boldly stepping to her side, raised his hat and said:

"Ah there, Bedelia! Don't you want to come and play in my yard?"

The policeman was still looking. The persecuted young woman had but to **beckon** a finger and Soapy would be practically **en route** for his insular **haven**. Already he imagined he could feel the cozy warmth of the **station-house**. The young woman faced him and, stretching out a hand, caught Soapy's coat sleeve.

---

masher [mǽʃəːr] n.
(속어) 난봉꾼, 플레이보이
contiguity [kɑ̀ntəgjúː)iti / kɔ̀n-]
n. 접촉, 접근, 인접
conscientious [kɑ̀nʃiénʃəs] adj.
양심적인, 성실한, 진지한

cant [kænt] n.
경사, 기욺
sidle [sáidl] v.
옆걸음질치다, 가만가만 다가가다
smirk [sməːrk] v.
능글맞게 웃다, 부자연한 웃음을 웃다
brazenly [bréizənli] adv.
뻔뻔스럽게, 철면피하게
impudent [ímpjədənt] adj.
뻔뻔스러운, 건방진, 버릇없는
contemptible [kəntémptəbəl]
adj. 멸시할 만한, 비열한
litany [lítəni] n.
장황한 이야기

beckon [békən] v.
(손짓, 고갯짓, 몸짓으로) 신호하다, 부르다
en route [ɑːnrúːt] adj.
도중의, 가는 길의
haven [héivən] n.
안식처, 피난처
station house:
경찰서

pail [peil] n.
버킷, 한 통의 분량
suds [sʌdz] n.
(속어) 맥주
doom [du:m] v.
~할 운명에 있다

libretto [librétou] n.
리브레토, 오페라 가사, 대본
enchantment [entʃǽntmənt, -tʃɑ́:nt-] n.
매혹, 마법, 마술
render [réndə:r] v.
~이 되게 하다
immune [imjú:n] adj.
면한, 면제된
transplendent [trænsplendənt] adj.
가장 화려한
catch at a straw:
아무리 하찮은 기회라도 놓치지 않다; 지푸라기라도 잡다 (a drowning man will catch at a straw)
disorderly conduct:
풍기문란
gibberish [dʒíbəriʃ, gíb-] n.
뭐가 뭔지 알 수 없는 말; 횡설수설
welkin [wélkin] n.
(고어·시어) 창공, 하늘

"Sure, Mike," she said joyfully, "if you'll blow me to a **pail** of **suds**. I'd have spoke to you sooner, but the cop was watching."

With the young woman playing the clinging ivy to his oak Soapy walked past the policeman overcome with gloom. He seemed **doomed** to liberty.

At the next corner he shook off his companion and ran. He halted in the district where by night are found the lightest streets, hearts, vows and **librettos**. Women in furs and men in greatcoats moved gaily in the wintry air. A sudden fear seized Soapy that some dreadful **enchantment** had **rendered** him **immune** to arrest. The thought brought a little of panic upon it, and when he came upon another policeman lounging grandly in front of a **transplendent** theatre he **caught at** the immediate **straw** of "**disorderly conduct.**"

On the sidewalk Soapy began to yell drunken **gibberish** at the top of his harsh voice. He danced, howled, raved and otherwise disturbed the **welkin**.

The policeman twirled his club, turned his back to Soapy and remarked to a citizen.

"'Tis one of them Yale lads celebratin' the goose egg they give to the Hartford College. Noisy; but no harm. We've instructions to lave them be."

disconsolate [diskánsəlit / -kón-] adj.
불행한, 절망적인
unavailing [ʌ̀nəvéiliŋ] adj.
효과 없는, 헛된
racket [rǽkit] n.
큰 소리, 소음, 야단 법석
unattainable [ʌ̀nətéinəbəl] adj.
도달하기 어려운, 성취할 수 없는
Arcadia [ɑːrkéidiə] n.
아르카디아(옛 그리스 산속의 이상향(理想鄕))

sneer [sniə:r] v.
빈정대다
add insult to ~:
"add insult to injury"(상처에 모욕을 가하다; 설상가상이 다)를 고쳐 씀
petit larceny(petty larceny): 경절도죄
presentiment [prizéntəmənt] n. 예감, 육감

opera cloak:
야회용 여성 외투

Disconsolate, Soapy ceased his **unavailing racket**. Would never a policeman lay hands on him? In his fancy the Island seemed an **unattainable Arcadia**. He buttoned his thin coat against the chilling wind.

In a cigar store he saw a well-dressed man lighting a cigar at a swinging light. His silk umbrella he had set by the door on entering. Soapy stepped inside, secured the umbrella and sauntered off with it slowly. The man at the cigar light followed hastily.

"My umbrella," he said, sternly.

"Oh, is it?" **sneered** Soapy, **adding insult to petit larceny**. "Well, why don't you call a policeman? I took it. Your umbrella! Why don't you call a cop? There stands one on the corner."

The umbrella owner slowed his steps. Soapy did likewise, with a **presentiment** that luck would again run against him. The policeman looked at the two curiously.

"Of course," said the umbrella man—"that is—well, you know how these mistakes occur—I—if it's your umbrella I hope you'll excuse me—I picked it up this morning in a restaurant—If you recognise it as yours, why—I hope you'll—"

"Of course it's mine," said Soapy, viciously.

The ex-umbrella man retreated. The policeman hurried to assist a tall blonde in an **opera**

cloak across the street in front of a street car that was approaching two blocks away.

Soapy walked eastward through a street damaged by improvements. He hurled the umbrella wrathfully into an excavation. He muttered against the men who wear helmets and carry clubs. Because he wanted to fall into their clutches, they seemed to regard him as a king who could do no wrong.

At length Soapy reached one of the avenues to the east where the **glitter** and **turmoil** was but faint. He set his face down this toward Madison Square, for the **homing instinct** survives even when the home is a park bench.

But on an unusually quiet corner Soapy came to a standstill. Here was an old church, **quaint** and rambling and gabled. Through one violet-stained window a soft light glowed, where, no doubt, the organist loitered over the keys, making sure of his mastery of the coming **Sabbath anthem**. For there drifted out to Soapy's ears sweet music that caught and held him transfixed against the convolutions of the iron fence.

The moon was above, lustrous and serene; vehicles and pedestrians were few; sparrows twittered sleepily in the eaves—for a little while the scene might have been a country churchyard. And the anthem that the organist

---

at length:
드디어, 마침내
glitter [glítər] n.
반짝임, 빛남
turmoil [tə́ːrmɔil] n.
소동, 혼란, 불안
homing instinct:
귀소 본능
quaint [kweint] adj.
예스러운, 고아한
Sabbath [sǽbəə] n.
안식일
anthem [ǽnθəm] n.
성가, 찬송가

cement [simént] v.
결합하다, 굳게 하다
immaculate [imǽkjəlit] adj.
티 하나 없는, 깨끗한

conjunction [kəndʒʌ́ŋkʃən] n.
연결관계
receptive [riséptiv] adj.
잘 받아들이는, 감수성이 풍부한
tumble [tʌ́mb-əl] v.
넘어지다, 굴러 떨어지다

instantaneous [ìnstəntéiniəs] adj. 순간적인, 즉각적인, 동시적인
mire [maiər] n.
늪
make a man of someone:
성숙하고 책임있는 사람이 되다
resurrect [rèzərékt] v.
부활시키다, 되살리다
solemn [sáləm / sɔ́l-] adj.
진지한, 엄숙한
roaring [rɔ́:riŋ] adj.
번창한, 활기찬

played **cemented** Soapy to the iron fence, for he had known it well in the days when his life contained such things as mothers and roses and ambitions and friends and **immaculate** thoughts and collars.

The **conjunction** of Soapy's **receptive** state of mind and the influences about the old church wrought a sudden and wonderful change in his soul. He viewed with swift horror the pit into which he had **tumbled**, the degraded days, unworthy desires, dead hopes, wrecked faculties and base motives that made up his existence.

And also in a moment his heart responded thrillingly to this novel mood. An **instantaneous** and strong impulse moved him to battle with his desperate fate. He would pull himself out of the **mire**; he would **make a man of himself** again; he would conquer the evil that had taken possession of him. There was time; he was comparatively young yet; he would **resurrect** his old eager ambitions and pursue them without faltering. Those **solemn** but sweet organ notes had set up a revolution in him. To-morrow he would go into the **roaring** downtown district and find work. A fur importer had once offered him a place as driver. He would find him to-morrow and ask for the position. He would be somebody in the world.

He would—

Soapy felt a hand laid on his arm. He looked quickly around into the broad face of a policeman.

"What are you doin' here?" asked the officer.

"Nothin'," said Soapy.

"Then come along," said the policeman.

"Three months on the Island," said the Magistrate in the Police Court the next morning.

... He would pull himself out of the mire; he would make a man of himself again; he would conquer the evil that had taken possession of him. There was time; he was comparatively young yet; he would resurrect his old eager ambitions and pursue them without faltering. Those solemn but sweet organ notes had set up a revolution in him.

The Skylight Room

stammer [stǽməːr] v.
더듬으며 말하다
entertain [èntərtéin] v.
마음에 품다, 생각하다

First Mrs. Parker would show you the double parlours. You would not dare to interrupt her description of their advantages and of the merits of the gentleman who had occupied them for eight years. Then you would manage to **stammer** forth the confession that you were neither a doctor nor a dentist. Mrs. Parker's manner of receiving the admission was such that you could never afterward **entertain** the same feeling toward your parents, who had neglected to train you up in one of the professions that fitted Mrs. Parker's parlours.

Next you ascended one flight of stairs and looked at the second-floor-back at $8. Convinced by her second-floor manner that it was worth

babble [bǽbəl] v.
떠듬거리며 말하다

scorn [skɔːrn] n.
경멸, 멸시, 비웃음
lambrequin [lǽmbəːrkin, -brə-]
n. (창, 문 등에) 드리운 장식 천
eviction [ivíkʃən] n.
퇴거시킴, 쫓아냄

cicerone [sìsəróuni, tʃìtʃə-] n.
관광 안내인, 가이드
honk [hɔːŋk, hɑŋk, / hɔŋk] v.
(기러기와 같은) 소리를 내다

the $12 that Mr. Toosenberry always paid for it until he left to take charge of his brother's orange plantation in Florida near Palm Beach, where Mrs. McIntyre always spent the winters that had the double front room with private bath, you managed to **babble** that you wanted something still cheaper.

If you survived Mrs. Parker's **scorn**, you were taken to look at Mr. Skidder's large hall room on the third floor. Mr. Skidder's room was not vacant. He wrote plays and smoked cigarettes in it all day long. But every room-hunter was made to visit his room to admire the **lambrequins**. After each visit, Mr. Skidder, from the fright caused by possible **eviction**, would pay something on his rent.

Then—oh, then—if you still stood on one foot, with your hot hand clutching the three moist dollars in your pocket, and hoarsely proclaimed your hideous and culpable poverty, nevermore would Mrs. Parker be **cicerone** of yours. She would **honk** loudly the word "Clara," she would show you her back, and march downstairs. Then Clara, the coloured maid, would escort you up the carpeted ladder that served for the fourth flight, and show you the Skylight Room. It occupied 7×8 feet of floor space at the middle of the hall. On each side of it was a dark lumber closet or storeroom.

cot [kɑt / kɔt] n.
간이 침대
skylight [skáilàit] n.
천장에 낸 채광창
infinity [infínəti] n.
무한대; 무한한 공간, 시간 또는 양

lug [lʌg] v.
질질 끌어서 나르다, 힘겹게 옮기다

incredulous [inkrédʒələs] adj.
믿으려 하지 않는, 의심하는
stare [stɛəːr] n.
응시, 빤히 쳐다보기

The Skylight Room 87

In it was an iron **cot**, a washstand and a chair. A shelf was the dresser. Its four bare walls seemed to close in upon you like the sides of a coffin. Your hand crept to your throat, you gasped, you looked up as from a well—and breathed once more. Through the glass of the little **skylight** you saw a square of blue **infinity**.

"Two dollars, suh," Clara would say in her half-contemptuous, half-Tuskegeenial tones.

One day Miss Leeson came hunting for a room. She carried a typewriter made to be **lugged** around by a much larger lady. She was a very little girl, with eyes and hair that had kept on growing after she had stopped and that always looked as if they were saying: "Goodness me! Why didn't you keep up with us?"

Mrs. Parker showed her the double parlours. "In this closet," she said, "one could keep a skeleton or anaesthetic or coal—"

"But I am neither a doctor nor a dentist," said Miss Leeson, with a shiver.

Mrs. Parker gave her the **incredulous**, pitying, sneering, icy **stare** that she kept for those who failed to qualify as doctors or dentists, and led the way to the second floor back.

"Eight dollars?" said Miss Leeson. "Dear me! I'm not Hetty if I do look green. I'm just a poor little working girl. Show me something higher and lower."

Mr. Skidder jumped and strewed the floor with cigarette stubs at the rap on his door.

"Excuse me, Mr. Skidder," said Mrs. Parker, with her demon's smile at his pale looks. "I didn't know you were in. I asked the lady to have a look at your lambrequins."

"They're too lovely for anything," said Miss Leeson, smiling in exactly the way the angels do.

After they had gone Mr. Skidder got very busy erasing the tall, black-haired **heroine** from his latest (unproduced) play and inserting a small, **roguish** one with heavy, bright hair and **vivacious** features.

"Anna Held'll jump at it," said Mr. Skidder to himself, putting his feet up against the lambrequins and disappearing in a cloud of smoke like an aerial cuttlefish.

Presently the **tocsin** call of "Clara!" sounded to the world the state of Miss Leeson's purse. A dark **goblin** seized her, mounted a **Stygian** stairway, thrust her into a vault with a glimmer of light in its top and muttered the menacing and **cabalistic** words "Two dollars!"

"I'll take it!" sighed Miss Leeson, sinking down upon the **squeaky** iron bed.

Every day Miss Leeson went out to work. At night she brought home papers with

---

heroine [hérouin] n.
(극·소설 등의) 여주인공
roguish [róugiʃ] adj.
장난기 있는, 짓궂은
vivacious [vivéiʃəs, vai-] adj.
쾌활한, 활발한, 명랑한

tocsin [táksin / tɔ́k-] n.
경종, 경보
goblin [gáblin / gɔ́b-] n.
악귀, 도깨비
Stygian [stídʒiən] adj.
어두운, 음침한
cabalistic [kæbəlístik] adj.
비밀스러운, 신비주의적인
squeaky [skwíːki] adj.
삐걱거리는

stoop [stu:p] n.
현관 입구의 계단, 포치
roomer [rú(:)mə:r] n.
셋방 든 사람, 하숙인

sniff [snif] v.
코방귀 뀌다, 코를 훌쩍이다
Coney:
코니아일랜드 (Coney Island)
group [gru:p] v.
떼를 짓다, 모이다

flush [flʌʃ] adj.
불그레한, 혈색 좋은

handwriting on them and made copies with her typewriter. Sometimes she had no work at night, and then she would sit on the steps of the high **stoop** with the other **roomers**. Miss Leeson was not intended for a skylight room when the plans were drawn for her creation. She was gay-hearted and full of tender, whimsical fancies. Once she let Mr. Skidder read to her three acts of his great (unpublished) comedy, "It's No Kid; or, The Heir of the Subway."

There was rejoicing among the gentlemen roomers whenever Miss Leeson had time to sit on the steps for an hour or two. But Miss Longnecker, the tall blonde who taught in a public school and said, "Well, really!" to everything you said, sat on the top step and **sniffed**. And Miss Dorn, who shot at the moving ducks at **Coney** every Sunday and worked in a department store, sat on the bottom step and sniffed. Miss Leeson sat on the middle step and the men would quickly **group** around her.

Especially Mr. Skidder, who had cast her in his mind for the star part in a private, romantic (unspoken) drama in real life. And especially Mr. Hoover, who was forty-five, fat, **flush** and foolish. And especially very young Mr. Evans, who set up a hollow cough to induce her to ask him to leave off cigarettes. The men voted her "the funniest and jolliest ever," but the sniffs

implacable [implǽkəbəl, -pléik-] adj.
달랠 수 없는, 무자비한

epicedian [èpəsí:diən] adj.
만가의, 애도하는
bane [bein] n.
파멸, 죽음
calamity [kəlǽməti] n.
재난, 불행, 비운
corpulence [kɔ́:rpjələns] n.
비만, 비대
try out:
착수해보다, 시험해보다
Momus [móuməs] n.
(그리스 신화) 모모스; 비난과 조소의 신
remand [rimǽnd, -má:nd] v.
돌려 보내다, 귀환을 명하다
avaunt [əvɔ́:nt, əvá:nt] int.
(고어·우스개) 가라, 물러가라
perdition [pərdíʃən] n.
멸망, 파멸, 지옥

firmament [fə́:rməmənt] n.
하늘, 창공

skyscraper [skáiskrèipə:r] n.
초고층 빌딩, 마천루

twinkle [twíŋk-əl] v.
반짝반짝 빛나다

on the top step and the lower step were **implacable**.

• • • • • • • •

I pray you let the drama halt while Chorus stalks to the footlights and drops an **epicedian** tear upon the fatness of Mr. Hoover. Tune the pipes to the tragedy of tallow, the **bane** of bulk, the **calamity** of **corpulence**. **Tried out**, Falstaff might have rendered more romance to the ton than would have Romeo's rickety ribs to the ounce. A lover may sigh, but he must not puff. To the train of **Momus** are the fat men **remanded**. In vain beats the faithfullest heart above a 52-inch belt. **Avaunt**, Hoover! Hoover, forty-five, flush and foolish, might carry off Helen herself; Hoover, forty-five, flush, foolish and fat is meat for **perdition**. There was never a chance for you, Hoover.

As Mrs. Parker's roomers sat thus one summer's evening, Miss Leeson looked up into the **firmament** and cried with her little gay laugh:

"Why, there's Billy Jackson! I can see him from down here, too."

All looked up—some at the windows of **skyscrapers**, some casting about for an airship, Jackson-guided.

"It's that star," explained Miss Leeson, pointing with a tiny finger. "Not the big one that **twinkles**—the steady blue one near it. I can

The Skylight Room 91

see it every night through my skylight. I named it Billy Jackson."

"Well, really!" said Miss Longnecker. "I didn't know you were an **astronomer**, Miss Leeson."

"Oh, yes," said the small **stargazer**, "I know as much as any of them about the style of sleeves they're going to wear next fall in Mars."

"Well, really!" said Miss Longnecker. "The star you refer to is Gamma, of the **constellation** Cassiopeia. It is nearly of the second **magnitude**, and its **meridian** passage is—"

"Oh," said the very young Mr. Evans, "I think Billy Jackson is a much better name for it."

"Same here," said Mr. Hoover, loudly breathing defiance to Miss Longnecker. "I think Miss Leeson has just as much right to name stars as any of those old **astrologers** had."

"Well, really!" said Miss Longnecker.

"I wonder whether it's a **shooting star**," remarked Miss Dorn. "I hit nine ducks and a rabbit out of ten in the gallery at Coney Sunday."

"He doesn't show up very well from down here," said Miss Leeson. "You ought to see him from my room. You know you can see stars even in the daytime from the bottom of a well. At night my room is like the shaft of a coal mine, and it makes Billy Jackson look like the big diamond pin that Night fastens her kimono with."

---

astronomer [əstránəmər / -trón-] n.
천문학자
stargazer [stɑ::rgeizər] n.
별을 쳐다보는 사람, 천문학자, 몽상가

constellation [kànstəléiʃən / kɔ̀n-] n.
별자리, 성좌
magnitude [mǽgnətjùːd] n.
등급, 광도
meridian [mərídiən] n.
자오선

astrologer [əstrálədʒər / -trɔ́l-] n.
점성가

shooting star:
유성, 별똥별

insolent [ínsələnt] adj.
뻐기는, 거만한, 무례한

avalanche [ǽvəlæntʃ / -là:nʃ] n.
눈사태
pirouette [pìruét] v.
발끝으로 맴돌다, 급선회하다

fragile [frǽdʒəl / -dʒail] adj.
허약한, 깨지기 쉬운, 섬세한
Erebus [érəbəs] n.
이승과 저승과의 사이에 있는 암흑계

There came a time after that when Miss Leeson brought no formidable papers home to copy. And when she went out in the morning, instead of working, she went from office to office and let her heart melt away in the drip of cold refusals transmitted through **insolent** office boys. This went on.

There came an evening when she wearily climbed Mrs. Parker's stoop at the hour when she always returned from her dinner at the restaurant. But she had had no dinner.

As she stepped into the hall Mr. Hoover met her and seized his chance. He asked her to marry him, and his fatness hovered above her like an **avalanche**. She dodged, and caught the balustrade. He tried for her hand, and she raised it and smote him weakly in the face. Step by step she went up, dragging herself by the railing. She passed Mr. Skidder's door as he was red-inking a stage direction for Myrtle Delorme (Miss Leeson) in his (unaccepted) comedy, to "**pirouette** across stage from L to the side of the Count." Up the carpeted ladder she crawled at last and opened the door of the skylight room.

She was too weak to light the lamp or to undress. She fell upon the iron cot, her **fragile** body scarcely hollowing the worn springs. And in that **Erebus** of the skylight room, she slowly raised her heavy eyelids, and smiled.

For Billy Jackson was shining down on her, calm and bright and constant through the skylight. There was no world about her. She was sunk in a pit of blackness, with but that small square of **pallid** light framing the star that she had so whimsically and oh, so **ineffectually** named. Miss Longnecker must be right; it was Gamma, of the constellation Cassiopeia, and not Billy Jackson. And yet she could not let it be Gamma.

As she lay on her back she tried twice to raise her arm. The third time she got two thin fingers to her lips and blew a kiss out of the black pit to Billy Jackson. Her arm fell back limply.

"Good-bye, Billy," she **murmured** faintly. "You're millions of miles away and you won't even twinkle once. But you kept where I could see you most of the time up there when there wasn't anything else but darkness to look at, didn't you? . . . Millions of miles . . . Good-bye, Billy Jackson."

Clara, the coloured maid, found the door locked at 10 the next day, and they forced it open. Vinegar, and the slapping of wrists and burnt feathers proving of no avail, some one ran to 'phone for an ambulance.

In due time it backed up to the door with

---

pallid [pǽlid] adj.
창백한
ineffectually [ìniféktʃuəli] adv.
효과 없이, 헛되이

murmur [mə́:rmə:r] v.
낮게 속삭이다, 중얼거리다

much gong-clanging, and the capable young **medico**, in his white linen coat, ready, active, confident, with his smooth face half **debonair**, half grim, danced up the steps.

"Ambulance call to 49," he said briefly. "What's the trouble?"

"Oh, yes, doctor," sniffed Mrs. Parker, as though her trouble that there should be trouble in the house was the greater. "I can't think what can be the matter with her. Nothing we could do would **bring** her **to**. It's a young woman, a Miss Elsie—yes, a Miss Elsie Leeson. Never before in my house—"

"What room?" cried the doctor in a terrible voice, to which Mrs. Parker was a stranger.

"The skylight room. It—"

Evidently the ambulance doctor was familiar with the location of skylight rooms. He was gone up the stairs, four at a time. Mrs. Parker followed slowly, as her dignity demanded.

On the first landing she met him coming back bearing the astronomer in his arms. He stopped and let loose the practised **scalpel** of his tongue, not loudly. Gradually Mrs. Parker **crumpled** as a stiff garment that slips down from a nail. Ever afterward there remained **crumples** in her mind and body. Sometimes her curious roomers would ask her what the doctor said to her.

"Let that be," she would answer. "If I can get forgiveness for having heard it I will be satisfied."

The ambulance physician strode with his burden through the pack of hounds that follow the curiosity chase, and even they fell back along the sidewalk abashed, for his face was that of one who bears his own dead.

They noticed that he did not lay down upon the bed prepared for it in the ambulance the form that he carried, and all that he said was: "Drive like h—l, Wilson," to the driver.

That is all. Is it a story? In the next morning's paper I saw a little news item, and the last sentence of it may help you (as it helped me) to **weld** the incidents together.

It **recounted** the reception into Bellevue Hospital of a young woman who had been removed from No. 49 East —— street, suffering from **debility** induced by starvation. It concluded with these words:

"Dr. William Jackson, the ambulance physician who attended the case, says the patient will recover."

The Handbook of Hymen

weather bureau:
기상청
meteorological
[mìːtiərəlɑ́dʒikəl / -lɔ́dʒ-] adj.
기상의, 기상학의

'Tis the opinion of myself, Sanderson Pratt, who sets this down, that the educational system of the United States should be in the hands of the **weather bureau**. I can give you good reasons for it; and you can't tell me why our college professors shouldn't be transferred to the **meteorological** department. They have been learned to read; and they could very easily glance at the morning papers and then wire in to the main office what kind of weather to expect. But there's the other side of the proposition. I am going on to tell you how the weather furnished me and Idaho Green with

prospect [prəspékt] v.
(광산, 석유 등을 찾아) 답사하다, 시굴하다
grubstake [grʌ́bstèik] v.
(발견한 이익의 일부를 받는다는 조건으로) 자금·의복·식료 따위를 공급하다
grub[grʌb] n.
(속어) 음식물
premonition [prìːməníʃən] n.
예감, 징후, 전조

flurry [flə́ːri, flʌ́ri] n.
(비·눈 따위를 동반한) 질풍, 돌풍
element [éləmənt] n.
자연력, 폭풍우, 악천후
cut up:
장난치다, 짓궂게 굴다

instigate [ínstəgèit] v.
부추기다, 선동하다

an elegant education.

We was up in the Bitter Root Mountains over the Montana line **prospecting** for gold. A chin-whiskered man in Walla-Walla, carrying a line of hope as excess baggage, had **grubstaked** us; and there we was in the foothills pecking away, with enough **grub** on hand to last an army through a peace conference.

Along one day comes a mail-rider over the mountains from Carlos, and stops to eat three cans of greengages, and leave us a newspaper of modern date. This paper prints a system of **premonitions** of the weather, and the card it dealt Bitter Root Mountains from the bottom of the deck was "warmer and fair, with light westerly breezes."

That evening it began to snow, with the wind strong in the east. Me and Idaho moved camp into an old empty cabin higher up the mountain, thinking it was only a November **flurry**. But after falling three foot on a level it went to work in earnest; and we knew we was snowed in. We got in plenty of firewood before it got deep, and we had grub enough for two months, so we let the **elements** rage and **cut up** all they thought proper.

If you want to **instigate** the art of manslaughter just shut two men up in a eighteen by twenty-foot cabin for a month. Human nature

stand [stænd] v.
참다, 견디다
skillet [skílit] n.
프라이팬
edict [í:dikt] n.
칙령, 포고, 명령

emanate [émənèit] v.
(생각·명령 등이) 나오다, 퍼지다
cud [kʌd] n.
되새김질 거리

cur [kə:r] n.
잡종개, 망나니
inmate [ínmèit] n.
주거인, 동거인

implement [ímpləmənt] n.
도구, 기구

won't **stand** it.

When the first snowflakes fell me and Idaho Green laughed at each other's jokes and praised the stuff we turned out of a **skillet** and called bread. At the end of three weeks Idaho makes this kind of a **edict** to me. Says he:

"I never exactly heard sour milk dropping out of a balloon on the bottom of a tin pan, but I have an idea it would be music of the spears compared to this attenuated stream of asphyxiated thought that **emanates** out of your organs of conversation. The kind of half-masticated noises that you emit every day puts me in mind of a cow's **cud**, only she's lady enough to keep hers to herself, and you ain't."

"Mr. Green," says I, "you having been a friend of mine once, I have some hesitations in confessing to you that if I had my choice for society between you and a common yellow, three-legged **cur** pup, one of the **inmates** of this here cabin would be wagging a tail just at present."

This way we goes on for two or three days, and then we quits speaking to one another. We divides up the cooking **implements**, and Idaho cooks his grub on one side of the fireplace, and me on the other. The snow is up to the windows, and we have to keep a fire all day.

You see me and Idaho never had any education beyond reading and doing "if John had

The Handbook of Hymen

intrinsic [intrínsik] adj.
본질적인, 본래 갖추어진
knock around:
정처 없이 돌아다니다, 방랑하다
snowbound [snoubaund] adj.
눈에 갇힌
meditation [mèdətéiʃ-ən] n.
명상, 묵상, 고찰
drawback [drɔ́ːbæ̀k] n.
결점, 약점
bott [bɑt / bɔt] n.
보트병, 말 피부병의 일종
buckboard [bʌ́kbɔ̀ːrd] n.
4륜 짐마차

three apples and James five" on a slate. We never felt any special need for a university degree, though we had acquired a species of **intrinsic** intelligence in **knocking around** the world that we could use in emergencies. But, **snowbound** in that cabin in the Bitter Roots, we felt for the first time that if we had studied Homer or Greek and fractions and the higher branches of information, we'd have had some resources in the line of **meditation** and private thought. I've seen them Eastern college fellows working in camps all through the West, and I never noticed but what education was less of a **drawback** to 'em than you would think. Why, once over on Snake River, when Andrew McWilliams' saddle horse got the **botts**, he sent a **buckboard** ten miles for one of these strangers that claimed to be a botanist. But that horse died.

One morning Idaho was poking around with a stick on top of a little shelf that was too high to reach. Two books fell down to the floor. I started toward 'em, but caught Idaho's eye. He speaks for the first time in a week.

burn one's finger:
(쓸데없이 참섭하거나 성급히
행동하거나 하여) 데다, 혼나다
in spite of:
~에도 불구하고
square [skwɛəːr] adj.
공정한, 올바른

"Don't **burn your fingers**," says he. "**In spite of** the fact that you're only fit to be the companion of a sleeping mud-turtle, I'll give you a **square** deal. And that's more than your parents did when they turned you loose in the

sociability [sòuʃəbíləti] n.
사교성
bedside manner:
환자를 대하는 의사의 태도
seven-up [sév-ənʌ́p] n.
7점을 먼저 따면 이기는 카드 놀이

nugget [nʌ́git] n.
금괴(金塊), 귀금속 덩어리

indispensable [ìndis-pénsəbəl] adj.
불가결의, 절대 필요한
stump [stʌmp] v.
맞서다, 도전하다
veto [víːtou] n.
거부권
aqueduct [ǽkwədʌ̀kt] n.
수로

world with the **sociability** of a rattle-snake and the **bedside manner** of a frozen turnip. I'll play you a game of **seven-up**, the winner to pick up his choice of the book, the loser to take the other."

We played; and Idaho won. He picked up his book; and I took mine. Then each of us got on his side of the house and went to reading.

I never was as glad to see a ten-ounce **nugget** as I was that book. And Idaho looked at his like a kid looks at a stick of candy.

Mine was a little book about five by six inches called "Herkimer's Handbook of **Indispensable** Information." I may be wrong, but I think that was the greatest book that ever was written. I've got it to-day; and I can **stump** you or any man fifty times in five minutes with the information in it. Talk about Solomon or the New York *Tribune*! Herkimer had cases on both of 'em. That man must have put in fifty years and travelled a million miles to find out all that stuff. There was the population of all cities in it, and the way to tell a girl's age, and the number of teeth a camel has. It told you the longest tunnel in the world, the number of the stars, how long it takes for chicken pox to break out, what a lady's neck ought to measure, the **veto** powers of Governors, the dates of the Roman **aqueducts**, how many pounds of rice

The Handbook of Hymen 101

going without three beers a day would buy, the average annual temperature of Augusta, Maine, the quantity of seed required to plant an acre of carrots in drills, **antidotes** for poisons, the number of hairs on a blond lady's head, how to preserve eggs, the height of all the mountains in the world, and the dates of all wars and battles, and how to restore drowned persons, and **sunstroke**, and the number of tacks in a pound, and how to make dynamite and flowers and beds, and what to do before the doctor comes—and a hundred times as many things besides. If there was anything Herkimer didn't know I didn't miss it out of the book.

I sat and read that book for four hours. All the wonders of education was compressed in it. I forgot the snow, and I forgot that me and old Idaho was **on the outs**. He was sitting still on a stool reading away with a kind of partly soft and partly mysterious look shining through his tan-bark whiskers.

"Idaho," says I, "what kind of a book is yours?"

Idaho must have forgot, too, for he answered moderate, without any **slander** or **malignity**.

"Why," says he, "this here seems to be a volume by Homer K. M."

"Homer K. M. what?" I asks.

"Why, just Homer K. M.," says he.

"You're a liar," says I, a little **riled** that Idaho

---

antidote [ǽntidòut] n.
해독제
sunstroke [sʌ́nstròuk] n.
일사병

on the outs:
사이가 틀어져 있다

slander [slǽndəːr / slɑ́ːn-] n.
중상, 비방
malignity [məlígnəti] n.
악의, 원한

rile [rail] v.
화나게 하다, 짜증나게 하다

should try to put me up a tree. "No man is going 'round signing books with his initials. If it's Homer K. M. Spoopendyke, or Homer K. M. McSweeney, or Homer K. M. Jones, why don't you say so like a man instead of biting off the end of it like a calf chewing off the tail of a shirt on a clothes-line?"

"I put it to you straight, Sandy," says Idaho, quiet. "It's a poem book," says he, "by Homer K. M. I couldn't get **colour** out of it at first, but there's a **vein** if you follow it up. I wouldn't have missed this book for a pair of red blankets."

"You're welcome to it," says I. "What I want is a **disinterested** statement of facts for the mind to work on, and that's what I seem to find in the book I've drawn."

"What you've got," says Idaho, "is **statistics**, the lowest grade of information that exists. They'll poison your mind. Give me old K. M.'s system of surmises. He seems to be a kind of a wine agent. His regular toast is 'nothing doing,' and he seems to have a **grouch**, but he keeps it so well lubricated with **booze** that his worst kicks sound like an invitation to split a **quart**. But it's poetry," says Idaho, "and I have sensations of scorn for that **truck** of yours that tries to convey sense in feet and inches. When it comes to explaining the instinct of philosophy

---

color [kʌ́lər] n.
특색, 문채, 개성
vein [vein] n.
성격, 경향, 기질

disinterested [disíntəristid, -rèst-] adj.
청렴한, 공평한

statistics [stətístiks] n.
통계, 통계학
grouch [grautʃ] n.
불평, 투덜거림
booze [bu:z] n.
술, 알코올 음료
quart [kwɔ:rt] n.
쿼트(1갤런의 1/4 또는 2파인트), 1쿼트의 음료
truck [trʌk] n.
잡동사니, 허튼 소리

The Handbook of Hymen 103

through the art of nature, old K. M. has got your man beat by drills, rows, paragraphs, chest measurement, and average annual rainfall."

So that's the way me and Idaho had it. Day and night all the excitement we got was studying our books. That snowstorm sure fixed us with a fine lot of **attainments apiece**. By the time the snow melted, if you had stepped up to me suddenly and said: "Sanderson Pratt, what would it cost per square foot to lay a roof with twenty by twenty-eight tin at nine dollars and fifty cents per box?" I'd have told you as quick as light could travel the length of a spade handle at the rate of one hundred and ninety-two thousand miles per second. How many can do it? You wake up 'most any man you know in the middle of the night, and ask him quick to tell you the number of bones in the human skeleton exclusive of the teeth, or what percentage of the vote of the Nebraska Legislature **overrules** a veto. Will he tell you? Try him and see.

About what benefit Idaho got out of his poetry book I didn't exactly know. Idaho **boosted** the wine agent every time he opened his mouth; but I wasn't so sure.

This Homer K. M., from what leaked out of his **libretto** through Idaho, seemed to me to be a kind of a dog who looked at life like it was

---

attainment [ətéinmənt] n.
학식, 재능, 조예
apiece [əpí:s] adv.
각자에게
overrule [òuvərú:l] v.
파기하다, 무효로 하다

boost [bu:st] v.
격려하다, 선전하다

libretto [librétou] n.
리브레토, 오페라 가사, 대본

a tin can tied to his tail. After running himself half to death, he sits down, hangs his tongue out, and looks at the can and says:

"Oh, well, since we can't shake the **growler**, let's get it filled at the corner, and all have a drink on me."

Besides that, it seems he was a Persian; and I never hear of Persia producing anything worth mentioning unless it was Turkish rugs and Maltese cats.

That spring me and Idaho struck **pay ore**. It was a habit of ours to sell out quick and keep moving. We unloaded on our grubstaker for eight thousand dollars apiece; and then we drifted down to this little town of Rosa, on the Salmon river, to rest up, and get some human grub, and have our whiskers harvested.

Rosa was no mining-camp. It laid in the valley, and was as free of **uproar** and **pestilence** as one of them rural towns in the country. There was a three-mile trolley line **champing** its bit in the environs; and me and Idaho spent a week riding on one of the cars, dropping off at nights at the Sunset View Hotel. Being now well read as well as travelled, we was soon **pro re nata** with the best society in Rosa, and was invited out to the most dressed-up and **high-toned** entertainments. It was at a piano recital and quail-eating contest in the city hall,

---

growler [gráulər] n.
으르렁거리는 사람, 딱딱거리는 사람

pay [pei] adj.
채산이 맞는, 수지맞는
ore [ɔ:r] n.
광석

uproar [ʎprɔ́:r] n.
소란, 소동
pestilence [péstələns] n.
역병, 폐해
champ [tʃæmp] v.
(말이 재갈을) 씹다
pro re nata:
현 상황에서는, 필요에 따라
high-toned [háitóund] adj.
고상한, 고결한, 뛰어난

fire company: 소방대	

for the benefit of the **fire company**, that me and Idaho first met Mrs. De Ormond Sampson, the queen of Rosa society.

Mrs. Sampson was a widow, and owned the only two-story house in town. It was painted yellow, and whichever way you looked from you could see it as plain as egg on the chin of an O'Grady on a Friday. Twenty-two men in Rosa besides me and Idaho was trying to **stake a claim** on that yellow house.

stake a claim:
소유권을 주장하다

There was a dance after the song books and quail bones had been **raked** out of the Hall. Twenty-three of the **bunch** galloped over to Mrs. Sampson and asked for a dance. I sidestepped the **two-step**, and asked permission to escort her home. That's where I made a hit.

rake [reik] v.
갈퀴로 긁다, 긁어 내다, 긁어 모으다
bunch [bʌntʃ] n.
무리, 집단
two-step [túːstèp] n.
투스텝 (2박자의 사교 댄스)

On the way home says she:

"Ain't the stars lovely and bright to-night, Mr. Pratt?"

"For the chance they've got," says I, "they're **humping** themselves in a mighty creditable way. That big one you see is sixty-six million miles distant. It took thirty-six years for its light to reach us. With an eighteen-foot telescope you can see forty-three millions of 'em, including them of the thirteenth magnitude, which, if one was to go out now, you would keep on seeing it for twenty-seven hundred years."

hump [hʌmp] v.
노력하다, 열심히 하다

"My!" says Mrs. Sampson. "I never knew

account for:
설명하다
sweat gland:
땀샘
perspiratory [pərspáirətɔ̀:ri / -spáiərətəri] adj.
발한의, 땀의
end to end:
끝과 끝을 붙여서
irrigation ditch:
관개용 수로

sapheaded [sǽphèdid] adj.
바보 같은, 얼간이 같은
plugugly [plʌ́gʌ̀gli] n.
깡패, 건달
converse [kənvə́:rs] v.
대화하다

tabulate [tǽbjəlèit] v.
(일람)표로 만들다
compile [kəmpáil] v.
수집하다, 집계하다
lutheran [lú:θərən] adj.
Martin Luther의, 루터 교회의

that before. How warm it is! I'm as damp as I can be from dancing so much."

"That's easy to **account for**," says I, "when you happen to know that you've got two million **sweat glands** working all at once. If every one of your **perspiratory** ducts, which are a quarter of an inch long, was placed **end to end**, they would reach a distance of seven miles."

"Lawsy!" says Mrs. Sampson. "It sounds like an **irrigation ditch** you was describing, Mr. Pratt. How do you get all this knowledge of information?"

"From observation, Mrs. Sampson," I tells her. "I keep my eyes open when I go about the world."

"Mr. Pratt," says she, "I always did admire a man of education. There are so few scholars among the **sap-headed plug-uglies** of this town that it is a real pleasure to **converse** with a gentleman of culture. I'd be gratified to have you call at my house whenever you feel so inclined."

And that was the way I got the goodwill of the lady in the yellow house. Every Tuesday and Friday evening I used to go there and tell her about the wonders of the universe as discovered, **tabulated**, and **compiled** from nature by Herkimer. Idaho and the other gay **Lutherans** of the town got every minute of the rest of the week that they could.

I never imagined that Idaho was trying to work on Mrs. Sampson with old K. M.'s rules of **courtship** till one afternoon when I was on my way over to take her a basket of wild hog-plums. I met the lady coming down the lane that led to her house. Her eyes was **snapping**, and her hat made a dangerous dip over one eye.

"Mr. Pratt," she opens up, "this Mr. Green is a friend of yours, I believe."

"For nine years," says I.

"Cut him out," says she. "He's no gentleman!"

"Why ma'am," says I, "he's a plain **incumbent** of the mountains, with **asperities** and the usual failings of a **spendthrift** and a liar, but I never on the most momentous occasion had the heart to deny that he was a gentleman. It may be that in **haberdashery** and the sense of arrogance and display Idaho offends the eye, but inside, ma'am, I've found him **impervious** to the lower grades of crime and obesity. After nine years of Idaho's society, Mrs. Sampson," I **winds up**, "I should hate to **impute** him, and I should hate to see him imputed."

"It's right **plausible** of you, Mr. Pratt," says Mrs. Sampson, "to take up the **curmudgeons** in your friend's behalf; but it don't alter the fact that he has made proposals to me

obnoxious [əbnákʃəs / -nɔ́k-] adj. 밉살스러운, 불쾌한
ruffle [rʌ́f-əl] v. 헝클어 놓다, 성나게 하다
ignominy [ígnəmìni] n. 치욕, 불명예
deride [diráid] v. 조소하다, 비웃다
prey [prei] n. 희생자, 피해자
spurious [spjú-əriəs] adj. 가짜의, 위조의, 겉치레의
demeanor [dimí:nər] n. 태도, 품행
irreligious [ìrilídʒəs] adj. 무종교의, 반종교적인, 불경건한

nom de plume [nàmdəplú:m / nɔ̀m-] n. (French) 필명, 작가의 가명

cavort [kəvɔ́:rt] v. 날뛰다, 껑충거리다
claret [klǽrit] n. 프랑스 Bordeaux산 붉은 포도주

sufficiently **obnoxious** to **ruffle** the **ignominy** of any lady."

"Why, now, now, now!" says I. "Old Idaho do that! I could believe it of myself, sooner. I never knew but one thing to **deride** in him; and a blizzard was responsible for that. Once while we was snowbound in the mountains he became a **prey** to a kind of **spurious** and uneven poetry, which may have corrupted his **demeanour**."

"It has," says Mrs. Sampson. "Ever since I knew him he has been reciting to me a lot of **irreligious** rhymes by some person he calls Ruby Ott, and who is no better than she should be, if you judge by her poetry."

"Then Idaho has struck a new book," says I, "for the one he had was by a man who writes under the **nom de plume** of K. M."

"He'd better have stuck to it," says Mrs. Sampson, "whatever it was. And to-day he caps the vortex. I get a bunch of flowers from him, and on 'em is pinned a note. Now, Mr. Pratt, you know a lady when you see her; and you know how I stand in Rosa society. Do you think for a moment that I'd skip out to the woods with a man along with a jug of wine and a loaf of bread, and go singing and **cavorting** up and down under the trees with him? I take a little **claret** with my meals, but I'm not in the habit

brush [brʌʃ] n.
숲, 잡목림
raise Cain:
소동을 일으키다
verse [vəːrs] n.
운문, 시

rhyme [raim] n.
운, 압운; 운문, 시
figurative [fígjərətiv] adj.
비유적인
overlook [òuvərlúk] v.
관대히 봐주다, 눈감아주다
extricate [ékstrəkèit] v.
구출하다, 탈출시키다, 해방하다
equator [ikwéitər] n.
적도
altitude [ǽltətjùːd] n.
높이, 고도
latitude [lǽtətjùːd] n.
위도

of packing a jug of it into the **brush** and **raising Cain** in any such style as that. And of course he'd bring his book of **verses** along, too. He said so. Let him go on his scandalous picnics alone! Or let him take his Ruby Ott with him. I reckon she wouldn't kick unless it was on account of there being too much bread along. And what do you think of your gentleman friend now, Mr. Pratt?"

"Well, 'm," says I, "it may be that Idaho's invitation was a kind of poetry, and meant no harm. May be it belonged to the class of **rhymes** they call **figurative**. They offend law and order, but they get sent through the mails on the grounds that they mean something that they don't say. I'd be glad on Idaho's account if you'd **overlook** it," says I, "and let us **extricate** our minds from the low regions of poetry to the higher planes of fact and fancy. On a beautiful afternoon like this, Mrs. Sampson," I goes on, "we should let our thoughts dwell accordingly. Though it is warm here, we should remember that at the **equator** the line of perpetual frost is at an **altitude** of fifteen thousand feet. Between the **latitudes** of forty degrees and forty-nine degrees it is from four thousand to nine thousand feet."

"Oh, Mr. Pratt," says Mrs. Sampson, "it's such a comfort to hear you say them beautiful facts

jar [dʒɑːr] n.	
귀에 거슬리는 소리	
minx [miŋks] n.	
왈가닥, 말괄량이	
inhumanity [ìnhjuːmǽnəti] n.	
몰인정, 무자비	
ribaldry [ríb-əldri] n.	
품위가 낮음, 상스러움	
ring [riŋ] n.	
나이테	

after getting such a **jar** from that **minx** of a Ruby's poetry!"

"Let us sit on this log at the roadside," says I, "and forget the **inhumanity** and **ribaldry** of the poets. It is in the glorious columns of ascertained facts and legalised measures that beauty is to be found. In this very log we sit upon, Mrs. Sampson," says I, "is statistics more wonderful than any poem. The **rings** show it was sixty years old. At the depth of two thousand feet it would become coal in three thousand years. The deepest coal mine in the world is at Killingworth, near Newcastle. A box four feet long, three feet wide, and two feet eight inches deep will hold one ton of coal. If an artery is cut, compress it above the wound. A man's leg contains thirty bones. The Tower of London was burned in 1841."

"... and let us extricate our minds from the low regions of poetry to the higher planes of fact and fancy. ..."

"Go on, Mr. Pratt," says Mrs. Sampson. "Them ideas is so **original** and **soothing**. I think statistics are just as lovely as they can be."

original [ərídʒənəl] adj.
독창적인, 창의성이 풍부한
soothing [súːðiŋ] adj.
진정시키는, 누그러뜨리는

But it wasn't till two weeks later that I got all that was coming to me out of Herkimer.

One night I was waked up by folks **hollering** "Fire!" all around. I jumped up and dressed and went out of the hotel to enjoy the scene. When I seen it was Mrs. Sampson's house, I gave forth a kind of yell, and I was there in two minutes.

holler [hálər / hɔ́l-] v.
외치다, 고함치다

The whole lower story of the yellow house

was in flames, and every masculine, feminine, and canine in Rosa was there, **screeching** and barking and **getting in the way** of the firemen. I saw Idaho trying to get away from six firemen who were holding him. They was telling him the whole place was on fire down-stairs, and no man could go in it and come out alive.

"Where's Mrs. Sampson?" I asks.

"She hasn't been seen," says one of the firemen. "She sleeps up-stairs. We've tried to get in, but we can't, and our company hasn't got any ladders yet."

I runs around to the light of the big **blaze**, and pulls the Handbook out of my inside pocket. I kind of laughed when I felt it in my hands—I **reckon** I was some **daffy** with the sensation of excitement.

"Herky, old boy," I says to it, as I flipped over the pages, "you ain't ever lied to me yet, and you ain't ever throwed me down at a scratch yet. Tell me what, old boy, tell me what!" says I.

I turned to "What to do in Case of Accidents," on page 117. I run my finger down the page, and struck it. Good old Herkimer, he never overlooked anything! It said:

Suffocation from Inhaling Smoke or Gas.—There is nothing better than **flaxseed**. Place a few seed in the outer corner of the eye.

I shoved the Handbook back in my pocket, and grabbed a boy that was running by.

"Here," says I, giving him some money, "run to the drug store and bring a dollar's worth of flaxseed. Hurry, and you'll get another one for yourself. Now," I **sings out** to the crowd, "we'll have Mrs. Sampson!" And I throws away my coat and hat.

Four of the firemen and citizens grabs hold of me. It's sure death, they say, to go in the house, for the floors was beginning to fall through.

"How in blazes," I sings out, kind of laughing yet, but not feeling like it, "do you expect me to put flaxseed in a eye without the eye?"

I **jabbed** each elbow in a fireman's face, kicked the bark off of one citizen's shin, and **tripped** the other one with a side hold. And then I busted into the house. If I die first I'll write you a letter and tell you if it's any worse down there than the inside of that yellow house was; but don't believe it yet. I was a heap more cooked than the hurry-up orders of broiled chicken that you get in restaurants. The fire and smoke had me down on the floor twice, and was about to shame Herkimer, but the firemen helped me with their little stream of water, and I got to Mrs. Sampson's room. She'd lost conscientiousness from the smoke, so I wrapped her in the bed clothes and got her on my shoulder. Well, the floors wasn't as bad as they said, or I never could have done it—not **by no means**.

I carried her out fifty yards from the house and laid her on the grass. Then, of course, every one of them other twenty-two plaintiff's to the lady's hand crowded around with tin **dippers** of water ready to save her. And up runs the boy with the flaxseed.

I unwrapped the covers from Mrs. Sampson's head. She opened her eyes and says:

"Is that you, Mr. Pratt?"

"S-s-sh," says I. "Don't talk till you've had the remedy."

I runs my arm around her neck and raises her head, gentle, and breaks the bag of flaxseed with the other hand; and as easy as I could I bends over and slips three or four of the seeds in the outer corner of her eye.

Up gallops the village doc by this time, and snorts around, and grabs at Mrs. Sampson's pulse, and wants to know what I mean by any such sandblasted nonsense.

"Well, old Jalap and Jerusalem oakseed," says I, "I'm no regular **practitioner**, but I'll show you my authority, anyway."

---

by no means:
절대 아닌

dipper [dípər] n.
버킷, 양동이

practitioner [præktíʃənər] n.
개업한 의사나 변호사

fetch [fetʃ] v.
가져오다, 데려오다

hike [haik] v.
갑자기 올리다, 증가시키다

They **fetched** my coat, and I gets out the Handbook.

"Look on page 117," says I, "at the remedy for suffocation by smoke or gas. Flaxseed in the outer corner of the eye, it says. I don't know whether it works as a smoke consumer or whether it **hikes** the compound gastro-hip-popotamus nerve into action, but Herkimer says it, and he was called to the case first. If you want to make it a consultation, there's no objection."

Old doc takes the book and looks at it by means of his specs and a fireman's lantern.

"Well, Mr. Pratt," says he, "you evidently got on the wrong line in reading your diagnosis. The recipe for suffocation says: 'Get the patient into fresh air as quickly as possible, and place in a reclining position.' The flaxseed remedy is for 'Dust and Cinders in the Eye,' on the line above. But, after all—"

"See here," interrupts Mrs. Sampson, "I reckon I've got something to say in this consultation. That flaxseed done me more good than anything I ever tried." And then she raises up her head and lays it back on my arm again, and says: "Put some in the other eye, Sandy dear."

And so if you was to stop off at Rosa to-morrow, or any other day, you'd see a fine new yellow house with Mrs. Pratt, that was Mrs.

morocco [mərákou / -rɔ́k-] n.
모로코 가죽 (무두질한 염소 가죽)

pertain [pərtéin] v.
속하다, 관계하다

Sampson, embellishing and adorning it. And if you was to step inside you'd see on the marble-top centre table in the parlour "Herkimer's Handbook of Indispensable Information," all rebound in red **morocco**, and ready to be consulted on any subject **pertaining** to human happiness and wisdom.

Jeff Peters as a Personal Magnet

Jeff Peters has been engaged in as many schemes for making money as there are recipes for cooking rice in Charleston, S.C.

Best of all I like to hear him tell of his earlier days when he sold **liniments** and cough cures on street corners, living **hand to mouth, heart to heart** with the people, throwing heads or tails with fortune for his last coin.

"I struck Fisher Hill, Arkansaw," said he, "in a buckskin suit, **moccasins**, long hair and a thirty-carat diamond ring that I got from an actor in Texarkana. I don't know what he ever did with the pocket knife I **swapped** him for it.

Jeff Peters as a Personal Magnet

best bet:
최선의 방책이나 수단
resurrection [rèzərékʃ-ən] n.
소생, 부활
bitter [bítər] n.
쓴 술(향미 또는 강장제용)

ingredient [ingrí:diənt] n.
성분, 재료
valise [vəlí:s / -lí:z] n.
여행가방
rosy [róuzi] adj.
장밋빛의, 유망한, 밝은

fake [feik] n.
위조품, 가짜
extract [ékstrækt] n.
추출물, 진액

malarial [məlé-əriəl] adj.
말라리아의

"I was Dr. Waugh-hoo, the celebrated Indian medicine man. I carried only one **best bet** just then, and that was **Resurrection Bitters**. It was made of life-giving plants and herbs accidentally discovered by Ta-qua-la, the beautiful wife of the chief of the Choctaw Nation, while gathering truck to garnish a platter of boiled dog for the annual corn dance.

"Business hadn't been good at the last town, so I only had five dollars. I went to the Fisher Hill druggist and he credited me for half a gross of eight-ounce bottles and corks. I had the labels and **ingredients** in my **valise**, left over from the last town. Life began to look **rosy** again after I got in my hotel room with the water running from the tap, and the Resurrection Bitters lining up on the table by the dozen.

"**Fake**? No, sir. There was two dollars' worth of fluid **extract** of cinchona and a dime's worth of aniline in that half-gross of bitters. I've gone through towns years afterwards and had folks ask for 'em again.

"I hired a wagon that night and commenced selling the bitters on Main Street. Fisher Hill was a low, **malarial** town; and a compound hypothetical pneumocardiac anti-scorbutic tonic was just what I diagnosed the crowd as needing. The bitters started off like

lapel [ləpél] n. (양복의) 접은 옷깃	
constable [kánstəbl / kʎn-] n. 순경 illegitimate [ìlidʒítəmit] adj. 불법의, 위법의 by the name of: ~이라는 이름으로, ~이라 불리는	
landlord [lǽndlɔ̀:rd] n. 주인, 경영자	
regalia [rigéiliə, -ljə] n. 고급 여송연	

sweetbreads-on-toast at a vegetarian dinner. I had sold two dozen at fifty cents apiece when I felt somebody pull my coat tail. I knew what that meant; so I climbed down and sneaked a five dollar bill into the hand of a man with a German silver star on his **lapel**.

"'**Constable**,' says I, 'it's a fine night.'

"'Have you got a city license,' he asks, 'to sell this **illegitimate** essence of spooju that you flatter **by the name of** medicine?'

"'I have not,' says I. 'I didn't know you had a city. If I can find it to-morrow I'll take one out if it's necessary.'

"'I'll have to close you up till you do,' says the constable.

"I quit selling and went back to the hotel. I was talking to the **landlord** about it.

"'Oh, you won't stand no show in Fisher Hill,' says he. 'Dr. Hoskins, the only doctor here, is a brother-in-law of the Mayor, and they won't allow no fake doctor to practice in town.'

"'I don't practice medicine,' says I, 'I've got a State peddler's license, and I take out a city one wherever they demand it.'

"I went to the Mayor's office the next morning and they told me he hadn't showed up yet. They didn't know when he'd be down. So Doc Waugh-hoo hunches down again in a hotel chair and lights a jimpson-weed **regalia**, and waits.

> by and by:
> 이윽고, 곧

"**By and by** a young man in a blue necktie slips into the chair next to me and asks the time.

"'Half-past ten,' says I, 'and you are Andy Tucker. I've seen you work. Wasn't it you that put up the Great Cupid Combination package on the Southern States? Let's see, it was a Chilian diamond engagement ring, a wedding ring, a potato masher, a bottle of soothing syrup and Dorothy Vernon—all for fifty cents.'

"Andy was pleased to hear that I remembered him. He was a good street man; and he was more than that—he respected his profession, and he was satisfied with 300 per cent. profit. He had plenty of offers to go into the illegitimate drug and garden seed business; but he was never to be **tempted** off of the straight path.

> tempt [tempt] v.
> 마음을 끌다, 유혹하다, 부추기다

"I wanted a partner, so Andy and me agreed to go out together. I told him about the situation in Fisher Hill and how finances was low **on account of** the local mixture of politics and **jalap**. Andy had just got in on the train that morning. He was pretty low himself, and was going to **canvass** the town for a few dollars to build a new battleship by popular subscription at Eureka Springs. So we went out and sat on the porch and talked it over.

> on account of:
> ~ 때문에
> jalap [dʒǽləp] n.
> 할라파(멕시코산 풀); 그 뿌리
> canvass [kǽnvəs] v.
> 조사하다, 점검하다

"The next morning at eleven o'clock when I

was sitting there alone, an Uncle Tom shuffles into the hotel and asked for the doctor to come and see Judge Banks, who, it seems, was the mayor and a **mighty** sick man.

"'I'm no doctor,' says I. 'Why don't you go and get the doctor?'

"'Boss,' says he. 'Doc Hoskins am done gone twenty miles in de country to see some sick persons. He's de only doctor in de town, and Massa Banks am powerful bad off. He sent me to ax you to please, suh, come.'

"'As man to man,' says I, 'I'll go and look him over.' So I put a bottle of Resurrection Bitters in my pocket and goes up on the hill to the mayor's mansion, the finest house in town, with a **mansard** roof and two cast iron dogs on the lawn.

"This Mayor Banks was in bed all but his whiskers and feet. He was making internal noises that would have had everybody in San Francisco hiking for the parks. A young man was standing by the bed holding a cup of water.

"'Doc,' says the Mayor, 'I'm awful sick. I'm about to die. Can't you do nothing for me?'

"'Mr. Mayor,' says I, 'I'm not a regular pre-ordained **disciple** of S. Q. Lapius. I never took a course in a medical college,' says I. 'I've just come as a fellow man to see if I could be

---

mighty [máiti] adv.
대단히, 몹시, 아주

mansard [mǽnsɑːrd] n.
망사르드 지붕(이중 경사의 지붕)

disciple [disáipəl] n.
제자, 문하생, 신봉자

of assistance.'

"'I'm deeply obliged,' says he. 'Doc Waugh-hoo, this is my nephew, Mr. Biddle. He has tried to **alleviate** my **distress**, but without success. Oh, Lordy! Ow-ow-ow!!' he **sings out**.

"I nods at Mr. Biddle and sets down by the bed and feels the mayor's pulse. 'Let me see your liver—your tongue, I mean,' says I. Then I turns up the lids of his eyes and looks close at the pupils of 'em.

"'How long have you been sick?' I asked.

"'I was taken down—ow-ouch—last night,' says the Mayor. 'Gimme something for it, doc, won't you?'

"'Mr. Fiddle,' says I, 'raise the window shade a bit, will you?'

"'Biddle,' says the young man. 'Do you feel like you could eat some ham and eggs, Uncle James?'

"'Mr. Mayor,' says I, after laying my ear to his right shoulder blade and listening, 'you've got a bad **attack** of super-inflammation of the right **clavicle** of the **harpsichord**!'

"'Good Lord!' says he, with a groan, 'Can't you rub something on it, or set it or anything?'

"I picks up my hat and starts for the door.

"'You ain't going, doc?' says the Mayor with a **howl**. 'You ain't going away and leave me to die with this—superfluity of the clapboards,

---

alleviate [əlí:vièit] v.
경감하다, 완화하다, 누그러뜨리다
distress [distrés] n.
고통, 괴로움
sing out:
외치다, 고함치다

attack [ətǽk] n.
발병, 발작
clavicle [klǽvikəl] n.
쇄골(鎖骨)
harpsichord [há:rpsikɔ̀:rd] n.
하프시코드(16-18세기에 쓰인 피아노의 전신)

howl [haul] n.
울음소리, 고함, 신음

are you?'

"'Common humanity, Dr. Whoa-ha,' says Mr. Biddle, 'ought to prevent your deserting a fellow human in distress.'

"'Dr. Waugh-hoo, when you get through plowing,' says I. And then I walks back to the bed and throws back my long hair.

"'Mr. Mayor,' says I, 'there is only one hope for you. Drugs will do you no good. But there is another power higher yet, although drugs are high enough,' says I.

"'And what is that?' says he.

"'Scientific demonstrations,' says I. 'The triumph of mind over **sarsaparilla**. The belief that there is no pain and sickness except what is produced when we ain't feeling well. Declare yourself **in arrears**. Demonstrate.'

"'What is this **paraphernalia** you speak of, Doc?' says the Mayor. 'You ain't a Socialist, are you?'

"'I am speaking,' says I, 'of the great doctrine of psychic financiering—of the enlightened school of long-distance, sub-conscientious treatment of **fallacies** and **meningitis**—of that wonderful in-door sport known as personal magnetism.'

"'Can you work it, doc?' asks the Mayor.

"'I'm one of the Sole **Sanhedrims** and Ostensible **Hooplas** of the Inner Pulpit,' says

---

sarsaparilla [sɑ̀:rs-əpərílə] n.
사르사파릴라(향미용으로 쓰이는 남아메리카 열대 식물)
in arrears:
체납된, 납기일이 지난

paraphernalia [pæ̀rəfərnéiljə] n. 도구 일체, 설비

fallacy [fǽləsi] n.
잘못된 생각, 착오
meningitis [mènindʒáitis] n.
수막염

Sanhedrim [sænhédrin, sɑn-, -hí:d-, sǽnidrim] n.
고대 예루살렘의 최고 평의회 겸 최고 재판소
hoopla [hú:plɑ̀:] n.
열광, 대소동

medium [míːdiəm] n.
무당, 영매
séance [séiɑːns] n.
회의, 집회, 강령회

"'I am speaking,' says I, 'of the great doctrine of psychic financiering—of the enlightened school of long-distance, sub-conscientious treatment of fallacies and meningitis—of that wonderful in-door sport known as personal magnetism.'

I. 'The lame talk and the blind rubber whenever I make a pass at 'em. I am a **medium**, a coloratura hypnotist and a spirituous control. It was only through me at the recent **seances** at Ann Arbor that the late president of the Vinegar Bitters Company could revisit the earth to communicate with his sister Jane. You see me peddling medicine on the street,' says I, 'to the poor. I don't practice personal magnetism on them. I do not drag it in the dust,' says I, 'because they haven't got the dust.'

"'Will you treat my case?' asks the Mayor.

"'Listen,' says I. 'I've had a good deal of trouble with medical societies everywhere I've been. I don't practice medicine. But, to save your life, I'll give you the psychic treatment if you'll agree as mayor not to push the license question.'

"'Of course I will,' says he. 'And now get to work, doc, for them pains are coming on again.'

"'My fee will be $250.00, cure guaranteed in two treatments,' says I.

"'All right,' says the Mayor. 'I'll pay it. I guess my life's worth that much.'

"I sat down by the bed and looked him straight in the eye.

"'Now,' says I, 'get your mind off the disease. You ain't sick. You haven't got a heart or a clavicle or a funny bone or brains or anything.

You haven't got any pain. Declare error. Now you feel the pain that you didn't have leaving, don't you?'

"'I do feel some little better, doc,' says the Mayor, 'darned if I don't. Now state a few lies about my not having this swelling in my left side, and I think I could be propped up and have some sausage and buckwheat cakes.'

"I made a few passes with my hands.

"'Now,' says I, 'the inflammation's gone. The right lobe of the **perihelion** has subsided. You're getting sleepy. You can't hold your eyes open any longer. For the present the disease is checked. Now, you are asleep.'

"The Mayor shut his eyes slowly and began to snore.

"'You observe, Mr. Tiddle,' says I, 'the wonders of modern science.'

"'Biddle,' says he, 'When will you give uncle the rest of the treatment, Dr. Pooh-pooh?'

"'Waugh-hoo,' says I. 'I'll come back at eleven to-morrow. When he wakes up give him eight drops of **turpentine** and three pounds of steak. Good morning.'

"The next morning I was back **on time**. 'Well, Mr. Riddle,' says I, when he opened the bedroom door, 'and how is uncle this morning?'

"'He seems much better,' says the young man.

"The mayor's color and pulse was fine. I

gave him another treatment, and he said the last of the pain left him.

"'Now,' says I, 'you'd better stay in bed for a day or two, and you'll be all right. It's a good thing I happened to be in Fisher Hill, Mr. Mayor,' says I, 'for all the remedies in the **cornucopia** that the regular schools of medicine use couldn't have saved you. And now that error has flew and pain proved a **perjurer**, let's allude to a cheerfuller subject—say the fee of $250. No checks, please, I hate to write my name on the back of a check almost as bad as I do on the front.'

"'I've got the cash here,' says the mayor, pulling a pocket book from under his pillow.

"He counts out five fifty-dollar notes and holds 'em in his hand.

"'Bring the receipt,' he says to Biddle.

"I signed the receipt and the mayor handed me the money. I put it in my inside pocket careful.

"'Now do your duty, officer,' says the mayor, grinning much unlike a sick man.

"Mr. Biddle lays his hand on my arm.

"'You're **under arrest**, Dr. Waugh-hoo, **alias** Peters,' says he, 'for practising medicine without authority under the State law.'

"'Who are you?' I asks.

"'I'll tell you who he is,' says Mr. Mayor,

scheme [ski:m] n.
계획, 책략, 음모

sitting up in bed. 'He's a detective employed by the State Medical Society. He's been following you over five counties. He came to me yesterday and we fixed up this **scheme** to catch you. I guess you won't do any more doctoring around these parts, Mr. Fakir. What was it you said I had, doc?' the mayor laughs, 'compound—well, it wasn't softening of the brain, I guess, anyway.'

"'A detective,' says I.

"'Correct,' says Biddle. 'I'll have to **turn you over** to the sheriff.'

turn over:
넘기다, 맡기다

"'Let's see you do it,' says I, and I grabs Biddle by the throat and half throws him out the window, but he pulls a gun and sticks it under my chin, and I stand still. Then he puts handcuffs on me, and takes the money out of my pocket.

"'I witness,' says he, 'that they're the same bills that you and I marked, Judge Banks. I'll turn them over to the sheriff when we get to his office, and he'll send you a receipt. They'll have to be used as evidence in the case.'

"'All right, Mr. Biddle,' says the mayor. 'And now, Doc Waugh-hoo,' he goes on, 'why don't you demonstrate? Can't you pull the cork out of your magnetism with your teeth and **hocus-pocus** them handcuffs off?'

hocus-pocus [houkəspoukəs] v.
장난치다, 속이다

"'Come on, officer,' says I, dignified. 'I may

as well make the best of it.' And then I turns to old Banks and rattles my chains.

"'Mr. Mayor,' says I, 'the time will come soon when you'll believe that personal magnetism is a success. And you'll be sure that it succeeded in this case, too.'

"And I guess it did.

"When we got nearly to the gate, I says: 'We might meet somebody now, Andy. I reckon you better take 'em off, and—' Hey? Why, of course it was Andy Tucker. That was his scheme; and that's how we got the capital to go into business together."

'the time will come soon when you'll believe that personal magnetism is a success. And you'll be sure that it succeeded in this case, too.'

Shearing the Wolf

eloquent [éləkwənt] adj.
웅변의, 달변인, 설득력 있는

hiatus [haiéitəs] n.
틈, 중단
levy [lévi] v.
거두어들이다, 징수하다
contribution [kàntrəbjú:ʃən / kɔ̀n-] n.
기부, 세금
conscience [kánʃəns / kɔ́n-] n.
양심, 도덕심

Jeff Peters was always **eloquent** when the ethics of his profession was under discussion.

"The only times," said he, "that me and Andy Tucker ever had any **hiatuses** in our cordial intents was when we differed on the moral aspects of grafting. Andy had his standards and I had mine. I didn't approve of all of Andy's schemes for **levying contributions** from the public, and he thought I allowed my **conscience** to interfere too often for the financial good of the firm. We had high arguments sometimes. Once one word led on to another till he said I reminded him of Rockefeller.

"'I don't know how you mean that, Andy,'

taunt [tɔ:nt, tɑ:nt] n.
비웃음, 조롱
subpoena [səbpí:nə] n.
소환장, 호출장

drover [dróuvər] n.
가축 몰이꾼, 가축 상인
cessation [seséiʃən] n.
정지, 휴지, 중지
hostility [hɑstíləti / hɔs-] n.
적대 행위
concession [kənséʃən] n.
허가, 면허, 이권
prospectus [prəspéktəs] n.
설립 취지서, 내용 설명서

quoit [kwait / -ɔit] n.
고리던지기

notorious [noutɔ́:riəs] adj.
소문난, 유명한, 이름난

says I, 'but we have been friends too long for me to take offense, at a **taunt** that you will regret when you cool off. I have yet,' says I, 'to shake hands with a **subpœna** server.'

"One summer me and Andy decided to rest up a spell in a fine little town in the mountains of Kentucky called Grassdale. We was supposed to be horse **drovers**, and good decent citizens besides, taking a summer vacation. The Grassdale people liked us, and me and Andy declared a **cessation** of **hostilities**, never so much as floating the fly leaf of a rubber **concession prospectus** or flashing a Brazilian diamond while we was there.

"One day the leading hardware merchant of Grassdale drops around to the hotel where me and Andy stopped, and smokes with us, sociable, on the side porch. We knew him pretty well from pitching **quoits** in the afternoons in the court house yard. He was a loud, red man, breathing hard, but fat and respectable beyond all reason.

"After we talk on all the **notorious** themes of the day, this Murkison—for such was his entitlements—takes a letter out of his coat pocket in a careful, careless way and hands it to us to read.

"'Now, what do you think of that?' says he, laughing—'a letter like that to ME!'

green goods:
위조 지폐
expert [ékspə:rt] n.
전문가, 숙련자
Treasury [tréʒ-əri] n.
재무부

confide [kənfáid] v.
털어놓다
rascal [ræskəl / rá:s-] n.
악당, 건달

"Me and Andy sees at a glance what it is; but we pretend to read it through. It was one of them old time typewritten **green goods** letters explaining how for $1,000 you could get $5,000 in bills that an **expert** couldn't tell from the genuine; and going on to tell how they were made from plates stolen by an employee of the **Treasury** at Washington.

"'Think of 'em sending a letter like that to ME!' says Murkison again.

"'Lot's of good men get 'em,' says Andy. 'If you don't answer the first letter they let you drop. If you answer it they write again asking you to come on with your money and do business.'

"'But think of 'em writing to ME!' says Murkison.

"A few days later he drops around again.

"'Boys,' says he, 'I know you are all right or I wouldn't **confide** in you. I wrote to them **rascals** again just for fun. They answered and told me to come on to Chicago. They said telegraph to J. Smith when I would start. When I get there I'm to wait on a certain street corner till a man in a gray suit comes along and drops a newspaper in front of me. Then I am to ask him how the water is, and he knows it's me and I know it's him.'

"'Ah, yes,' says Andy, gaping, 'it's the same

abattoir [ǽbətwɑ̀:r] n. 도살장, 투기장	
satchel [sǽtʃ-əl] n. 작은 가방	
brown paper: 갈색 포장지	

old game. I've often read about it in the papers. Then he conducts you to the private **abattoir** in the hotel, where Mr. Jones is already waiting. They show you brand new real money and sell you all you want at five for one. You see 'em put it in a **satchel** for you and know it's there. Of course it's **brown paper** when you come to look at it afterward.'

"'Oh, they couldn't switch it on me,' says Murkison. 'I haven't built up the best paying business in Grassdale without having **witticisms** about me. You say it's real money they show you, Mr. Tucker?'

witticism [wítəsìz-əm] n. 재담, 익살, 명언

"'I've always—I see by the papers that it always is,' says Andy.

"'Boys,' says Murkison, 'I've got it in my mind that them fellows can't fool me. I think I'll put a couple of thousand in my jeans and go up there and put it all over 'em. If Bill Murkison gets his eyes once on them bills they show him he'll never take 'em off of 'em. They offer $5 for $1, and they'll have to **stick to** the bargain if I tackle 'em. That's the kind of trader Bill Murkison is. Yes, I jist believe I'll drop up Chicago way and take a 5 to 1 shot on J. Smith. I guess the water'll be fine enough.'

stick to: 끝까지 지키다, 벗어나지 않다

"Me and Andy tries to get this financial **misquotation** out of Murkison's head, but we might as well have tried to keep the man who rolls

misquotation [mìskwoutéiʃən] n. 잘못된 인용

swindler [swíndlər] n. 사기꾼	

peanuts with a toothpick from betting on Bryan's election. No, sir; he was going to perform a public duty by catching these green goods **swindlers** at their own game. Maybe it would teach 'em a lesson.

heresy [hérəsi] n.
이교, 이단
ratiocination [ræ̀ʃiásənèiʃən] n. 추론, 추리

"After Murkison left us me and Andy sat a while preponderging over our silent meditations and **heresies** of reason. In our idle hours we always improved our higher selves by **ratiocination** and mental thought.

impugn [ìmpjú:n] v.
비난하다
molar [móulər] n.
어금니
chew the rag:
지껄이다, 떠들다
conscientious [kànʃiénʃəs̀] adj.
양심적인, 성실한, 진지한

"'Jeff,' says Andy after a long time, 'quite unseldom I have seen fit to **impugn** your **molars** when you have been **chewing the rag** with me about your **conscientious** way of doing business. I may have been often wrong. But here is a case where I think we can agree. I feel that it would be wrong for us to allow Mr. Murkison to go alone to meet those Chicago green goods men. There is but one way it can end. Don't you think we would both feel better if we was to intervene in some way and prevent the doing of this deed?'

"I got up and shook Andy Tucker's hand hard and long.

retract [ritrǽkt] v.
취소하다, 철회하다
nucleus [njú:kliəs] n.
중심, 핵심
do a person credit:
남의 명예가 되다, 남을 명예롭게 하다

"'Andy,' says I, 'I may have had one or two hard thoughts about the heartlessness of your corporation, but I **retract** 'em now. You have a kind **nucleus** at the interior of your exterior after all. It **does you credit**. I was just

praiseworthy [préizwə̀:rði] adj.
칭찬할 만한, 기특한
come off:
성공하다, 잘 되어 가다

fanatic [fənǽtik] n.
광신자, 열광자
bigotry [bígətri] n.
고집 불통, 편협
unscrupulous [ʌnskrúːpjələs] adj.
부도덕한, 파렴치한
trickster [tríkstəːr] n.
사기꾼, 협잡꾼
menace [ménəs] n.
위험, 위협, 협박

consent [kənsént] v.
동의하다, 찬성하다, 승인하다
waft [wɑːft, wæft] v.
떠돌다, 부유하다
ignis fatuus [ígnəs-fǽtʃuəs] n.
도깨비불, 현혹시키는 것
regalement [rigeilmənt] n.
대접, 향응, 진미

thinking the same thing that you have expressed. It would not be honorable or **praiseworthy**,' says I, 'for us to let Murkison go on with this project he has taken up. If he is determined to go let us go with him and prevent this swindle from **coming off**.'

"Andy agreed with me; and I was glad to see that he was in earnest about breaking up this green goods scheme.

"'I don't call myself a religious man,' says I, 'or a **fanatic** in moral **bigotry**, but I can't stand still and see a man who has built up a business by his own efforts and brains and risk be robbed by an **unscrupulous trickster** who is a **menace** to the public good.'

"'Right, Jeff,' says Andy. 'We'll stick right along with Murkison if he insists on going and block this funny business. I'd hate to see any money dropped in it as bad as you would.'

"Well, we went to see Murkison.

"'No, boys,' says he. 'I can't **consent** to let the song of this Chicago siren **waft** by me on the summer breeze. I'll fry some fat out of this **ignis fatuus** or burn a hole in the skillet. But I'd be plumb diverted to death to have you all go along with me. Maybe you could help some when it comes to cashing in the ticket to that 5 to 1 shot. Yes, I'd really take it as a pastime and **regalement** if you boys would go along too.'

light out: 급히 떠나다	"Murkison gives it out in Grassdale that he is going for a few days with Mr. Peters and Mr. Tucker to look over some iron ore property in West Virginia. He wires J. Smith that he will set foot in the spider web on a given date; and the three of us **lights out** for Chicago.
premonition [prìːmənίʃən] n. 예감, 징후, 전조	"On the way Murkison amuses himself with **premonitions** and advance pleasant recollections.
	"'In a gray suit,' says he, 'on the southwest corner of Wabash avenue and Lake street. He drops the paper, and I ask how the water is. Oh, my, my, my!' And then he laughs all over for five minutes.
cogitation [kɑdʒəteiʃən / kɔdʒ-] n. 심사 숙고, 명상, 고찰	"Sometimes Murkison was serious and tried to talk himself out of his **cogitations**, whatever they was.
prey [prei] v. 약탈하다, 휩쓸다	"'Boys,' says he, 'I wouldn't have this to get out in Grassdale for ten times a thousand dollars. It would ruin me there. But I know you all are all right. I think it's the duty of every citizen,' says he, 'to try to do up these robbers that **prey** upon the public. I'll show 'em whether the water's fine. Five dollars for one—that's what J. Smith offers, and he'll have to keep his contract if he does business with Bill Murkison.'

"We got into Chicago about 7 p.m. Murkison was to meet the gray man at half past 9. We ued dinner at a hotel and then went up to Murkison's room to wait for the time to come.

"'Now, boys,' says Murkison, 'let's get our **gumption** together and **inoculate** a plan for defeating the enemy. Suppose while I'm exchanging airy bandage with the gray **capper** you **gents** come along, by accident, you know, and **holler**: "Hello, Murk!" and shake hands with symptoms of surprise and familiarity. Then I take the capper aside and tell him you all are Jenkins and Brown of Grassdale, groceries and feed, good men and maybe willing to take a chance while away from home.'

"'"Bring 'em along," he'll say, of course, "if they care to invest." Now, how does that scheme strike you?'

"'What do you say, Jeff?' says Andy, looking at me.

"'Why, I'll tell you what I say,' says I. 'I say let's settle this thing right here now. I don't see any use of wasting any more time.' I took a nickel-plated .38 out of my pocket and clicked the cylinder around a few times.

"'You **undevout, sinful, insidious hog**,' says I to Murkison, 'get out that two thousand and lay it on the table. Obey with velocity,' says I, 'for otherwise alternatives are **impending**. I am preferably a man of mildness, but now and then I find myself in the middle of **extremities**.

courthouse [kɔ́:rtháus] n.
법원
skin [skin] v.
강탈하다, 빼앗다, 사취하다
stand off:
물리치다, 막아내다
decent [dí:sənt] adj.
고상한, 기품있는
larceny [lá:rs-əni] n.
절도죄, 도둑질
contemptible [kəntémptəbəl]
adj. 멸시할 만한, 경멸할 만한,
비열한
scoundrel [skáundr-əl] n.
무뢰한, 악당
extortion [ikstɔ́:rʃən] n.
강탈, 빼앗음
wiretapper [wáiə:rtæpər] n.
도청자
out of business:
폐업하여, 가게 문을 닫는
squeal [skwi:l] v.
밀고하다, 고발하다
hock [hɑk / hɔk] v.
저당잡히다

Such men as you,' I went on after he had laid the money out, 'is what keeps the jails and **court houses** going. You come up here to rob these men of their money. Does it excuse you?' I asks, 'that they were trying to **skin** you? No, sir; you was going to rob Peter to **stand off** Paul. You are ten times worse,' says I, 'than that green goods man. You go to church at home and pretend to be a **decent** citizen, but you'll come to Chicago and commit **larceny** from men that have built up a sound and profitable business by dealing with such **contemptible scoundrels** as you have tried to be to-day. How do you know,' says I, 'that that green goods man hasn't a large family dependent upon his **extortions**? It's you supposedly respectable citizens who are always on the lookout to get something for nothing,' says I, 'that support the lotteries and wild-cat mines and stock exchanges and **wire tappers** of this country. If it wasn't for you they'd **go out of business**. The green goods man you was going to rob,' says I, 'studied maybe for years to learn his trade. Every turn he makes he risks his money and liberty and maybe his life. You come up here all sanctified and vanoplied with respectability and a pleasing post office address to swindle him. If he gets the money you can **squeal** to the police. If you get it he **hocks** the

Shearing the Wolf

gray suit to buy supper and says nothing. Mr. Tucker and me **sized** you **up**,' says I, 'and came along to see that you got what you deserved. Hand over the money,' says I, 'you grass fed **hypocrite**.'

"I put the two thousand, which was all in $20 bills, in my inside pocket.

"'Now get out your watch,' says I to Murkison. 'No, I don't want it,' says I. 'Lay it on the table and you sit in that chair till it ticks off an hour. Then you can go. If you make any noise or leave any sooner we'll handbill you all over Grassdale. I guess your high position there is worth more than $2,000 to you.'

"Then me and Andy left.

"On the train Andy was a long time silent. Then he says: 'Jeff, do you mind my asking you a question?'

"'Two,' says I, 'or forty.'

"'Was that the idea you had,' says he, 'when we started out with Murkison?'

"'Why, certainly,' says I. 'What else could it have been? Wasn't it yours, too?'

"In about half an hour Andy spoke again. I think there are times when Andy don't exactly understand my system of ethics and moral **hygiene**.

"'Jeff,' says he, 'some time when you have the leisure I wish you'd draw off a **diagram**

---

size up:
평가하다, 판단하다
hypocrite [hípəkrìt] n.
위선자

You are ten times worse,' says I, 'than that green goods man. You go to church at home and pretend to be a decent citizen, but you'll come to Chicago and commit larceny from men that have built up a sound and profitable business by dealing with such contemptible scoundrels as you have tried to be to-day.

hygiene [háidʒi:n] n.
위생학, 위생 상태

diagram [dáiəgræm] n.
그림, 약도

footnote [fútnòut] n.
각주(脚注)

and **foot-notes** of that conscience of yours. I'd like to have it to refer to occasionally.'"

A Service of Love

When one loves one's Art no service seems too hard.

That is our **premise**. This story shall draw a conclusion from it, and show at the same time that the premise is incorrect. That will be a new thing in logic, and a **feat** in story-telling somewhat older than the **great wall of China**.

Joe Larrabee came out of the post-oak flats of the Middle West **pulsing** with a genius for pictorial art. At six he drew a picture of the town pump with a prominent citizen passing it hastily. This **effort** was framed and hung in the drug store window by the side of the ear of corn with an uneven number of rows. At twenty he left for New York with a flowing

---

premise [prémis] n.
전제
feat [fi:t] n.
위업, 공적, 공훈
Great Wall of China:
만리장성

pulse [pʌls] v.
맥박치다, 고동하다
effort [éfərt] n.
노력의 결과, 작품, 역작

relative [rélətiv] n. 친척, 친족, 인척	
chip in: 기부하다, 추렴하다, 갹출하다	

necktie and a capital tied up somewhat closer.

Delia Caruthers did things in six octaves so promisingly in a pine-tree village in the South that her **relatives chipped in** enough in her chip hat for her to go "North" and "finish." They could not see her f—, but that is our story.

atelier [ǽtəljèi] n.
작업실, 화실, 아틀리에
chiaroscuro [kià:rəskjú:rou] n.
명암의 배합
oolong [ú:lɔ̀(:)ŋ, -làŋ] n.
우롱차, 오룡차
enamor [inǽmər] v.
반하게 하다, 매혹하다

Joe and Delia met in an **atelier** where a number of art and music students had gathered to discuss **chiaroscuro**, Wagner, music, Rembrandt's works, pictures, Waldteufel, wall paper, Chopin and **Oolong**.

Joe and Delia became **enamoured** one of the other, or each of the other, as you please, and in a short time were married—for (see above), when one loves one's Art no service seems too hard.

flat [flæt] n.
플랫식 주택
(각층에 1가구가 살게 만든 아파트)
sell all thou hast~:
마태복음 19장 21절 참조

Mr. and Mrs. Larrabee began housekeeping in a **flat**. It was a lonesome flat—something like the A sharp way down at the left-hand end of the keyboard. And they were happy; for they had their Art, and they had each other. And my advice to the rich young man would be—**sell all thou hast**, and give it to the poor—janitor for the privilege of living in a flat with your Art and your Delia.

indorse [indɔ́:rs], [in-] v.
인정하다, 승인하다
dictum [díktəm] n.
공식 견해, 언명, 단정

Flat-dwellers shall **indorse** my **dictum** that theirs is the only true happiness. If a home is happy it cannot fit too close—let the dresser

A Service of Love

escritoire [èskritwá:r] n.
책상

renown [rináun] n.
명성, 유명
repute [ripjú:t] n.
평판, 세평

mighty [máiti] adv.
대단히, 몹시, 아주
cynical [sínikəl] adj.
의심하는, 비웃는, 비꼬는
sandbag [sǽndbæ̀g] v.
맹렬히 공격하다

collapse and become a billiard table; let the mantel turn to a rowing machine, the **escritoire** to a spare bedchamber, the washstand to an upright piano; let the four walls come together, if they will, so you and your Delia are between. But if home be the other kind, let it be wide and long—enter you at the Golden Gate, hang your hat on Hatteras, your cape on Cape Horn and go out by the Labrador.

Joe was painting in the class of the great Magister—you know his fame. His fees are high; his lessons are light—his high-lights have brought him **renown**. Delia was studying under Rosenstock—you know his **repute** as a disturber of the piano keys.

They were **mighty** happy as long as their money lasted. So is every—but I will not be **cynical**. Their aims were very clear and defined. Joe was to become capable very soon of turning out pictures that old gentlemen with thin side-whiskers and thick pocketbooks would **sandbag** one another in his studio for the privilege of buying. Delia was to become familiar and then contemptuous with Music, so that when she saw the orchestra seats and boxes unsold she could have sore throat and lobster in a private dining-room and refuse to go on the stage.

But the best, in my opinion, was the home

ardent:[á:rdənt] adj.
열렬한, 정열적인
voluble [váljəbəl / vɔ́l-] adj.
말 잘하는, 능변인, 유창한
inconsiderable [ìnkən-sídərəbəl] adj.
중요치 않은, 하잘 것 없는

vulgarian [vʌlgɛ́əriən] n.
속물, 속인
chafing dish:
요리 보온용 기구

canvass [kǽnvəs] v.
얻으려 하다, 부탁하다
elated [iléitid] adj.
우쭐한, 의기양양한

life in the little flat—the **ardent, voluble** chats after the day's study; the cozy dinners and fresh, light breakfasts; the interchange of ambitions—ambitions interwoven each with the other's or else **inconsiderable**—the mutual help and inspiration; and—overlook my artlessness—stuffed olives and cheese sandwiches at 11 p.m.

But after a while Art flagged. It sometimes does, even if some switchman doesn't flag it. Everything going out and nothing coming in, as the **vulgarians** say. Money was lacking to pay Mr. Magister and Herr Rosenstock their prices. When one loves one's Art no service seems too hard. So, Delia said she must give music lessons to keep the **chafing dish** bubbling.

For two or three days she went out **canvassing** for pupils. One evening she came home **elated**.

"Joe, dear," she said, gleefully, "I've a pupil. And, oh, the loveliest people! General—General A. B. Pinkney's daughter—on Seventy-first street. Such a splendid house, Joe—you ought to see the front door! Byzantine I think you would call it. And inside! Oh, Joe, I never saw anything like it before.

"My pupil is his daughter Clementina. I dearly love her already. She's a delicate thing—dresses always in white; and the sweetest, simplest manners! Only eighteen years old. I'm to give three lessons a week; and, just think, Joe! $5 a lesson. I don't mind it a bit; for when I get two or three more pupils I can **resume** my lessons with Herr Rosenstock. Now, smooth out that **wrinkle** between your brows, dear, and let's have a nice supper."

"That's all right for you, Dele," said Joe, attacking a can of peas with a carving knife and a hatchet, "but how about me? Do you think I'm going to let you hustle for wages while I philander in the regions of high art? Not by the bones of Benvenuto Cellini! I guess I can sell papers or lay cobblestones, and bring in a dollar or two."

Delia came and hung about his neck.

"Joe, dear, you are silly. You must keep on at your studies. It is not as if I had quit my music and gone to work at something else. While I teach I learn. I am always with my music. And we can live as happily as millionaires on $15 a week. You mustn't think of leaving Mr. Magister."

"All right," said Joe, reaching for the blue scalloped vegetable dish. "But I hate for you to be giving lessons. It isn't Art. But you're a **trump** and a **dear** to do it."

"When one loves one's Art no service seems too hard," said Delia.

moneyed [mʌ́nid] adj.
부자의, 부유한

engaging [engéidʒiŋ] adj.
마음을 끄는, 매력적인
mistress [místris] n.
여주인, 안주인

"Magister praised the sky in that sketch I made in the park," said Joe. "And Tinkle gave me permission to hang two of them in his window. I may sell one if the right kind of a **moneyed** idiot sees them."

"I'm sure you will," said Delia, sweetly. "And now let's be thankful for Gen. Pinkney and this veal roast."

During all of the next week the Larrabees had an early breakfast. Joe was enthusiastic about some morning-effect sketches he was doing in Central Park, and Delia packed him off breakfasted, coddled, praised and kissed at 7 o'clock. Art is an **engaging mistress**. It was most times 7 o'clock when he returned in the evening.

At the end of the week Delia, sweetly proud but languid, triumphantly tossed three five-dollar bills on the 8×10 (inches) centre table of the 8×10 (feet) flat parlour.

"Sometimes," she said, a little wearily, "Clementina tries me. I'm afraid she doesn't practise enough, and I have to tell her the same things so often. And then she always dresses entirely in white, and that does get monotonous. But Gen. Pinkney is the dearest old man! I wish you could know him, Joe. He comes in sometimes when I am with Clementina at the piano—he is a widower, you know—and stands

goatee [goutíː] n.
염소 수염
semiquaver [sémikwèivər, sémai-ə] n.
16분 음표
demisemiquaver [dèmisémikwèivər] n.
32분 음표
wainscoting [weinskətiŋ, -skoutiŋ] n.
징두리 벽판, 징두리 널
astrakhan [ǽstrəkən, -kǽn] n.
아스트라한(러시아 Volga강 하구의 도시), 아스트라한 모조 직물
portiere [pɔːrtjéər, -tiéər] n.
(문간 등에 치는) 휘장, 막
legal tender:
법정 화폐, 법화
obelisk [ábəlìsk / ɔ́b-] n.
오벨리스크, 방첨탑

there pulling his white **goatee**. 'And how are the **semiquavers** and the **demisemiquavers** progressing?' he always asks.

"I wish you could see the **wainscoting** in that drawing-room, Joe! And those **Astrakhan** rug **portières**. And Clementina has such a funny little cough. I hope she is stronger than she looks. Oh, I really am getting attached to her, she is so gentle and high bred. Gen. Pinkney's brother was once Minister to Bolivia."

And then Joe, with the air of a Monte Cristo, drew forth a ten, a five, a two and a one—all **legal tender** notes—and laid them beside Delia's earnings.

"Sold that watercolour of the **obelisk** to a man from Peoria," he announced overwhelmingly.

"Don't joke with me," said Delia, "not from Peoria!"

"All the way. I wish you could see him, Dele. Fat man with a woollen muffler and a quill toothpick. He saw the sketch in Tinkle's window and thought it was a windmill at first. He was game, though, and bought it anyhow. He ordered another—an oil sketch of the Lackawanna freight depot—to take back with him. Music lessons! Oh, I guess Art is still in it."

"I'm so glad you've kept on," said Delia, heartily. "You're bound to win, dear. Thirty-three dollars! We never had so much to spend before.

filet mignon [fileimi:njɑn / fileimi:njɔn] n.
필레 미뇽; 원통형으로 두껍게 자른 소 등심살
champignon [ʃæmpínjən] n.
샴피뇽(송이과의 식용 버섯)

Welsh rabbit:
치즈 토스트의 일종
distracted [distrǽktid] adj.
당황한, 이성을 잃은

We'll have oysters to-night."

"And **filet mignon** with **champignons**," said Joe. "Where is the olive fork?"

On the next Saturday evening Joe reached home first. He spread his $18 on the parlour table and washed what seemed to be a great deal of dark paint from his hands.

Half an hour later Delia arrived, her right hand tied up in a shapeless bundle of wraps and bandages.

"How is this?" asked Joe after the usual greetings. Delia laughed, but not very joyously.

"Clementina," she explained, "insisted upon a **Welsh rabbit** after her lesson. She is such a queer girl. Welsh rabbits at 5 in the afternoon. The General was there. You should have seen him run for the chafing dish, Joe, just as if there wasn't a servant in the house. I know Clementina isn't in good health; she is so nervous. In serving the rabbit she spilled a great lot of it, boiling hot, over my hand and wrist. It hurt awfully, Joe. And the dear girl was so sorry! But Gen. Pinkney!—Joe, that old man nearly went **distracted**. He rushed downstairs and sent somebody—they said the furnace man or somebody in the basement—out to a drug store for some oil and things to bind it up with. It doesn't hurt so much now."

"What's this?" asked Joe, taking the hand

tenderly and pulling at some white strands beneath the bandages.

"It's something soft," said Delia, "that had oil on it. Oh, Joe, did you sell another sketch?" She had seen the money on the table.

"Did I?" said Joe; "just ask the man from Peoria. He got his depot to-day, and he isn't sure but he thinks he wants another parkscape and a view on the Hudson. What time this afternoon did you burn your hand, Dele?"

"Five o'clock, I think," said Dele, **plaintively**. "The iron—I mean the rabbit came off the fire about that time. You ought to have seen Gen. Pinkney, Joe, when—"

"Sit down here a moment, Dele," said Joe. He drew her to the couch, sat beside her and put his arm across her shoulders.

"What have you been doing for the last two weeks, Dele?" he asked.

She **braved** it for a moment or two with an eye full of love and stubbornness, and murmured a phrase or two vaguely of Gen. Pinkney; but at length down went her head and out came the truth and tears.

"I couldn't get any pupils," she confessed. "And I couldn't bear to have you give up your lessons; and I got a place ironing shirts in that big Twenty-fourth street laundry. And I think I did very well to make up both General

plaintively [pléintivli] adv.
애처롭게, 슬프게

brave [breiv] v.
무릅쓰다, 용감하게 맞서다

Pinkney and Clementina, don't you, Joe? And when a girl in the laundry set down a hot iron on my hand this afternoon I was all the way home making up that story about the Welsh rabbit. You're not angry, are you, Joe? And if I hadn't got the work you mightn't have sold your sketches to that man from Peoria."

"He wasn't from Peoria," said Joe, slowly.

"Well, it doesn't matter where he was from. How clever you are, Joe—and—kiss me, Joe—and what made you ever suspect that I wasn't giving music lessons to Clementina?"

"I didn't," said Joe, "until to-night. And I wouldn't have then, only I sent up this cotton waste and oil from the engine-room this afternoon for a girl upstairs who had her hand burned with a smoothing-iron. I've been firing the engine in that laundry for the last two weeks."

"And then you didn't—"

"My purchaser from Peoria," said Joe, "and Gen. Pinkney are both creations of the same art—but you wouldn't call it either painting or music."

And then they both laughed, and Joe began:

"When one loves one's Art no service seems—"

But Delia stopped him with her hand on his lips. "No," she said—"just 'When one loves.'"

The Green Door

consummation [kɑ̀nsəméiʃən / kɔ̀n-] n.
완성, 달성, 성취, 마무리
vaudeville [vɔ́:dəvil, vóud-] n.
보드빌 (노래, 춤 등을 섞은 쇼)
ejaculate [idʒǽkjəlèit] v.
(갑자기) 소리치다, 외치다
parallelogram [pæ̀rəléləgræ̀m] n. 평행 사변형

Suppose you should be walking down Broadway after dinner, with ten minutes allotted to the **consummation** of your cigar while you are choosing between a diverting tragedy and something serious in the way of **vaudeville**. Suddenly a hand is laid upon your arm. You turn to look into the thrilling eyes of a beautiful woman, wonderful in diamonds and Russian sables. She thrusts hurriedly into your hand an extremely hot buttered roll, flashes out a tiny pair of scissors, snips off the second button of your overcoat, meaningly **ejaculates** the one word, "**parallelogram**!" and swiftly flies down a cross street, looking back fearfully over her shoulder.

sheepishly [ʃíːpiʃli] adv.
소심하게, 수줍게

plentiful [pléntifəl] adj.
많은, 충분한, 풍부한
Golden Fleece:
(그리스 신화) 금 양털
Holy Grail:
성배(聖杯), 예수가 최후의 만찬에 썼다는 잔
ladylove [léidilʌv] n.
애인, 연인
prodigal son:
돌아온 탕아
(누가복음 15:11-32 참조)

tierce [tiəːrs] n.
(펜싱) 제3의 자세

That would be pure adventure. Would you accept it? Not you. You would flush with embarrassment; you would **sheepishly** drop the roll and continue down Broadway, fumbling feebly for the missing button. This you would do unless you are one of the blessed few in whom the pure spirit of adventure is not dead.

True adventurers have never been **plentiful**. They who are set down in print as such have been mostly business men with newly invented methods. They have been out after the things they wanted—**golden fleeces**, **holy grails**, **lady loves**, treasure, crowns and fame. The true adventurer goes forth aimless and uncalculating to meet and greet unknown fate. A fine example was the **Prodigal Son**—when he started back home.

Half-adventurers—brave and splendid figures—have been numerous. From the Crusades to the Palisades they have enriched the arts of history and fiction and the trade of historical fiction. But each of them had a prize to win, a goal to kick, an axe to grind, a race to run, a new thrust in **tierce** to deliver, a name to carve, a crow to pick—so they were not followers of true adventure.

In the big city the twin spirits Romance and Adventure are always abroad seeking worthy wooers. As we roam the streets they slyly peep at us and challenge us in twenty different **guises**. Without knowing why, we look up suddenly to see in a window a face that seems to belong to our gallery of intimate portraits; in a sleeping thoroughfare we hear a cry of **agony** and fear coming from an empty and shuttered house; instead of at our familiar curb, a cab-driver deposits us before a strange door, which one, with a smile, opens for us and bids us enter; a slip of paper, written upon, flutters down to our feet from the high lattices of Chance; we exchange glances of instantaneous hate, affection and fear with hurrying strangers in the passing crowds; a sudden **souse** of rain—and our umbrella may be sheltering the daughter of the Full Moon and first cousin of the **Sidereal** System; at every corner handkerchiefs drop, fingers **beckon**, eyes besiege, and the lost, the lonely, the rapturous, the mysterious, the perilous, changing clues of adventure are slipped into our fingers. But few of us are willing to hold and follow them. We are grown stiff with the **ramrod** of convention down our backs. We pass on; and some day we come, at the end of a very dull life, to reflect that our romance has been a pallid thing of a marriage or two, a satin rosette kept in a safe-deposit drawer, and a lifelong feud with a steam radiator.

---

guise [gaiz] n.
외관, 모습, 겉보기
agony [ǽgəni] n.
고민, 고통
souse [saus] n.
물에 담금, 흠뻑 젖음
sidereal [saidí-əriəl] adj.
별의, 항성의
beckon [békən] v.
(손짓, 고갯짓, 몸짓으로) 신호하다, 부르다
ramrod [rǽmrɑd / -rɔ̀d] n.
포(砲)에 탄약을 재는 도구; 꽂을대

at every corner handkerchiefs drop, fingers beckon, eyes besiege, and the lost, the lonely, the rapturous, the mysterious, the perilous, changing clues of adventure are slipped into our fingers. But few of us are willing to hold and follow them.

egregious [igríːdʒəs, -dʒiəs] adj. 지독한, 어처구니없는
station house: 경찰서
dupe [djuːp] n. 잘 속는 사람
trickster [tríkstəːr] n. 사기꾼, 협잡꾼
allurement [əlúərmənt] n. 매력, 유혹
undiminished [ʌndimíniʃt] adj. 줄지 않은, 쇠퇴하지 않은
ardour [áːrdər] n. 열정, 열의

specious [spíːʃəs] adj. 허울 좋은, 겉만 번드르르한,
table d'hôte [táːb-əldóut, tǽb-] n. (호텔 등의) 공동식탁

serenely [siríːnli] adv. 조용하게, 평온하게

Rudolf Steiner was a true adventurer. Few were the evenings on which he did not go forth from his hall bedchamber in search of the unexpected and the **egregious**. The most interesting thing in life seemed to him to be what might lie just around the next corner. Sometimes his willingness to tempt fate led him into strange paths. Twice he had spent the night in a **station-house**; again and again he had found himself the **dupe** of ingenious and mercenary **tricksters**; his watch and money had been the price of one flattering **allurement**. But with **undiminished ardour** he picked up every glove cast before him into the merry lists of adventure.

One evening Rudolf was strolling along a crosstown street in the older central part of the city. Two streams of people filled the sidewalks—the home-hurrying, and that restless contingent that abandons home for the **specious** welcome of the thousand-candle-power *table d'hôte*.

The young adventurer was of pleasing presence, and moved **serenely** and watchfully. By daylight he was a salesman in a piano store. He wore his tie drawn through a topaz ring instead of fastened with a stick pin; and once he had written to the editor of a magazine that "Junie's Love Test" by Miss Libbey, had been the book that had most influenced his life.

During his walk a violent chattering of teeth in a glass case on the sidewalk seemed at first to draw his attention (with a **qualm**), to a restaurant before which it was set; but a second glance revealed the electric letters of a dentist's sign high above the next door. A giant negro, fantastically dressed in a red embroidered coat, yellow trousers and a military cap, discreetly distributed cards to those of the passing crowd who consented to take them.

This mode of dentistic advertising was a common sight to Rudolf. Usually he passed the dispenser of the dentist's cards without reducing his store; but to-night the African slipped one into his hand so deftly that he retained it there smiling a little at the successful feat.

When he had travelled a few yards further he glanced at the card **indifferently**. Surprised, he turned it over and looked again with interest. One side of the card was blank; on the other was written in ink three words, "The Green Door." And then Rudolf saw, three steps in front of him, a man throw down the card the negro had given him as he passed. Rudolf picked it up. It was printed with the dentist's name and address and the usual schedule of "plate work" and "bridge work" and "crowns," and **specious** promises of "painless" operations.

pedestrian [pədéstriən] n.
보행자
legend [lédʒ-ənd] n.
기입, 적힌 내용

arch [ɑ:rtʃ] adj.
장난기 있는, 교활한
sprite [sprait] n.
요정, 도깨비
follower [fɑ́louə:r / fɔ́l-] n.
추종자, 신봉자, 지지자
quest [kwest] n.
모험, 여행, 원정
suavely [swɑ:vli] adv.
온화하게, 점잖게
akin [əkín] adj.
가까운, 유사한
jabber [dʒǽbər] n.
재잘거림, 중얼거림

The adventurous piano salesman halted at the corner and considered. Then he crossed the street, walked down a block, recrossed and joined the upward current of people again. Without seeming to notice the negro as he passed the second time, he carelessly took the card that was handed him. Ten steps away he inspected it. In the same handwriting that appeared on the first card "The Green Door" was inscribed upon it. Three or four cards were tossed to the pavement by **pedestrians** both following and leading him. These fell blank side up. Rudolf turned them over. Every one bore the printed **legend** of the dental "parlours."

Rarely did the **arch sprite** Adventure need to beckon twice to Rudolf Steiner, his true **follower**. But twice it had been done, and the **quest** was on.

Rudolf walked slowly back to where the giant negro stood by the case of rattling teeth. This time as he passed he received no card. In spite of his gaudy and ridiculous garb, the Ethiopian displayed a natural barbaric dignity as he stood, offering the cards **suavely** to some, allowing others to pass unmolested. Every half minute he chanted a harsh, unintelligible phrase **akin** to the **jabber** of car conductors and grand opera. And not only did he withhold a card this time,

countenance [káuntənəns] n.
얼굴 표정, 안색
contemptuous [kəntémptʃuəs] adj. 얕보는, 경멸하는
disdain [disdéin] n.
경멸, 모멸
throng [θrɔ(:)ŋ, θrɑŋ] n.
군중, 인파
deficient [difíʃənt] adj.
부족한, 모자란
enigma [inígmə] n.
수수께끼

but it seemed to Rudolf that he received from the shining and massive black **countenance** a look of cold, almost **contemptuous disdain**.

The look stung the adventurer. He read in it a silent accusation that he had been found wanting. Whatever the mysterious written words on the cards might mean, the black had selected him twice from the **throng** for their recipient; and now seemed to have condemned him as **deficient** in the wit and spirit to engage the **enigma**.

Standing aside from the rush, the young man made a rapid estimate of the building in which he conceived that his adventure must lie. Five stories high it rose. A small restaurant occupied the basement.

polyglot [páliglàt / póliglòt] adj.
여러 언어에 통하는, 여러 언어의
babel [béibəl, bǽb-] n.
떠들썩한 말소리 또는 장소
abode [əbóud] n.
주거, 거처
palmist [pá:mist] n.
수상가, 손금쟁이
domesticity [dòumestísəti] n.
가정 생활

The first floor, now closed, seemed to house millinery or furs. The second floor, by the winking electric letters, was the dentist's. Above this a **polyglot babel** of signs struggled to indicate the **abodes** of **palmists**, dressmakers, musicians and doctors. Still higher up draped curtains and milk bottles white on the window sills proclaimed the regions of **domesticity**.

After concluding his survey Rudolf walked briskly up the high flight of stone steps into the house. Up two flights of the carpeted stairway he continued; and at its top paused. The

wan [wɑn / wɔn] adj.
창백한
halo [héilou] n.
둥근 빛, 후광
contumelious [kàntjumí:ljəs / kɔ̀n-] adj.
오만 불손한, 무례한

gamester [géimstər] n.
도박꾼, 노름꾼
cunning [kʌ́niŋ] adj.
교활한, 간사한
rogue [roug] n.
악한, 불량배
temerarious [tèməréəriəs] adj.
무모한, 대담 무쌍한

rustle [rʌ́s-əl] n.
바스락 거림, 옷 스치는 소리
totter [tátə:r / tɔ́tə:r] v.
비틀거리다, 비트적거리다

hallway there was dimly lighted by two pale jets of gas—one far to his right, the other nearer, to his left. He looked toward the nearer light and saw, within its **wan halo**, a green door. For one moment he hesitated; then he seemed to see the **contumelious** sneer of the African juggler of cards; and then he walked straight to the green door and knocked against it.

Moments like those that passed before his knock was answered measure the quick breath of true adventure. What might not be behind those green panels! **Gamesters** at play; **cunning rogues** baiting their traps with subtle skill; beauty in love with courage, and thus planning to be sought by it; danger, death, love, disappointment, ridicule—any of these might respond to that **temerarious** rap.

A faint **rustle** was heard inside, and the door slowly opened. A girl not yet twenty stood there, white-faced and **tottering**. She loosed the knob and swayed weakly, groping with one hand. Rudolf caught her and laid her on a faded couch that stood against the wall. He closed the door and took a swift glance around the room by the light of a flickering gas jet. Neat, but extreme poverty was the story that he read.

The girl lay still, as if in a faint. Rudolf looked around the room excitedly for a barrel.

derby [dá:rbi / dá:r-] n.
중산모
tendril [téndril] n.
덩굴손
wofully [wóufəl] adv.
슬프게, 애처롭게

himmel:
(German) 하늘, 천국, 신

People must be rolled upon a barrel who—no, no; that was for drowned persons. He began to fan her with his hat. That was successful, for he struck her nose with the brim of his **derby** and she opened her eyes. And then the young man saw that hers, indeed, was the one missing face from his heart's gallery of intimate portraits. The frank, grey eyes, the little nose, turning pertly outward; the chestnut hair, curling like the **tendrils** of a pea vine, seemed the right end and reward of all his wonderful adventures. But the face was **wofully** thin and pale.

The girl looked at him calmly, and then smiled.

"Fainted, didn't I?" she asked, weakly. "Well, who wouldn't? You try going without anything to eat for three days and see!"

"**Himmel**!" exclaimed Rudolf, jumping up. "Wait till I come back."

He dashed out the green door and down the stairs. In twenty minutes he was back again, kicking at the door with his toe for her to open it. With both arms he hugged an array of wares from the grocery and the restaurant. On the table he laid them—bread and butter, cold meats, cakes, pies, pickles, oysters, a roasted chicken, a bottle of milk and one of red-hot tea.

unerring [ʌnə́:riŋ] adj. 실수하지 않는

"This is ridiculous," said Rudolf, blusteringly, "to go without eating. You must quit making election bets of this kind. Supper is ready." He helped her to a chair at the table and asked: "Is there a cup for the tea?" "On the shelf by the window," she answered. When he turned again with the cup he saw her, with eyes shining rapturously, beginning upon a huge Dill pickle that she had rooted out from the paper bags with a woman's **unerring** instinct. He took it from her, laughingly, and poured the cup full of milk. "Drink that first" he ordered, "and then you shall have some tea, and then a chicken wing. If you are very good you shall have a pickle to-morrow. And now, if you'll allow me to be your guest we'll have supper."

He drew up the other chair. The tea brightened the girl's eyes and brought back some of her colour. She began to eat with a sort of dainty ferocity like some starved wild animal. She seemed to regard the young man's presence and the aid he had rendered her as a natural thing—not as though she undervalued the conventions; but as one whose great stress gave her the right to put aside the artificial for the human. But gradually, with the return of strength and comfort, came also a sense of the little conventions that belong; and she began to tell him her little story. It was one of a thousand such as the city **yawns** at every day—the shop girl's story of **insufficient** wages, further reduced by "fines" that go to **swell** the store's profits; of time lost through illness; and then of lost positions, lost hope, and—the knock of the adventurer upon the green door.

But to Rudolf the history sounded as big as the Iliad or the crisis in "Junie's Love Test."

"To think of you going through all that," he exclaimed.

"It was something fierce," said the girl, solemnly.

"And you have no relatives or friends in the city?"

"None whatever."

"I am all alone in the world, too," said Rudolf, after a pause.

"I am glad of that," said the girl, promptly; and somehow it pleased the young man to hear that she approved of his **bereft** condition.

Very suddenly her eyelids dropped and she sighed deeply.

"I'm awfully sleepy," she said, "and I feel so good."

Then Rudolf rose and took his hat. "I'll say good-night. A long night's sleep will be fine for you."

He held out his hand, and she took it and said "good-night." But her eyes asked a question so

---

yawn [jɔ:n] v.
하품하다
insufficient [ìnsəfíʃənt] adj.
불충분한, 부족한
swell [swel] v.
부풀다, 늘다, 증대하다

bereft [biréft] adj.
빼앗긴, 잃은

eloquently, so frankly and pathetically that he answered it with words.

"Oh, I'm coming back to-morrow to see how you are getting along. You can't get rid of me so easily."

Then, at the door, as though the way of his coming had been so much less important than the fact that he had come, she asked: "How did you come to knock at my door?"

He looked at her for a moment, remembering the cards, and felt a sudden jealous pain. What if they had fallen into other hands as adventurous as his? Quickly he decided that she must never know the truth. He would never let her know that he was aware of the strange **expedient** to which she had been driven by her great distress.

"One of our piano tuners lives in this house," he said. "I knocked at your door by mistake."

The last thing he saw in the room before the green door closed was her smile.

At the head of the stairway he paused and looked curiously about him. And then he went along the hallway to its other end; and, coming back, ascended to the floor above and continued his puzzled explorations. Every door that he found in the house was painted green.

Wondering, he descended to the sidewalk. The fantastic African was still there. Rudolf

expedient [ikspí:diənt] n.
수단, 방책, 임시조처

confronted him with his two cards in his hand.

"Will you tell me why you gave me these cards and what they mean?" he asked.

In a broad, good-natured grin the negro exhibited a splendid advertisement of his master's profession.

"Dar it is, boss," he said, pointing down the street. "But I 'spect you is a little late for de fust act."

Looking the way he pointed Rudolf saw above the entrance to a theatre the blazing electric sign of its new play, "The Green Door."

"I'm informed dat it's a fust-rate show, sah," said the negro. "De agent what represents it pussented me with a dollar, sah, to distribute a few of his cards along with de doctah's. May I offer you one of de doctah's cards, suh?"

At the corner of the block in which he lived Rudolf stopped for a glass of beer and a cigar. When he had come out with his lighted weed he buttoned his coat, pushed back his hat and said, stoutly, to the lamp post on the corner:

"All the same, I believe it was the hand of Fate that **doped out** the way for me to find her."

Which conclusion, under the circumstances, certainly admits Rudolf Steiner to the ranks of the true followers of Romance and Adventure.

Looking the way he pointed Rudolf saw above the entrance to a theatre the blazing electric sign of its new play, "The Green Door."

dope out:
찾아내다, 알아내다

PHŒBE

attribute [ətríbju:t] v.
~에 기인한다고 생각하다, ~의 결과라고 생각하다
aforesaid [əfɔːrsed] adj.
앞서 말한, 전술한

insolence [ínsələns] n.
오만, 무례
phraseology [frèiziálədʒi / -ɔ́l-] n.
표현, 문구, 어법

"You are a man of many novel adventures and varied enterprises," I said to Captain Patricio Maloné. "Do you believe that the possible element of good luck or bad luck—if there is such a thing as luck—has influenced your career or persisted for or against you to such an extent that you were forced to **attribute** results to the operation of the **aforesaid** good luck or bad luck?"

This question (of almost the dull **insolence** of legal **phraseology**) was put while we sat in Rousselin's little red-tiled café near Congo Square in New Orleans.

Brown-faced, white-hatted, finger-ringed captains of adventure came often to Rousselin's for the cognac. They came from sea and land, and were **chary** of **relating** the things they had seen—not because they were more wonderful than the fantasies of the Ananiases of print, but because they were so different. And I was a perpetual wedding-guest, always striving to cast my buttonhole over the finger of one of these mariners of fortune. This Captain Maloné was a Hiberno-Iberian creole who had gone **to and fro** in the earth and walked up and down in it. He looked like any other well-dressed man of thirty-five whom you might meet, except that he was hopelessly weather-tanned, and wore on his chain an ancient ivory-and-gold Peruvian **charm** against evil, which has nothing at all to do with this story.

"My answer to your question," said the captain, smiling, "will be to tell you the story of Bad-Luck Kearny. That is, if you don't mind hearing it."

My reply was to pound on the table for Rousselin.

"Strolling along Tchoupitoulas Street one night," began Captain Maloné, "I noticed, without especially **taxing** my interest, a small man walking rapidly toward me. He stepped upon a wooden cellar door, crashed through it, and disappeared. I rescued him from a heap of soft coal below. He dusted himself briskly,

swear [swɛər] v.
욕하다, 악담하다
gratitude [grǽtətjùːd] n.
감사, 사의
vile [vail] adj.
초라한, 빈약한, 변변치 못한
vermouth [vərmúːə] n.
베르무트 (백 포도주에 향료를 섞은 술)
bitter [bítər] n.
쓴 술
be at bay:
궁지에 몰린
crowd [kraud] v.
강요하다, 요구하다

pan [pæn] v.
(흙·모래를) 냄비로 일다, (사금을) 가려내다
calico [kǽlikòu] n.
캘리코, 옥양목
melodeon [milóudiən] n.
멜로디온
concession [kənséʃən] n.
허가, 면허, 이권
reptile [réptil, -tail] n.
비열한 인간, 엉큼한 사람

swearing fluently in a mechanical tone, as an underpaid actor recites the gypsy's curse. **Gratitude** and the dust in his throat seemed to call for fluids to clear them away. His desire for liquidation was expressed so heartily that I went with him to a café down the street where we had some vile **vermouth** and **bitters**.

"Looking across that little table I had my first clear sight of Francis Kearny. He was about five feet seven, but as tough as a cypress knee. His hair was darkest red, his mouth such a mere slit that you wondered how the flood of his words came rushing from it. His eyes were the brightest and lightest blue and the hopefulest that I ever saw. He gave the double impression that he **was at bay** and that you had better not **crowd** him further.

"'Just in from a gold-hunting expedition on the coast of Costa Rica,' he explained. 'Second mate of a banana steamer told me the natives were **panning** out enough from the beach sands to buy all the rum, red **calico**, and parlour **melodeons** in the world. The day I got there a syndicate named Incorporated Jones gets a government **concession** to all minerals from a given point. For the next choice I take coast fever and count green and blue lizards for six weeks in a grass hut. I had to be notified when I was well, for the **reptiles** were actually

tramp [træmp] n.
부정기 화물선
packet [pǽkit] n.
우편선, 정기선
be along:
오다, 도착하다

there. Then I shipped back as third cook on a Norwegian **tramp** that blew up her boiler two miles below Quarantine. I was due to bust through that cellar door here to-night, so I hurried the rest of the way up the river, roustabouting on a lower coast **packet** that made up a landing for every fisherman that wanted a plug of tobacco. And now I'm here for what comes next. And it'll **be along**, it'll be along,' said this queer Mr. Kearny; 'it'll be along on the beams of my bright but not very particular star.'

"From the first the personality of Kearny charmed me. I saw in him the bold heart, the restless nature, and the **valiant** front against the **buffets** of fate that make his countrymen such valuable **comrades** in risk and adventure. And just then I was wanting such men. Moored at a fruit company's **pier** I had a 500-ton steamer ready to sail the next day with a cargo of sugar, lumber, and corrugated iron for a port in—well, let us call the country Esperando—it has not been long ago, and the name of Patricio Maloné is still spoken there when its unsettled politics are discussed. Beneath the sugar and iron were packed a thousand Winchester rifles. In Aguas Frias, the capital, Don Rafael Valdevia, Minister of War, Esperando's greatest-hearted and most able patriot, awaited my coming. No

valiant [vǽljənt] adj.
용감한, 씩씩한
buffet [bʌ́fit] n.
타격, 시달림
comrade [kámræd, -rid / kɔ́m-]
n. 동료, 동지, 친구, 전우
pier [piər] n.
부두, 선창

insignificant [ìnsignífikənt] adj. 하찮은, 시시한
uprising [ʌ́pràiziŋ] n. 반란, 폭동
clamor [klǽmər] n. 함성, 와글거림
din [din] n. 소음, 시끄러운 소리
execrable [éksikrəbəl] adj. 형편 없는, 질 나쁜
tarpaulin [tɑ:rpɔ́:lin] n. 타르칠한 방수포
tyrant [tái-ərənt] n. 폭군, 독재자
roustabout [ráustəbàut] n. 부두 노동자
minion [mínjən] n. (권력자의) 앞잡이, 부하
despot [déspət, -pɑt / -pɔt] n. 전제 군주, 독재자

Don Rafael Valdevia was one. His great ambition was to raise Esperando into peace and honest prosperity and the respect of the serious nations. So he waited for my rifles in Aguas Frias.

doubt you have heard, with a smile, of the **insignificant** wars and **uprisings** in those little tropic republics. They make but a faint **clamour** against the **din** of great nations' battles; but down there, under all the ridiculous uniforms and petty diplomacy and senseless countermarching and intrigue, are to be found statesmen and patriots. Don Rafael Valdevia was one. His great ambition was to raise Esperando into peace and honest prosperity and the respect of the serious nations. So he waited for my rifles in Aguas Frias. But one would think I am trying to win a recruit in you! No; it was Francis Kearny I wanted. And so I told him, speaking long over our **execrable** vermouth, breathing the stifling odour from garlic and **tarpaulins**, which, as you know, is the distinctive flavour of cafés in the lower slant of our city. I spoke of the **tyrant** President Cruz and the burdens that his greed and insolent cruelty laid upon the people. And at that Kearny's tears flowed. And then I dried them with a picture of the fat rewards that would be ours when the oppressor should be overthrown and the wise and generous Valdevia in his seat. Then Kearny leaped to his feet and wrung my hand with the strength of a **roustabout**. He was mine, he said, till the last **minion** of the hated **despot** was hurled from the highest

| Cordilleras: 아메리카 대륙을 남북으로 가로지르는 산맥
| overturn [òuvərtə́:rn] v. 뒤집어 엎다, 전복시키다

peaks of the **Cordilleras** into the sea.

"I paid the score, and we went out. Near the door Kearny's elbow **overturned** an upright glass showcase, smashing it into little bits. I paid the storekeeper the price he asked.

"'Come to my hotel for the night,' I said to Kearny. 'We sail to-morrow at noon.'

"He agreed; but on the sidewalk he fell to cursing again in the dull, monotonous, glib way that he had done when I pulled him out of the coal cellar.

"'Captain,' said he, 'before we go any further, it's no more than fair to tell you that I'm known from **Baffin's Bay** to **Terra del Fuego** as "Bad-Luck" Kearny. And I'm It. Everything I get into goes up in the air except a balloon. Every bet I ever made I lost except when I **coppered** it. Every boat I ever sailed on sank except the submarines. Everything I was ever interested in went to pieces except a patent bombshell that I invented. Everything I ever took hold of and tried to run I ran into the ground except when I tried to **plough**. And that's why they call me Bad-Luck Kearny. I thought I'd tell you.'

"'Bad luck,' said I, 'or what goes by that name, may now and then **tangle** the affairs of any man. But if it **persists** beyond the estimate of what we may call the "averages" there must

Baffin Bay: 배핀만; 대서양과 북극해 사이에 있는 만
Terra del Fuego: 티에라델푸에고; 남아메리카 대륙 남쪽 끝에 있는 군도 (스페인어로 불의 땅(Land of Fire))
copper [kápər / kɔ́pər] v. (반대에) 돈을 걸다
plough[plau] v. (쟁기·괭이로) 갈다, ~에 두둑을 만들다

tangle [tǽŋ-əl] v. 엉키게 하다, 얽히게 하다, 꼬이게 하다
persist [pə:rsíst, -zíst] v. 고집하다, 지속하다

be a cause for it.'

"'There is,' said Kearny **emphatically**, 'and when we walk another square I will show it to you.'

"Surprised, I kept by his side until we came to Canal Street and out into the middle of its great width.

"Kearny seized me by an arm and pointed a tragic fore-finger at a rather brilliant star that shone steadily about thirty degrees above the horizon.

"'That's Saturn,' said he, 'the star that **presides** over bad luck and evil and disappointment and nothing doing and trouble. I was born under that star. Every move I make, up **bobs** Saturn and blocks it. He's the **hoodoo** planet of the heavens. They say he's 73,000 miles in diameter and no solider of body than split-pea soup, and he's got as many disreputable and malignant **rings** as Chicago. Now, what kind of a star is that to be born under?'

"I asked Kearny where he had obtained all this astonishing knowledge.

"'From Azrath, the great **astrologer** of Cleveland, Ohio,' said he. 'That man looked at a glass ball and told me my name before I'd taken a chair. He **prophesied** the date of my birth and death before I'd said a word. And then he cast my **horoscope**, and the **sidereal**

sock [sɑk / sɔk] v.
충격을 주다
plexus [pléksəs] n.
망상조직, 복잡한 상태, 엉킴
implicate [ímpləkèit] v.
연루시키다, 얽히게 하다

deputy [dépjəti] adj.
대리의
sparkler [spá:rklə:r] n.
빛나는 것
hand out:
나누어 주다, 분배하다

phoebe [fí:bi] n.
포이베(달의 여신; Artemis, Diana); 토성의 최외각 위성
in charge:
관리하는, 감독하는
sway [swei] n.
지배, 영향, 통치

system **socked** me in the solar **plexus**. It was bad luck for Francis Kearny from A to Izard and for his friends that were **implicated** with him. For that I gave up ten dollars. This Azrath was sorry, but he respected his profession too much to read the heavens wrong for any man. It was night time, and he took me out on a balcony and gave me a free view of the sky. And he showed me which Saturn was, and how to find it in different balconies and longitudes.

"'But Saturn wasn't all. He was only the man higher up. He furnishes so much bad luck that they allow him a gang of **deputy sparklers** to help **hand** it **out**. They're circulating and revolving and hanging around the main supply all the time, each one throwing the hoodoo on his own particular district.

"'You see that ugly little red star about eight inches above and to the right of Saturn?' Kearny asked me. 'Well, that's her. That's **Phœbe**. She's got me **in charge**. "By the day of your birth," says Azrath to me, "your life is subjected to the influence of Saturn. By the hour and minute of it you must dwell under the **sway** and direct authority of Phœbe, the ninth satellite." So said this Azrath.' Kearny shook his fist viciously skyward. 'Curse her, she's done her work well,' said he. 'Ever since I was astrologized, bad luck has followed me like my

cripple [krípəl] v.
손상하다, 무력하게 하다

reassure [rìːəʃúəːr] v.
안심시키다, 기운을 돋우다

rudder [rʌ́dəːr] n.
(배의) 키, 방향타
tug [tʌg] n.
예인선

iota [aióutə] n.
아주 조금, 티끌만큼
weather [wéðəːr] v.
(폭풍우, 위험, 어려움 등을)
뚫고 나가다, 극복하다
baleful [béilfəl] adj.
해로운, 악의가 있는

shadow, as I told you. And for many years before. Now, Captain, I've told you my handicap as a man should. If you're afraid this evil star of mine might **cripple** your scheme, leave me out of it.'

"I **reassured** Kearny as well as I could. I told him that for the time we would banish both astrology and astronomy from our heads. The manifest valour and enthusiasm of the man drew me. 'Let us see what a little courage and diligence will do against bad luck,' I said. 'We will sail to-morrow for Esperando.'

"Fifty miles down the Mississippi our steamer broke her **rudder**. We sent for a **tug** to tow us back and lost three days. When we struck the blue waters of the Gulf, all the storm clouds of the Atlantic seemed to have concentrated above us. We thought surely to sweeten those leaping waves with our sugar, and to stack our arms and lumber on the floor of the Mexican Gulf.

"Kearny did not seek to cast off one **iota** of the burden of our danger from the shoulders of his fatal horoscope. He **weathered** every storm on deck, smoking a black pipe, to keep which alight rain and sea-water seemed but as oil. And he shook his fist at the black clouds behind which his **baleful** star winked its unseen eye. When the skies cleared one evening, he **reviled** his malignant guardian with grim humour.

"'On watch, aren't you, you red-headed **vixen**? Out making it hot for little Francis Kearny and his friends, **according to Hoyle**. **Twinkle, twinkle, little devil**! You're a lady, aren't you?—dogging a man with your bad luck just because he happened to be born while your boss was **floorwalker**. Get busy and sink the ship, you one-eyed **banshee**. Phœbe! H'm! Sounds as mild as a milkmaid. You can't judge a woman by her name. Why couldn't I have had a man star? I can't make the remarks to Phœbe that I could to a man. Oh, Phœbe, you be—blasted!'

"For eight days gales and squalls and waterspouts beat us from our course. Five days only should have landed us in Esperando. Our **Jonah** swallowed the bad credit of it with appealing frankness; but that scarcely lessened the hardships our cause was made to suffer.

"At last one afternoon we steamed into the calm **estuary** of the little Rio Escondido. Three miles up this we crept, feeling for the shallow channel between the low banks that were crowded to the edge with gigantic trees and riotous vegetation. Then our whistle gave a little **toot**, and in five minutes we heard a shout, and Carlos—my brave Carlos Quintana—crashed

---

revile [riváil] v.
욕하다

vixen [víksən] n.
암여우, 심술궂은 여자
according to Hoyle:
기존의 기준에 따라
Twinkle, twinkle, little devil:
영국 동요 "Twinkle, twinkle, little star" 참조
floorwalker [flɔ́ːrwɔ̀ːkər] n.
사회자, 매장 감독
banshee [bǽnʃiː] n.
울음 소리로 가족에게 죽을 사람이 있다는 것을 알린다는 여자 유령

Jonah [dʒóunə] n.
(구약성서) 요나; 불행을 가져오는 사람, 불길한 사람

estuary [éstʃuèri] n.
큰 강의 어귀
toot [tuːt] n.
(기적, 나팔 등의 소리)

through the tangled vines waving his cap madly for joy.

"A hundred yards away was his camp, where three hundred chosen patriots of Esperando were awaiting our coming. For a month Carlos had been **drilling** them there in the tactics of war, and filling them with the spirit of revolution and liberty.

"'My Captain—*compadre mio*!' shouted Carlos, while yet my boat was being lowered. 'You should see them in the drill by *companies*—in the column wheel—in the march by fours—they are superb! Also in the manual of arms—but, alas! performed only with sticks of bamboo. The guns, *capitan*—say that you have brought the guns!'

"'A thousand Winchesters, Carlos,' I called to him. 'And two **Gatlings**.'

"'*Valgame Dios*!' he cried, throwing his cap in the air. 'We shall sweep the world!'

"At that moment Kearny **tumbled** from the steamer's side into the river. He could not swim, so the crew threw him a rope and drew him back aboard. I caught his eye and his look of pathetic but still bright and **undaunted** consciousness of his guilty luck. I told myself that although he might be a man to **shun**, he was also one to be admired.

"I gave orders to the sailing-master that the

stout [staut] adj.
튼튼한, 견고한
flatboat [flǽtbout] n.
너벅선

zeal [ziːl] n.
열심, 열의
tackle [tǽk-əl] n.
도르래 장치
impetuously [impétʃuəsli] adv.
성급하게, 충동적으로
crackle [krǽkəl] n.
딱딱 소리
hemp [hemp] n.
삼, 대마
plummet [plʌ́mit] n.
무거운 짐, 중압물

arms, ammunition, and provisions were to be landed at once. That was easy in the steamer's boats, except for the two Gatling guns. For their transportation ashore we carried a **stout flatboat**, brought for the purpose in the steamer's hold.

"In the meantime I walked with Carlos to the camp and made the soldiers a little speech in Spanish, which they received with enthusiasm; and then I had some wine and a cigarette in Carlos's tent. Later we walked back to the river to see how the unloading was being conducted.

"The small arms and provisions were already ashore, and the petty officers had squads of men conveying them to camp. One Gatling had been safely landed; the other was just being hoisted over the side of the vessel as we arrived. I noticed Kearny darting about on board, seeming to have the ambition of ten men, and to be doing the work of five. I think his **zeal** bubbled over when he saw Carlos and me. A rope's end was swinging loose from some part of the **tackle**. Kearny leaped **impetuously** and caught it. There was a **crackle** and a hiss and a smoke of scorching **hemp**, and the Gatling dropped straight as a **plummet** through the bottom of the flatboat and buried itself in twenty feet of water and five feet of river mud.

poignant [pɔ́injənt] adj.
매서운, 통렬한
murmur [mə́:rmə:r] n.
속삭임, 중얼거림
malediction [mæ̀lədíkʃ-ən] n.
저주, 악담, 비방

indomitable [indɑ́mətəbəl / -dɔ́m-] adj.
꺾이지 않는, 굴복하지 않는
buffet [bʌ́fit] n.
타격, 시달림
martyr [mɑ́:rtə:r] n.
순교자
tribulation [trìbjəléiʃ-ən] n.
고난, 고생, 시련
prestige [prestí:dʒ, préstidʒ] n.
위신, 명성, 신망
slue [slu:] v.
돌리다, 회전시키다
lubber [lʌ́bər] n.
풋내기 선원
bowknot [bóunɑ̀t / -nɔ̀t] n.
나비 매듭

"I turned my back on the scene. I heard Carlos's loud cries as if from some extreme grief too **poignant** for words. I heard the complaining **murmur** of the crew and the **maledictions** of Torres, the sailing master—I could not bear to look.

"By night some degree of order had been restored in camp. Military rules were not drawn strictly, and the men were grouped about the fires of their several messes, playing games of chance, singing their native songs, or discussing with voluble animation the contingencies of our march upon the capital.

"To my tent, which had been pitched for me close to that of my chief lieutenant, came Kearny, **indomitable**, smiling, bright-eyed, bearing no traces of the **buffets** of his evil star. Rather was his aspect that of a heroic **martyr** whose **tribulations** were so high-sourced and glorious that he even took a splendour and a **prestige** from them.

"'Well, Captain,' said he, 'I guess you realize that Bad-Luck Kearny is still on deck. It was a shame, now, about that gun. She only needed to be **slewed** two inches to clear the rail; and that's why I grabbed that rope's end. Who'd have thought that a sailor—even a Sicilian **lubber** on a banana coaster—would have fastened a line in a **bow-knot**? Don't think I'm

dodge [dɑdʒ / dɔdʒ] v.
피하다, 비키다, 모면하다

incompetency [inkɑ́mpətənsi / -kɔ́m-] n.
무능력, 부적당

mishap [míshæp] n.
불운한 일, 재난

masculine [mǽskjəlin] adj.
남성의, 남자의

feminine [fémənin] adj.
여자의, 여성의

calamity [kəlǽməti] n.
재난, 불행, 비운

as to ~:
~에 관하여

trying to **dodge** the responsibility, Captain. It's my luck.'

"'There are men, Kearny,' said I gravely, 'who pass through life blaming upon luck and chance the mistakes that result from their own faults and **incompetency**. I do not say that you are such a man. But if all your **mishaps** are traceable to that tiny star, the sooner we endow our colleges with chairs of moral astronomy, the better.'

"'It isn't the size of the star that counts,' said Kearny; 'it's the quality. Just the way it is with women. That's why they gave the biggest planets **masculine** names, and the little stars **feminine** ones—to even things up when it comes to getting their work in. Suppose they had called my star Agamemnon or Bill McCarty or something like that instead of Phœbe. Every time one of those old boys touched their **calamity** button and sent me down one of their wireless pieces of bad luck, I could talk back and tell 'em what I thought of 'em in suitable terms. But you can't address such remarks to a Phœbe.'

"'It pleases you to make a joke of it, Kearny,' said I, without smiling. 'But it is no joke to me to think of my Gatling mired in the river ooze.'

"'**As to** that,' said Kearny, abandoning his light mood at once, 'I have already done what

splice [splais] v.
합쳐 잇다, (밧줄 따위를) 꼬아 잇다
hawser [hɔ́ːzər] n.
(계선용) 굵은 밧줄
rig [rig] v.
장비하다, 조립하다
terra firma [térəfɔ́ːrmə] n.
마른 땅, 육지
at outs (on the outs):
사이가 틀어진
waive [weiv] v.
보류하다, 미루다, 연기하다
drill [dril] v.
교련하다, 훈련하다
raw [rɔː] adj.
숙련되지않은, 경험이 많지 않은

detail [díːteil, ditéil] v.
파견하다
superstition [sùːpərstíʃən] n.
미신, 맹신

I could. I have had some experience in hoisting stone in quarries. Torres and I have already **spliced** three **hawsers** and stretched them from the steamer's stern to a tree on shore. We will **rig** a tackle and have the gun on **terra firma** before noon to-morrow.'

"One could not remain long **at outs** with Bad-Luck Kearny.

"'Once more,' said I to him, 'we will **waive** this question of luck. Have you ever had experience in **drilling raw** troops?'

"'I was first sergeant and drill-master,' said Kearny, 'in the Chilean army for one year. And captain of artillery for another.'

"'What became of your command?' I asked.

"'Shot down to a man,' said Kearny, 'during the revolutions against Balmaceda.'

"Somehow the misfortunes of the evil-starred one seemed to turn to me their comedy side. I lay back upon my goat's-hide cot and laughed until the woods echoed. Kearny grinned. 'I told you how it was,' he said.

"'To-morrow,' I said, 'I shall **detail** one hundred men under your command for manual-of-arms drill and company evolutions. You will rank as lieutenant. Now, for God's sake, Kearny,' I urged him, 'try to combat this **superstition** if it is one. Bad luck may be like any other visitor—preferring to stop where it is expected. Get your mind off stars. Look upon Esperando as your planet of good fortune.'

"'I thank you, Captain,' said Kearny quietly. 'I will try to make it the best handicap I ever ran.'

"By noon the next day the submerged Gatling was rescued, as Kearny had promised. Then Carlos and Manuel Ortiz and Kearny (my lieutenants) distributed Winchesters among the troops and put them through an **incessant** rifle drill. We fired no shots, blank or solid, for of all coasts Esperando is the stillest; and we had no desire to sound any warnings in the ear of that corrupt government until they should carry with them the message of Liberty and the downfall of Oppression.

"In the afternoon came a mule-rider bearing a written message to me from Don Rafael Valdevia in the capital, Aguas Frias.

"Whenever that man's name comes to my lips, words of **tribute** to his greatness, his noble simplicity, and his conspicuous genius follow **irrepressibly**. He was a traveller, a student of peoples and governments, a master of sciences, a poet, an **orator**, a leader, a soldier, a critic of the world's campaigns and the **idol** of the people of Esperando. I had been honoured by his friendship for years. It was I who first turned his mind to the thought that

unscrupulous [ʌnskrúːpjələs] adj. 부도덕한, 파렴치한
tyrant [táiərənt] n. 폭군, 독재자
impartial [impáːrʃəl] adj. 공정한, 치우치지 않은, 편견이 없는
legislation [lèdʒisléiʃ-ən] n. 입법, 법률제정
coffer [kɔ́ːfər, káf-] n. 금고, 재원
portfolio [pɔ́ːrtfóuliòu] n. 장관의 지위

clamor [klǽmər] v. 외치다, 시끄럽게 요구하다
misrule [misrúːl] n. 실정, 혼란, 무정부 상태
dissatisfaction [dissæ̀tisfǽkʃən] n. 불만, 불평
lasso [lǽsou] v. 올가미 밧줄로 잡다
saviour [séivjəːr] n. 구조자, 구세주
halfhearted [hǽfhɑːrtid] adj. 마음이 내키지 않는, 할 마음이 없는

he should leave for his monument a new Esperando—a country freed from the rule of **unscrupulous tyrants**, and a people made happy and prosperous by wise and **impartial legislation**. When he had consented he threw himself into the cause with the undivided zeal with which he endowed all of his acts. The **coffers** of his great fortune were opened to those of us to whom were entrusted the secret moves of the game. His popularity was already so great that he had practically forced President Cruz to offer him the **portfolio** of Minister of War.

"The time, Don Rafael said in his letter, was ripe. Success, he prophesied, was certain. The people were beginning to **clamour** publicly against Cruz's **misrule**. Bands of citizens in the capital were even going about of nights hurling stones at public buildings and expressing their **dissatisfaction**. A bronze statue of President Cruz in the Botanical Gardens had been **lassoed** about the neck and overthrown. It only remained for me to arrive with my force and my thousand rifles, and for himself to come forward and proclaim himself the people's **saviour**, to overthrow Cruz in a single day. There would be but a **half-hearted** resistance from the six hundred government troops stationed in the capital. The country was ours.

He presumed that by this time my steamer had arrived at Quintana's camp. He proposed the eighteenth of July for the attack. That would give us six days in which to strike camp and march to Aguas Frias. In the meantime Don Rafael remained my good friend and *compadre en la causa de la libertad*.

"On the morning of the 14th we began our march toward the sea-following range of mountains, over the sixty-mile trail to the capital. Our small arms and provisions were laden on pack mules. Twenty men harnessed to each Gatling gun rolled them smoothly along the flat, **alluvial lowlands**. Our troops, well-shod and well-fed, moved with **alacrity** and heartiness. I and my three lieutenants were mounted on the tough mountain ponies of the country.

"A mile out of camp one of the pack mules, becoming stubborn, broke away from the train and plunged from the path into the **thicket**. The alert Kearny **spurred** quickly after it and intercepted its flight. Rising in his **stirrups**, he released one foot and bestowed upon the **mutinous** animal a hearty kick. The mule **tottered** and fell with a crash broadside upon the ground. As we gathered around it, it walled its great eyes almost humanly towards Kearny and expired. That was bad; but worse, to our minds, was the **concomitant** disaster. Part of

priceless [práislis] adj.
대단히 귀중한, 돈으로 살 수 없는
mala suerte:
(Spanish) 불운
abstract [æbstrǽkt] v.
제거하다, 감하다
beckon [békən] v.
(손짓, 고갯짓, 몸짓으로) 신호하다, 부르다

cause [kɔ:z] n.
이상, 목적, 대의 명분
calamity [kəlǽməti] n.
재난, 불행, 비운
sailing master:
항해장
passage [pǽsidʒ] n.
통행권, 뱃삯, 차비

the mule's burden had been one hundred pounds of the finest coffee to be had in the tropics. The bag burst and spilled the priceless brown mass of the ground berries among the dense vines and weeds of the swampy land. *Mala suerte!* When you take away from an Esperandan his coffee, you **abstract** his patriotism and 50 per cent. of his value as a soldier. The men began to rake up the precious stuff; but I **beckoned** Kearny back along the trail where they would not hear. The limit had been reached.

"I took from my pocket a wallet of money and drew out some bills.

"'Mr. Kearny,' said I, 'here are some funds belonging to Don Rafael Valdevia, which I am expending in his **cause**. I know of no better service it can buy for him than this. Here is one hundred dollars. Luck or no luck, we part company here. Star or no star, **calamity** seems to travel by your side. You will return to the steamer. She touches at Amotapa to discharge her lumber and iron, and then puts back to New Orleans. Hand this note to the **sailing-master**, who will give you **passage**.' I wrote on a leaf torn from my book, and placed it and the money in Kearny's hand.

"'Good-bye,' I said, extending my own. 'It is not that I am displeased with you; but there is no place in this **expedition** for—let us say, the **Señorita** Phœbe.' I said this with a smile, trying to **smooth** the thing for him. 'May you have better luck, *companero*.'

"Kearny took the money and the paper.

"'It was just a little touch,' said he, 'just a little lift with the toe of my boot—but what's the odds?—that blamed mule would have died if I had only dusted his ribs with a **powder puff**. It was my luck. Well, Captain, I would have liked to be in that little fight with you over in Aguas Frias. Success to the cause. *Adios!*'

"He turned around and set off down the trail without looking back. The unfortunate mule's pack-saddle was transferred to Kearny's pony, and we again took up the march.

"Four days we journeyed over the foot-hills and mountains, **fording** icy torrents, winding around the crumbling **brows** of ragged peaks, creeping along the rocky flanges that **overlooked** awful **precipices**, crawling breathlessly over tottering bridges that crossed bottomless **chasms**.

"On the evening of the seventeenth we camped by a little stream on the bare hills five miles from Aguas Frias. At daybreak we were to take up the march again.

"At midnight I was standing outside my tent

---

expedition [èkspədíʃən] n.
(집단, 단체의) 모험, 원정
senorita [sèinjɔríːtə, sìː-] n.
(Spanish) 아가씨, 영어의 Miss
smooth [smuːð] v.
부드럽게 하다, 세련되게 하다

powder puff:
퍼프, 분첩
adios [ӕdióus, àːdi-] int.
안녕

ford [fɔːrd] v.
(개울·여울목을) 걸어서 건너다
brow [brau] n.
산마루
overlook [òuvərlúk] v.
~이 바라보이다, ~이 내려다 보이다
precipice [présəpis] n.
벼랑, 절벽
chasm [kӕzəm] n.
깊게 갈라진 틈, 깊은 구렁

illimitable [illímitəbəl] adj. 무한한, 광대한, 끝없는	
zenith [zí:niə / zén-] n. 천정(天頂); 임의의 지점에서 똑바로 위에 있는 천구(天球)의 점	
sinister [sínistə:r] adj. 불길한, 사악한	
malignant [məlígnənt] adj. 해로운, 악의에 찬	
firmament [fə́:rməmənt] n. 하늘, 창공	
makeshift [méikʃift] n. 임시 변통의 수단, 미봉책, 대용품	
rebuff [ribʌ́f] n. 거절, 퇴짜	

inhaling the fresh cold air. The stars were shining bright in the cloudless sky, giving the heavens their proper aspect of **illimitable** depth and distance when viewed from the vague darkness of the blotted earth. Almost at its **zenith** was the planet Saturn; and with a half-smile I observed the **sinister** red sparkle of his **malignant** attendant—the demon star of Kearny's ill luck. And then my thoughts strayed across the hills to the scene of our coming triumph where the heroic and noble Don Rafael awaited our coming to set a new and shining star in the **firmament** of nations.

"I heard a slight rustling in the deep grass to my right. I turned and saw Kearny coming toward me. He was ragged and dew-drenched and limping. His hat and one boot were gone. About one foot he had tied some **makeshift** of cloth and grass. But his manner as he approached was that of a man who knows his own virtues well enough to be superior to **rebuffs**.

"'Well, sir,' I said, staring at him coldly, 'if there is anything in persistence, I see no reason why you should not succeed in wrecking and ruining us yet.'

"'I kept half a day's journey behind,' said Kearny, fishing out a stone from the covering of his lame foot, 'so the bad luck wouldn't touch

commissary [kámasèri / kómasəri] n.
식량

blunder [blʌ́ndər] n.
큰 실수
yonder [jándə:r / jón-] adv.
저쪽에, 저편에
defy [difái] v.
싸움을 걸다, 도전하다
spoil [spɔil] v.
망쳐놓다, 결단내다, 못쓰게 만들다
at any rate:
하여튼, 좌우간에
turn away:
쫓아내다, 보내다
rout [raut] v.
깨우다, 끌어내다

illumine [ilú:min] v.
비추다, 밝게 하다

you. I couldn't help it, Captain; I wanted to be in on this game. It was a pretty tough trip, especially in the department of the **commissary**. In the low grounds there were always bananas and oranges. Higher up it was worse; but your men left a good deal of goat meat hanging on the bushes in the camps. Here's your hundred dollars. You're nearly there now, captain. Let me in on the scrapping to-morrow.'

"'Not for a hundred times a hundred would I have the tiniest thing go wrong with my plans now,' I said, 'whether caused by evil planets or the **blunders** of mere man. But **yonder** is Aguas Frias, five miles away, and a clear road. I am of the mind to **defy** Saturn and all his satellites to **spoil** our success now. **At any rate**, I will not **turn away** to-night as weary a traveller and as good a soldier as you are, Lieutenant Kearny. Manuel Ortiz's tent is there by the brightest fire. **Rout** him out and tell him to supply you with food and blankets and clothes. We march again at daybreak.'

"Kearny thanked me briefly but feelingly and moved away.

"He had gone scarcely a dozen steps when a sudden flash of bright light **illumined** the surrounding hills; a sinister, growing, hissing sound like escaping steam filled my ears. Then followed a roar as of distant thunder, which

culminate [kʌ́lmənèit] v.
마침내 ~이 되다, ~으로 끝나다
wax [wæks] v.
~이 되다
glare [glɛər] n.
번쩍이는 빛, 눈부신 빛
precede [prisíːd] v.
선행하다, 앞서다, 먼저 일어나다

This terrifying noise culminated in a tremendous explosion, which seemed to rock the hills as an earthquake would; the illumination waxed to a glare so fierce that I clapped my hands to my eyes to save them. I thought the end of the world had come.

meteor [míːtiər, -tiɔ̀ːr] n.
운석, 별똥별

grew louder every instant. This terrifying noise **culminated** in a tremendous explosion, which seemed to rock the hills as an earthquake would; the illumination **waxed** to a **glare** so fierce that I clapped my hands to my eyes to save them. I thought the end of the world had come. I could think of no natural phenomenon that would explain it. My wits were staggering. The deafening explosion trailed off into the rumbling roar that had **preceded** it; and through this I heard the frightened shouts of my troops as they stumbled from their resting-places and rushed wildly about. Also I heard the harsh tones of Kearny's voice crying: 'They'll blame it on me, of course, and what the devil it is, it's not Francis Kearny that can give you an answer.'

"I opened my eyes. The hills were still there, dark and solid. It had not been, then, a volcano or an earthquake. I looked up at the sky and saw a comet-like trail crossing the zenith and extending westward—a fiery trail waning fainter and narrower each moment.

"'A **meteor**!' I called aloud. 'A meteor has fallen. There is no danger.'

"And then all other sounds were drowned by a great shout from Kearny's throat. He had raised both hands above his head and was standing tiptoe.

"'PHŒBE'S GONE!' he cried, with all his lungs. 'She's **busted** and gone to hell. Look, Captain, the little red-headed hoodoo has blown herself to **smithereens**. She found Kearny too tough to handle, and she puffed up with **spite** and **meanness** till her boiler blew up. It's be Bad-Luck Kearny no more. Oh, let us be joyful!

"'**Humpty Dumpty** sat on a wall;
     Humpty busted, and that'll be all!'

"I looked up, wondering, and picked out Saturn in his place. But the small red twinkling **luminary** in his vicinity, which Kearny had pointed out to me as his evil star, had vanished. I had seen it there but half an hour before; there was no doubt that one of those awful and mysterious **spasms** of nature had **hurled** it from the heavens.

"I clapped Kearny on the shoulder.

"'Little man,' said I, 'let this clear the way for you. It appears that astrology has failed to **subdue** you. Your horoscope must be cast **anew** with **pluck** and loyalty for controlling stars. I play you to win. Now, get to your tent, and sleep. Daybreak is the word.'

"At nine o'clock on the morning of the eighteenth of July I rode into Aguas Frias with Kearny at my side. In his clean linen suit and with his military poise and keen eye he was a model of a fighting adventurer. I had visions of him riding as commander of President Valdevia's body-guard when the plums of the new republic should begin to fall.

"Carlos followed with the troops and supplies. He was to halt in a wood outside the town and remain concealed there until he received the word to advance.

"Kearny and I rode down the Calle Ancha toward the *residencia* of Don Rafael at the other side of the town. As we passed the superb white buildings of the University of Esperando, I saw at an open window the gleaming spectacles and bald head of Herr Bergowitz, professor of the natural sciences and friend of Don Rafael and of me and of the cause. He waved his hand to me, with his broad, **bland** smile.

"There was no excitement apparent in Aguas Frias. The people went about leisurely as at all times; the market was **thronged** with bareheaded women buying fruit and *carne*; we heard the twang and tinkle of string bands in the **patios** of the *cantinas*. We could see that it was a **waiting game** that Don Rafael was playing.

"His *residencia* was a large but low building around a great courtyard in grounds crowded with ornamental trees and tropic shrubs. At

---

bland [blænd] adj.
온후한, 부드러운

throng [θrɔ(:)ŋ, θrɑŋ] v.
떼지어 모이다, 쇄도하다, 북적거리다
patio [pǽtiòu, pɑ́:-] n.
파티오; 스페인식 집의 안뜰
cantina [kæntí:nə] n.
술집
waiting game:
대기 전술

his door an old woman who came informed us that Don Rafael had not yet arisen.

"'Tell him,' said I, 'that Captain Maloné and a friend wish to see him at once. Perhaps he has overslept.'

"She came back looking frightened.

"'I have called,' she said, 'and rung his bell many times, but he does not answer.'

"I knew where his sleeping-room was. Kearny and I pushed by her and went to it. I put my shoulder against the thin door and forced it open.

"In an armchair by a great table covered with maps and books sat Don Rafael with his eyes closed. I touched his hand. He had been dead many hours. On his head above one ear was a wound caused by a heavy blow. It had ceased to bleed long before.

"I made the old woman call a ***mozo***, and **dispatched** him in haste to **fetch** Herr Bergowitz.

"He came, and we stood about as if we were half stunned by the awful shock. Thus can the letting of a few drops of blood from one man's veins drain the life of a nation.

"Presently Herr Bergowitz **stooped** and picked up a darkish stone the size of an orange which he saw under the table. He examined it closely through his great glasses with the eye of science.

---

mozo [mouzou] n.
하인
dispatch [dispætʃ] v.
급파하다
fetch [fetʃ] v.
가져오다, 데려오다

stoop [stu:p] v.
몸을 굽히다, 웅크리다

fragment [frǽgmənt] n.
파편, 조각

babble [bǽbəl] v.
분명치 않은 소리를 내다, 중얼중얼 말하다
compendium [kəmpéndiəm] n.
대요, 개략, 일람표
fiery [fáiəri] adj.
불의, 불붙은
dissolution [dìsəlúːʃən] n.
붕괴, 소멸, 사멸
doom [duːm] n.
파멸, 멸망
last word:
최후의 단정, 결정적인 일

"Undoubtedly Phœbe had been feminine. Even when hurtling on her way to fiery dissolution and everlasting doom, the last word had been hers."

"'A **fragment**,' said he, 'of a detonating meteor. The most remarkable one in twenty years exploded above this city a little after midnight this morning.'

"The professor looked quickly up at the ceiling. We saw the blue sky through a hole the size of an orange nearly above Don Rafael's chair.

"I heard a familiar sound, and turned. Kearny had thrown himself on the floor and was **babbling** his **compendium** of bitter, blood-freezing curses against the star of his evil luck.

"Undoubtedly Phœbe had been feminine. Even when hurtling on her way to **fiery dissolution** and everlasting **doom**, the **last word** had been hers."

Captain Maloné was not unskilled in narrative. He knew the point where a story should end. I sat reveling in his effective conclusion when he aroused me by continuing:

"Of course," said he, "our schemes were at an end. There was no one to take Don Rafael's place. Our little army melted away like dew before the sun.

"One day after I had returned to New Orleans I related this story to a friend who holds a professorship in Tulane University.

"When I had finished he laughed and asked whether I had any knowledge of Kearny's luck afterward. I told him no, that I had seen him no more; but that when he left me, he had expressed confidence that his future would be successful now that his unlucky star had been overthrown.

"'No doubt,' said the professor, 'he is happier not to know one fact. If he **derives** his bad luck from Phœbe, the ninth **satellite** of Saturn, that **malicious** lady is still engaged in overlooking his career. The star close to Saturn that he imagined to be her was near that planet simply by the chance of its **orbit**—probably at different times he has **regarded** many other stars that happened to be in Saturn's neighbourhood as his evil one. The real Phœbe is visible only through a very good telescope.'

"About a year afterward," continued Captain Maloné, "I was walking down a street that crossed the Poydras Market. An immensely stout, pink-faced lady in black satin crowded me from the narrow sidewalk with a frown. Behind her trailed a little man laden **to the gunwales** with bundles and bags of goods and vegetables.

"It was Kearny—but changed. I stopped and shook one of his hands, which still clung to a bag of garlic and red peppers.

"'How is the luck, old *companero*?' I asked him. I had not the heart to tell him the truth

---

derive [diráiv] v.
논리적으로 도출하다, 추론하다
satellite [sǽt-əlàit] n.
위성
malicious [məlíʃəs] adj.
악의적인, 심술궂은
orbit [ɔ́:rbit] n.
궤도
regard [rigá:rd] v.
주목해서 보다, 주시하다

to the gunwales:
가득 찬

about his star.

"'Well,' said he, 'I am married, as you may guess.'

"'Francis!' called the big lady, in deep tones, 'are you going to stop in the street talking all day?'

"'I am coming, Phœbe dear,' said Kearny, hastening after her."

Captain Maloné ceased again.

"After all, do you believe in luck?" I asked.

"Do you?" answered the captain, with his ambiguous smile shaded by the brim of his soft straw hat.

"'I am coming, Phœbe dear,' said Kearny, hastening after her."

The Pendulum

"Eighty-first street—let 'em out, please," yelled the shepherd in blue.

A flock of citizen sheep **scrambled** out and another flock scrambled aboard. Ding-ding! The cattle cars of the Manhattan Elevated rattled away, and John Perkins drifted down the stairway of the station with the released flock.

John walked slowly toward his flat. Slowly, because in the **lexicon** of his daily life there was no such word as "perhaps." There are no surprises awaiting a man who has been married two years and lives in a flat. As he walked John Perkins **prophesied** to himself with gloomy and **downtrodden cynicism** the foregone conclusions of the monotonous day.

---

scramble [skrǽmb-əl] v.
급히 움직이다, 앞을 다투다, 허둥지둥 하다

lexicon [léksəkən] n.
사전, 어휘
prophesy [práfəsài / prɔ́] v.
예언하다, 예측하다
downtrodden [dauntrɑdn / dauntrɔdn] adj.
짓밟힌, 유린된, 억압된
cynicism [sínəsìzəm] n.
냉소, 비꼬는 버릇

butterscotch [bʌ́tərskàtʃ / -skɔ̀tʃ] n.
버터와 황갈색 설탕을 넣은 시럽, 소스, 또는 캔디
pot roast:
냄비구이 쇠고기t
delirium tremen:
진전섬망
frolic [frɑ́lik / frɔ́l-] v.
들떠서 떠들다, 야단법석떨다, 장난치다
dumbwaiter [dʌ́mwèitər] n.
음식용 소형 엘리베이터

Katy would meet him at the door with a kiss flavored with cold cream and **butter-scotch**. He would remove his coat, sit upon a macadamized lounge and read, in the evening paper, of Russians and Japs slaughtered by the deadly linotype. For dinner there would be **pot roast**, a salad flavored with a dressing warranted not to crack or injure the leather, stewed rhubarb and the bottle of strawberry marmalade blushing at the certificate of chemical purity on its label. After dinner Katy would show him the new patch in her crazy quilt that the iceman had cut for her off the end of his four-in-hand. At half-past seven they would spread newspapers over the furniture to catch the pieces of plastering that fell when the fat man in the flat overhead began to take his physical culture exercises. Exactly at eight Hickey & Mooney, of the vaudeville team (unbooked) in the flat across the hall, would yield to the gentle influence of **delirium tremens** and begin to overturn chairs under the delusion that Hammerstein was pursuing them with a five-hundred-dollar-a-week contract. Then the gent at the window across the air-shaft would get out his flute; the nightly gas leak would steal forth to **frolic** in the highways; the **dumbwaiter** would slip off its trolley; the janitor would drive Mrs. Zanowitski's five children once more

The Pendulum

across the Yalu, the lady with the champagne shoes and the Skye terrier would trip downstairs and paste her Thursday name over her bell and letter-box—and the evening routine of the Frogmore flats would be under way.

John Perkins knew these things would happen. And he knew that at a quarter past eight he would **summon** his nerve and reach for his hat, and that his wife would deliver this speech in a **querulous** tone:

"Now, where are you going, I'd like to know, John Perkins?"

"Thought I'd drop up to McCloskey's," he would answer, "and play a game or two of **pool** with the fellows."

Of late such had been John Perkins's habit. At ten or eleven he would return. Sometimes Katy would be asleep; sometimes waiting up, ready to melt in the **crucible** of her **ire** a little more gold plating from the wrought steel chains of **matrimony**. For these things Cupid will have to answer when he stands at the **bar** of justice with his victims from the Frogmore flats.

To-night John Perkins encountered a tremendous **upheaval** of the commonplace when he reached his door. No Katy was there with her affectionate, confectionate kiss. The three rooms seemed in **portentous** disorder. All about lay her things in confusion. Shoes in

---

summon [sʌ́mən] v.
(용기, 힘 등을) 불러일으키다
querulous [kwérjələs] adj.
불평하는, 불만이 많은

pool [puːl] n.
포켓볼

of late:
요즘, 최근에
crucible [krúːsəbl] n.
도가니; 호된 시련
ire [áiər] n.
노여움, 분노
matrimony [mǽtrəmòuni] n.
결혼, 결혼 생활
bar [bɑːr] n.
법정, 심판

upheaval [ʌvphíːvəl] n.
대변동, 동란, 격변
portentous [pɔːrténtəs] adj.
전조의, 불길한

perturbation [pə̀:rtərbéiʃən] n.
동요, 혼란, 불안

To-night John Perkins encountered a tremendous upheaval of the commonplace when he reached his door.

quinsy [kwínzi] n.
편도선염, 후두염

the middle of the floor, curling tongs, hair bows, kimonos, powder box, jumbled together on dresser and chairs—this was not Katy's way. With a sinking heart John saw the comb with a curling cloud of her brown hair among its teeth. Some unusual hurry and **perturbation** must have possessed her, for she always carefully placed these combings in the little blue vase on the mantel to be some day formed into the coveted feminine "rat."

Hanging conspicuously to the gas jet by a string was a folded paper. John seized it. It was a note from his wife running thus:

*Dear John: I just had a telegram saying mother is very sick. I am going to take the 4.30 train. Brother Sam is going to meet me at the depot there. There is cold mutton in the ice box. I hope it isn't her **quinsy** again. Pay the milkman 50 cents. She had it bad last spring. Don't forget to write to the company about the gas meter, and your good socks are in the top drawer. I will write to-morrow.*

Hastily,   KATY.

Never during their two years of matrimony had he and Katy been separated for a night. John read the note over and over in a dumbfounded way. Here was a break in a routine

wrapper [rǽpəːr] n.
실내복
desolation [dèsəléiʃən] n.
공허함, 황량함

Everything in the room spoke of a loss, of an essence gone, of its soul and life departed. John Perkins stood among the dead remains with a queer feeling of desolation in his heart.

that had never varied, and it left him dazed.

There on the back of a chair hung, pathetically empty and formless, the red **wrapper** with black dots that she always wore while getting the meals. Her week-day clothes had been tossed here and there in her haste. A little paper bag of her favorite butter-scotch lay with its string yet unwound. A daily paper sprawled on the floor, gaping rectangularly where a railroad time-table had been clipped from it. Everything in the room spoke of a loss, of an essence gone, of its soul and life departed. John Perkins stood among the dead remains with a queer feeling of **desolation** in his heart.

He began to set the rooms tidy as well as he could. When he touched her clothes a thrill of something like terror went through him. He had never thought what existence would be without Katy. She had become so thoroughly annealed into his life that she was like the air he breathed—necessary but scarcely noticed. Now, without warning, she was gone, vanished, as completely absent as if she had never existed. Of course it would be only for a few days, or at most a week or two, but it seemed to him as if the very hand of death had pointed a finger at his secure and uneventful home.

John dragged the cold mutton from the ice-box, made coffee and sat down to a lonely meal

dismantle [dismǽntl] v. 허물다, 부수다, 분해하다 lares and penastes: 라레스와 페나테스 (가정의 수호신); 가정	

face to face with the strawberry marmalade's shameless certificate of purity. Bright among withdrawn blessings now appeared to him the ghosts of pot roasts and the salad with tan polish dressing. His home was **dismantled**. A quinsied mother-in-law had knocked his **lares and penates** sky-high. After his solitary meal John sat at a front window.

He did not care to smoke. Outside the city roared to him to come join in its dance of folly and pleasure. The night was his. He might go forth unquestioned and **thrum** the strings of **jollity** as free as any gay bachelor there. He might **carouse** and wander and **have his fling** until dawn if he liked; and there would be no wrathful Katy waiting for him, bearing the **chalice** that held the dregs of his joy. He might play pool at McCloskey's with his roistering friends until **Aurora** dimmed the electric bulbs if he chose. The **hymeneal** strings that had **curbed** him always when the Frogmore flats had **palled** upon him were loosened. Katy was gone.

John Perkins was not accustomed to analyzing his emotions. But as he sat in his Katy-bereft 10×12 parlor he hit unerringly upon the keynote of his discomfort. He knew now that Katy was necessary to his happiness. His feeling for her, **lulled** into unconsciousness by the dull round

thrum [θrʌm] v. 퉁기다, 퉁겨 소리내다
jollity [dʒáləti / dʒɔ́-] n. 흥겨움, 유쾌함, 즐거움
carouse [kəráuz] v. 떠들썩하게 마시다, 흥청대다
have one's fling: 제멋대로 굴다, 방종하게 놀다
chalice [tʃǽlis] n. 술잔, 성배
Aurora [ərɔ́:rə, ɔ:rɔ́:-] n. 아우로라(새벽의 여신)
hymeneal [hàiməní:əl] adj. 결혼의, 혼인의
curb [kə:rb] v. 억제하다, 구속하다
pall [pɔ:l] v. 시시해지다, 흥미를 잃다

lull [lʌl] v. 가라앉다, 자다

din [din] n.
울리다, 울려퍼지다
florid [fló(:)rid, flár-] adj.
화려한, 찬란한, 현란한

double-dyed [dábəldáid] adj.
두 번 물들인, 철저한, 완전한
dub [dʌb] n.
서투른 사람
bum [bʌm] v.
놀고 지내다, 술에 빠지다
make up for:
보상하다

Momus [móuməs] n.
(그리스 신화) 모모스; 비난과 조소의 신
primrose [prímròuz] adj.
화려한, 즐거운
remorseful [rimɔ́:rsfəl] adj.
후회하는, 양심의 가책을 받는
cherub [tʃérəb] n. (pl. cherubim)
케루빔, 지품 천사
bounce [bauns] v.
내쫓다, 내던지다

of domesticity, had been sharply stirred by the loss of her presence. Has it not been **dinned** into us by proverb and sermon and fable that we never prize the music till the sweet-voiced bird has flown—or in other no less **florid** and true utterances?

"I'm a **double-dyed dub**," mused John Perkins, "the way I've been treating Katy. Off every night playing pool and **bumming** with the boys instead of staying home with her. The poor girl here all alone with nothing to amuse her, and me acting that way! John Perkins, you're the worst kind of a shine. I'm going to **make it up for** the little girl. I'll take her out and let her see some amusement. And I'll cut out the McCloskey gang right from this minute."

Yes, there was the city roaring outside for John Perkins to come dance in the train of **Momus**. And at McCloskey's the boys were knocking the balls idly into the pockets against the hour for the nightly game. But no **primrose** way nor clicking cue could woo the **remorseful** soul of Perkins the bereft. The thing that was his, lightly held and half scorned, had been taken away from him, and he wanted it. Backward to a certain man named Adam, whom the **cherubim bounced** from the orchard, could Perkins, the remorseful, trace his descent.

Near the right hand of John Perkins stood

a chair. On the back of it stood Katy's blue shirtwaist. It still **retained** something of her contour. Midway of the sleeves were fine, individual wrinkles made by the movements of her arms in working for his comfort and pleasure. A delicate but impelling odor of bluebells came from it. John took it and looked long and **soberly** at the **unresponsive grenadine**. Katy had never been unresponsive. Tears:—yes, tears—came into John Perkins's eyes. When she came back things would be different. He would make up for all his neglect. What was life without her?

The door opened. Katy walked in carrying a little hand satchel. John stared at her stupidly.

"My! I'm glad to get back," said Katy. "Ma wasn't sick to amount to anything. Sam was at the depot, and said she just had a little spell, and got all right soon after they telegraphed. So I took the next train back. I'm just dying for a cup of coffee."

Nobody heard the **click** and **rattle** of the **cogwheels** as the third-floor front of the Frogmore flats buzzed its machinery back into the Order of Things. A band slipped, a spring was touched, the gear was adjusted and the wheels revolve in their old orbit.

John Perkins looked at the clock. It was 8.15.

---

retain [ritéin] v.
보유하다, 유지하다
contour [kántuər / kɔ́n-] n.
윤곽, 외형
soberly [sóubə:rli] adv.
진지하게, 차분히
unresponsive [ʌ̀nrispánsiv / -pɔ́n-] adj.
반응이 느린, 둔감한, 냉정한
grenadine [grènədí:n] n.
올이 성긴 얇은 옷감

Tears:—yes, tears—came into John Perkins's eyes. When she came back things would be different. He would make up for all his neglect. What was life without her?

click [klik] n.
찰깍하는 소리
rattle [rǽtl] n.
덜거덕 소리
cogwheel [kághwìːl / kɔ́g-] n.
톱니바퀴

He reached for his hat and walked to the door.

"Now, where are you going, I'd like to know, John Perkins?" asked Katy, in a querulous tone.

"Thought I'd drop up to McCloskey's," said John, "and play a game or two of pool with the fellows."

Nobody heard the click and rattle of the cog-wheels as the third-floor front of the Frogmore flats buzzed its machinery back into the Order of Things.

The Ransom of Red Chief

It looked like a good thing: but wait till I tell you. We were down South, in Alabama—Bill Driscoll and myself—when this kidnapping idea struck us. It was, as Bill afterward expressed it, "during a moment of temporary mental apparition"; but we didn't find that out till later.

There was a town down there, as flat as a flannel-cake, and called Summit, of course. It contained inhabitants of as **undeleterious** and self-satisfied a class of peasantry as ever clustered around a **Maypole**.

Bill and me had a joint capital of about six

---

undeleterious [ʌndeləti̇əriəs] adj. 무해한, 위험하지 않은
maypole [méipòul] n. 오월제의 기둥
(꽃이나 리본 등으로 장식하여 메이 데이에 그 주위에서 춤을 춤)

hundred dollars, and we needed just two thousand dollars more to **pull off** a **fraudulent** town-lot scheme in Western Illinois with. We talked it over on the front steps of the hotel. Philoprogenitiveness, says we, is strong in semi-rural communities; therefore and for other reasons, a kidnapping project ought to do better there than in the radius of newspapers that send reporters out in plain clothes to stir up talk about such things. We knew that Summit couldn't get after us with anything stronger than **constables** and maybe some **lackadaisical bloodhounds** and a **diatribe** or two in the *Weekly Farmers' Budget*. So, it looked good.

We selected for our victim the only child of a prominent citizen named Ebenezer Dorset. The father was respectable and tight, a **mortgage fancier** and a stern, upright collection-plate passer and forecloser. The kid was a boy of ten, with **bas-relief** freckles, and hair the colour of the cover of the magazine you buy at the news-stand when you want to catch a train. Bill and me figured that Ebenezer would melt down for a **ransom** of two thousand dollars to a cent. But wait till I tell you.

About two miles from Summit was a little mountain, covered with a dense cedar **brake**. On the rear elevation of this mountain was a

---

pull off:
잘 해내다
fraudulent [frɔ́:dʒulənt] adj.
사기의, 부정한, 속이는
constable [kʌ́nstəbl / kʌ́n-] n.
순경
lackadaisical [læ̀kədéizik-əl] adj. 활기 없는, 열의 없는
bloodhound [blʌ́dhàund] n.
블러드하운드; 후각이 예민한 영국 경찰견, 집요한 추적자, 형사
diatribe [dáiətràib] n.
비난, 비방

mortgage [mɔ́:rgidʒ] n.
저당, 저당권
fancier [fǽnsiər] n.
애호가
bas-relief [bɑ̀:rilí:f, bæ̀s-] n.
얕은 부조, 얕은 돋을새김
ransom [rǽnsəm] n.
몸값

brake [breik] n.
숲, 덤불

cave. There we stored provisions.

One evening after sundown, we drove in a **buggy** past old Dorset's house. The kid was in the street, throwing rocks at a kitten on the opposite fence.

"Hey, little boy!" says Bill, "would you like to have a bag of candy and a nice ride?"

The boy catches Bill neatly in the eye with a piece of brick.

"That will cost the old man an extra five hundred dollars," says Bill, climbing over the wheel.

That boy **put up** a fight like a welter-weight **cinnamon bear**; but, at last, we got him down in the bottom of the buggy and drove away. We took him up to the cave, and I hitched the horse in the cedar **brake**. After dark I drove the buggy to the little village, three miles away, where we had hired it, and walked back to the mountain.

Bill was pasting **court-plaster** over the scratches and bruises on his features. There was a fire burning behind the big rock at the entrance of the cave, and the boy was watching a pot of boiling coffee, with two buzzard tail-feathers stuck in his red hair. He points a stick at me when I come up, and says:

"Ha! cursed **paleface**, do you dare to enter the camp of Red Chief, the terror of the **plains**?

---

buggy [bʌ́gi] n.
말 한 필이 끄는 경마차

put up:
실행하다, 수행하다
cinnamon bear:
갈색곰(북아메리카산)
brake [breik] n.
숲, 덤불

court plaster:
반창고

paleface [peilfeis] n.
(북미 인디언 용어) 백인
plain [plein] n.
평야, 평원, 광야

"He's all right now," says Bill, rolling up his trousers and examining some bruises on his shins. "We're playing Indian. We're making Buffalo Bill's show look like magic-lantern views of Palestine in the town hall. I'm Old Hank, the Trapper, Red Chief's **captive**, and I'm to be scalped at daybreak. By Geronimo! that kid can kick hard."

Yes, sir, that boy seemed to be **having the time of his life**. The fun of camping out in a cave had made him forget that he was a captive himself. He immediately **christened** me Snake-eye, the Spy, and announced that, when his **braves** returned from the **warpath**, I was to be broiled at the stake at the rising of the sun.

Then we had supper; and he filled his mouth full of bacon and bread and gravy, and began to talk. He made a during-dinner speech something like this:

"I like this fine. I never camped out before; but I had a pet 'possum once, and I was nine last birthday. I hate to go to school. Rats ate up sixteen of Jimmy Talbot's aunt's speckled hen's eggs. Are there any real Indians in these woods? I want some more gravy. Does the trees moving make the wind blow? We had five puppies. What makes your nose so red, Hank? My father has lots of money. Are the stars hot? I whipped Ed Walker twice, Saturday. I don't like girls. You dassent catch toads unless with a string. Do oxen make any noise? Why are oranges round? Have you got beds to sleep on in this cave? Amos Murray has got six toes. A parrot can talk, but a monkey or a fish can't. How many does it take to make twelve?"

Every few minutes he would remember that he was a **pesky redskin**, and pick up his stick rifle and tiptoe to the mouth of the cave to rubber for the scouts of the hated paleface. Now and then he would let out a **war-whoop** that made Old Hank the Trapper shiver. That boy had Bill terrorized from the start.

"Red Chief," says I to the kid, "would you like to go home?"

"Aw, what for?" says he. "I don't have any fun at home. I hate to go to school. I like to camp out. You won't take me back home again, Snake-eye, will you?"

"Not right away," says I. "We'll stay here in the cave a while."

"All right!" says he. "That'll be fine. I never had such fun in all my life."

We went to bed about eleven o'clock. We spread down some wide blankets and quilts and put Red Chief between us. We weren't afraid he'd run away. He kept us awake for three hours, jumping up and reaching for his rifle and **screeching**: "**Hist! pard**," in mine

crackle [krǽkəl] n.
딱딱 소리
twig [twig] n.
잔 가지, 가는 가지
rustle [rʌ́s-əl] n.
바스락 거림, 바스락하는 소리
stealthy [stélθi] adj.
남몰래 하는, 은밀한
ferocious [fəróuʃəs] adj.
사나운, 모진, 포악한
pirate [páiərət] n.
해적
whoop [hu(:)p, hwu(:)p] n.
야아하는 외침
yawp [jɔːp, jɑːp] n.
새된 소리, 날카로운 외침
indecent [indíːsnt] adj.
버릇없는, 품위없는, 꼴 사나운
incontinently [inkántənəntli / -kɔ́n-] adv.
자제할 수 없이

and Bill's ears, as the fancied **crackle** of a **twig** or the **rustle** of a leaf revealed to his young imagination the **stealthy** approach of the outlaw band. At last, I fell into a troubled sleep, and dreamed that I had been kidnapped and chained to a tree by a **ferocious pirate** with red hair.

Just at daybreak, I was awakened by a series of awful screams from Bill. They weren't yells, or howls, or shouts, or **whoops**, or **yawps**, such as you'd expect from a manly set of vocal organs—they were simply **indecent**, terrifying, humiliating screams, such as women emit when they see ghosts or caterpillars. It's an awful thing to hear a strong, desperate, fat man scream **incontinently** in a cave at daybreak.

I jumped up to see what the matter was. Red Chief was sitting on Bill's chest, with one hand twined in Bill's hair. In the other he had the sharp case-knife we used for slicing bacon; and he was industriously and realistically trying to take Bill's scalp, according to the sentence that had been pronounced upon him the evening before.

I got the knife away from the kid and made him lie down again. But, from that moment, Bill's spirit was broken. He laid down on his side of the bed, but he never closed an eye again in sleep as long as that boy was with us.

sunup [sÁnÀp] n.
일출, 해돋이

imp [imp] n.
개구쟁이

rowdy [ráudi] adj.
난폭한, 소란스러운
dote [dout] v.
맹목적으로 사랑하다
reconnoiter/reconnoitre
[rìːkənóitəːr, rèk-] v.
정찰하다, 답사하다
contiguous [kəntígjuəs] adj.
접촉하는, 인접한
yeomanry [jóumənri] n.
소지주들, 자작농
dastardly [dǽstərdli] adj.
비겁한, 비열한
courier [kúriər, kə́ːri-] n.
급사, 메신저

I dozed off for a while, but along toward **sunup** I remembered that Red Chief had said I was to be burned at the stake at the rising of the sun. I wasn't nervous or afraid; but I sat up and lit my pipe and leaned against a rock.

"What you getting up so soon for, Sam?" asked Bill.

"Me?" says I. "Oh, I got a kind of a pain in my shoulder. I thought sitting up would rest it."

"You're a liar!" says Bill. "You're afraid. You was to be burned at sunrise, and you was afraid he'd do it. And he would, too, if he could find a match. Ain't it awful, Sam? Do you think anybody will pay out money to get a little **imp** like that back home?"

"Sure," said I. "A **rowdy** kid like that is just the kind that parents **dote** on. Now, you and the Chief get up and cook breakfast, while I go up on the top of this mountain and **reconnoitre**."

I went up on the peak of the little mountain and ran my eye over the **contiguous** vicinity. Over toward Summit I expected to see the sturdy **yeomanry** of the village armed with scythes and pitchforks beating the countryside for the **dastardly** kidnappers. But what I saw was a peaceful landscape dotted with one man ploughing with a dun mule. Nobody was dragging the creek; no **couriers** dashed hither and yon, bringing tidings of no news to the distracted parents. There was a **sylvan** attitude of **somnolent** sleepiness pervading that section of the external outward surface of Alabama that lay exposed to my view. "Perhaps," says I to myself, "it has not yet been discovered that the wolves have borne away the tender **lambkin** from the **fold**. Heaven help the wolves!" says I, and I went down the mountain to breakfast.

When I got to the cave I found Bill backed up against the side of it, breathing hard, and the boy threatening to smash him with a rock half as big as a cocoanut.

"He put a red-hot boiled potato down my back," explained Bill, "and then mashed it with his foot; and I boxed his ears. Have you got a gun about you, Sam?"

I took the rock away from the boy and kind of patched up the argument. "I'll **fix you**," says the kid to Bill. "No man ever yet struck the Red Chief but what he got paid for it. You better **beware**!"

After breakfast the kid takes a piece of leather with strings wrapped around it out of his pocket and goes outside the cave unwinding it.

"What's he up to now?" says Bill, anxiously. "You don't think he'll run away, do you, Sam?"

"No fear of it," says I. "He don't seem to be

---

sylvan [sílvən] adj.
숲의, 목가적인
somnolent [sámnələnt / sɔ́m-] adj. 졸린, 잠이 오게 하는
lambkin [lǽmkin] n.
새끼 양
fold [fould] n.
우리; (우리 안의) 양떼

fix someone:
누군가에게 복수하거나 처벌을 가하다
beware [biwéər] v.
조심하다, 경계하다

homebody [houmbɑdi / houmbɔdi] n. 가정적인 사람, 잘 나다니지 않은 사람 on account of: ~ 때문에	much of a **home body**. But we've got to fix up some plan about the ransom. There don't seem to be much excitement around Summit **on account of** his disappearance; but maybe they haven't realized yet that he's gone. His folks may think he's spending the night with Aunt Jane or one of the neighbours. Anyhow, he'll be missed to-day. To-night we must get a message to his father demanding the two thousand dollars for his return."
sling [sliŋ] n. 투석기; 새총	Just then we heard a kind of war-whoop, such as David might have emitted when he knocked out the champion Goliath. It was a **sling** that Red Chief had pulled out of his pocket, and he was whirling it around his head. I dodged, and heard a heavy thud and a kind of sigh from Bill, like a horse gives out when you take his saddle off. A niggerhead rock the size of an egg had caught Bill just behind his left ear. He loosened himself all over and fell in the fire across the frying pan of hot water for washing the dishes. I dragged him out and poured cold water on his head for half an hour.
by and by: 이윽고, 곧 come to one's senses: 정신을 차리다	**By and by**, Bill sits up and feels behind his ear and says: "Sam, do you know who my favourite Biblical character is?" "Take it easy," says I. "You'll **come to your senses** presently." "King Herod," says he. "You won't go away

and leave me here alone, will you, Sam?"

I went out and caught that boy and shook him until his freckles rattled.

"If you don't **behave**," says I, "I'll take you straight home. Now, are you going to be good, or not?"

"I was only **funning**," says he **sullenly**. "I didn't mean to hurt Old Hank. But what did he hit me for? I'll behave, Snake-eye, if you won't send me home, and if you'll let me play the Black Scout to-day."

"I don't know the game," says I. "That's for you and Mr. Bill to decide. He's your **playmate** for the day. I'm going away for a while, on business. Now, you come in and make friends with him and say you are sorry for hurting him, or home you go, at once."

I made him and Bill shake hands, and then I took Bill aside and told him I was going to Poplar Cove, a little village three miles from the cave, and find out what I could about how the kidnapping had been regarded in Summit. Also, I thought it best to send a **peremptory** letter to old man Dorset that day, demanding the ransom and dictating how it should be paid.

"You know, Sam," says Bill, "I've stood by you **without batting an eye** in earthquakes, fire and flood—in poker games, dynamite outrages, police raids, train robberies and cyclones.

skyrocket [skaɪrɑkɪt /skaɪrɔkɪt]
n. 로켓 불꽃
get someone going:
흥분시키다, 화나게 하다

strut [strʌt] v.
뽐내며 걷다
decry [dikrái] v.
비난하다, 헐뜯다, 비방하다
parental [pəréntl] adj.
어버이의, 어버이다운
wildcat [wáildkæt] n.
난폭한 사람, 우악스런 사람

accede [æksí:d] v.
동의하다, 응하다

esquire [eskwáiər, éskwáiər]
n. 님, 귀하 (편지에서 Esq.로 약하여 쓰는 경칭)

I never lost my nerve yet till we kidnapped that two-legged **skyrocket** of a kid. He's **got me going**. You won't leave me long with him, will you, Sam?"

"I'll be back some time this afternoon," says I. "You must keep the boy amused and quiet till I return. And now we'll write the letter to old Dorset."

Bill and I got paper and pencil and worked on the letter while Red Chief, with a blanket wrapped around him, **strutted** up and down, guarding the mouth of the cave. Bill begged me tearfully to make the ransom fifteen hundred dollars instead of two thousand. "I ain't attempting," says he, "to **decry** the celebrated moral aspect of **parental** affection, but we're dealing with humans, and it ain't human for anybody to give up two thousand dollars for that forty-pound chunk of freckled **wildcat**. I'm willing to take a chance at fifteen hundred dollars. You can charge the difference up to me."

So, to relieve Bill, I **acceded**, and we collaborated a letter that ran this way:

Ebenezer Dorset, **Esq.**:

We have your boy concealed in a place far from Summit. It is useless for you or the most skilful detectives to attempt to find him.

Absolutely, the only terms on which you can have him restored to you are these: We demand fifteen hundred dollars in large bills for his return; the money to be left at midnight to-night at the same spot and in the same box as your reply—as hereinafter described. If you agree to these terms, send your answer in writing by a solitary messenger to-night at half-past eight o'clock. After crossing Owl Creek, on the road to Poplar Cove, there are three large trees about a hundred yards apart, close to the fence of the wheat field on the right-hand side. At the bottom of the fence-post, opposite the third tree, will be found a small pasteboard box.

The messenger will place the answer in this box and return immediately to Summit.

If you attempt any treachery or fail to comply with our demand as stated, you will never see your boy again.

If you pay the money as demanded, he will be returned to you safe and well within three hours. These terms are final, and if you do not accede to them no further communication will be attempted.

TWO DESPERATE MEN.

I addressed this letter to Dorset, and put it in my pocket. As I was about to start, the kid comes up to me and says:

stockade [stɑkéid / stɔk-] n.
방책, 울타리

foil [fɔil] v.
이기다, 무찌르다
pesky [péski] adj.
성가신, 귀찮은
savage [sǽvidʒ] n.
야만인, 미개인

hump [hʌmp] v.
노력하다, 열심히 하다
on time:
정각에, 제시간에

"Aw, Snake-eye, you said I could play the Black Scout while you was gone."

"Play it, of course," says I. "Mr. Bill will play with you. What kind of a game is it?"

"I'm the Black Scout," says Red Chief, "and I have to ride to the **stockade** to warn the settlers that the Indians are coming. I'm tired of playing Indian myself. I want to be the Black Scout."

"All right," says I. "It sounds harmless to me. I guess Mr. Bill will help you **foil** the **pesky savages**."

"What am I to do?" asks Bill, looking at the kid suspiciously.

"You are the hoss," says Black Scout. "Get down on your hands and knees. How can I ride to the stockade without a hoss?"

"You'd better keep him interested," said I, "till we get the scheme going. Loosen up."

Bill gets down on his all fours, and a look comes in his eye like a rabbit's when you catch it in a trap.

"How far is it to the stockade, kid?" he asks, in a husky manner of voice.

"Ninety miles," says the Black Scout. "And you have to **hump** yourself to get there **on time**. Whoa, now!"

The Black Scout jumps on Bill's back and digs his heels in his side.

"For Heaven's sake," says Bill, "hurry back, Sam, as soon as you can. I wish we hadn't made the ransom more than a thousand. Say, you quit kicking me or I'll get up and warm you good."

I walked over to Poplar Cove and sat around the postoffice and store, talking with the **chawbacons** that came in to trade. One whiskerando says that he hears Summit is all upset on account of Elder Ebenezer Dorset's boy having been lost or stolen. That was all I wanted to know. I bought some smoking tobacco, referred casually to the price of black-eyed peas, posted my letter **surreptitiously** and came away. The postmaster said the mail-carrier would come by in an hour to take the mail on to Summit.

When I got back to the cave Bill and the boy were not to be found. I explored the vicinity of the cave, and risked a **yodel** or two, but there was no response.

So I lighted my pipe and sat down on a mossy bank to await developments.

In about half an hour I heard the bushes rustle, and Bill **wabbled** out into the little **glade** in front of the cave. Behind him was the kid, stepping softly like a scout, with a broad grin on his face. Bill stopped, took off his hat and wiped his face with a red handkerchief. The kid stopped about eight feet behind him.

"Sam," says Bill, "I suppose you'll think I'm

renegade [rénigèid] n.
배반자, 반역자
proclivity [prouklívəti] n.
경향, 성벽, 기질
predominance [pridámənəns / -dɔ́m-] n.
우월, 우위, 탁월
martyr [mɑ́:rtə:r] n.
순교자
graft [græft, grɑ:ft] n.
부정 이득, 뇌물
depredation [dèprədéiʃən] n.
약탈, 파괴

palatable [pǽlətəbəl] adj.
맛있는
black-and-blue [blǽkəndblu:] adj. (얻어맞아) 검푸르게 멍든

a **renegade**, but I couldn't help it. I'm a grown person with masculine **proclivities** and habits of self-defense, but there is a time when all systems of egotism and **predominance** fail. The boy is gone. I have sent him home. All is off. There was **martyrs** in old times," goes on Bill, "that suffered death rather than give up the particular **graft** they enjoyed. None of 'em ever was subjugated to such supernatural tortures as I have been. I tried to be faithful to our articles of **depredation**; but there came a limit."

"What's the trouble, Bill?" I asks him.

"I was rode," says Bill, "the ninety miles to the stockade, not barring an inch. Then, when the settlers was rescued, I was given oats. Sand ain't a **palatable** substitute. And then, for an hour I had to try to explain to him why there was nothin' in holes, how a road can run both ways and what makes the grass green. I tell you, Sam, a human can only stand so much. I takes him by the neck of his clothes and drags him down the mountain. On the way he kicks my legs **black-and-blue** from the knees down; and I've got to have two or three bites on my thumb and hand cauterized.

"But he's gone"—continues Bill—"gone home. I showed him the road to Summit and kicked him about eight feet nearer there at one kick.

I'm sorry we lose the ransom; but it was either that or Bill Driscoll to the madhouse."

Bill is puffing and blowing, but there is a look of **ineffable** peace and growing content on his rose-pink features.

"Bill," says I, "there isn't any heart disease in your family, is there?

"No," says Bill, "nothing **chronic** except malaria and accidents. Why?"

"Then you might turn around," says I, "and have a look behind you."

Bill turns and sees the boy, and loses his **complexion** and sits down plump on the ground and begins to pluck aimlessly at grass and little sticks. For an hour I was afraid of his mind. And then I told him that my scheme was to put the whole job through immediately and that we would get the ransom and **be off** with it by midnight if old Dorset fell in with our proposition. So Bill braced up enough to give the kid a weak sort of a smile and a promise to play the Russian in a Japanese war with him as soon as he felt a little better.

I had a scheme for collecting that ransom without danger of being caught by **counterplots** that ought to commend itself to professional kidnappers. The tree under which the answer was to be left—and the money later on—was close to the road fence with big, bare fields on

> sirree [sərí:] int.
> (미국구어) (yes 또는 no 뒤에 붙여 강조하는 말), sir

all sides. If a gang of constables should be watching for any one to come for the note they could see him a long way off crossing the fields or in the road. But no, **sirree**! At half-past eight I was up in that tree as well hidden as a tree toad, waiting for the messenger to arrive.

Exactly on time, a half-grown boy rides up the road on a bicycle, locates the pasteboard box at the foot of the fence-post, slips a folded piece of paper into it and pedals away again back toward Summit.

> crabbed [krǽbid] adj.
> 난해한, 판독하기 어려운
> the sum and substance: 요지, 골자

I waited an hour and then concluded the thing was square. I slid down the tree, got the note, slipped along the fence till I struck the woods, and was back at the cave in another half an hour. I opened the note, got near the lantern and read it to Bill. It was written with a pen in a **crabbed** hand, and **the sum and substance** of it was this:

Two Desperate Men.

Gentlemen: I received your letter to-day by post, in regard to the ransom you ask for the return of my son. I think you are a little high in your demands, and I hereby make you a counter-proposition, which I am inclined to believe you will accept. You bring Johnny home and pay me two hundred and fifty dollars in cash, and I agree to take him off your hands. You had better come at night, for the neighbours believe he is lost, and I couldn't be responsible for what they would do to anybody they saw bringing him back. Very respectfully,

EBENEZER DORSET.

"Great pirates of Penzance!" says I; "of all the **impudent**—"

But I glanced at Bill, and hesitated. He had the most **appealing** look in his eyes I ever saw on the face of a dumb or a talking brute.

"Sam," says he, "what's two hundred and fifty dollars, after all? We've got the money. One more night of this kid will send me to a bed in **Bedlam**. Besides being a thorough gentleman, I think Mr. Dorset is a **spendthrift** for making us such a **liberal** offer. You ain't going to let the chance go, are you?"

"Tell you the truth, Bill," says I, "this little he **ewe lamb** has somewhat **got on my nerves** too. We'll take him home, pay the ransom and make our **get-away**."

We took him home that night. We got him to go by telling him that his father had bought a silver-mounted rifle and a pair of moccasins for him, and we were going to hunt bears the next day.

It was just twelve o'clock when we knocked

at Ebenezer's front door. Just at the moment when I should have been abstracting the fifteen hundred dollars from the box under the tree, according to the original proposition, Bill was counting out two hundred and fifty dollars into Dorset's hand.

When the kid found out we were going to leave him at home he started up a howl like a **calliope** and fastened himself as tight as a **leech** to Bill's leg. His father peeled him away gradually, like a porous plaster.

"How long can you hold him?" asks Bill.

"I'm not as strong as I used to be," says old Dorset, "but I think I can promise you ten minutes."

"Enough," says Bill. "In ten minutes I shall cross the Central, Southern and Middle Western States, and be **legging** it **trippingly** for the Canadian border."

And, as dark as it was, and as fat as Bill was, and as good a runner as I am, he was a good mile and a half out of Summit before I could catch up with him.

---

calliope [kǽliòup] n.
증기 풍금
leech [li:tʃ] n.
거머리

leg [leg] v.
걷다, 달리다
trippingly [trípiŋli] adv.
경쾌하게, 가볍게

The Duplicity of Hargraves

major [méidʒəːr] n.
소령
portico [pɔ́ːrtikòu] n.
포르티코, 기둥으로 받쳐진 지붕이 있는 현관

When **Major** Pendleton Talbot, of Mobile, sir, and his daughter, Miss Lydia Talbot, came to Washington to reside, they selected for a boarding place a house that stood fifty yards back from one of the quietest avenues. It was an old-fashioned brick building, with a **portico** upheld by tall white pillars. The yard was shaded by stately locusts and elms, and a catalpa tree in season rained its pink and white blossoms upon the grass. Rows of high box bushes lined the fence and walks. It was the Southern style and aspect of the place that pleased the eyes of the Talbots.

anecdote [ǽnikdòut] n.
일화
reminiscence [rèmənís-əns] n.
회고, 회상

till [til] v.
갈다, 경작하다
aristocracy [ærəstákrəsi / -tɔ́k-] n.
귀족, 귀족사회
scruple [skrú:p-əl] n.
도덕 관념, 양심의 가책
antiquated [ǽntikwèitid] adj.
오래된, 구식의
punctilious [pʌŋktíliəs] adj.
예의 범절에 까다로운, 형식에 치우친

archaic [ɑ:rkéiik] adj.
고풍의, 구식의, 낡은
genuflexion [ʤénjuflèkʃən] n.
절, 인사
christen [krísn] v.
이름을 붙이다, 명명하다

In this pleasant, private boarding house they engaged rooms, including a study for Major Talbot, who was adding the finishing chapters to his book, "**Anecdotes** and **Reminiscences** of the Alabama Army, Bench, and Bar."

Major Talbot was of the old, old South. The present day had little interest or excellence in his eyes. His mind lived in that period before the Civil War, when the Talbots owned thousands of acres of fine cotton land and the slaves to **till** them; when the family mansion was the scene of princely hospitality, and drew its guests from the **aristocracy** of the South. Out of that period he had brought all its old pride and **scruples** of honour, an **antiquated** and **punctilious** politeness, and (you would think) its wardrobe.

Such clothes were surely never made within fifty years. The major was tall, but whenever he made that wonderful, **archaic genuflexion** he called a bow, the corners of his frock coat swept the floor. That garment was a surprise even to Washington, which has long ago ceased to shy at the frocks and broadbrimmed hats of Southern congressmen. One of the boarders **christened** it a "Father Hubbard," and it certainly was high in the waist and full in the skirt.

But the major, with all his queer clothes,

| beloved [bilʌ́vid, -lʌ́vd] adj.
사랑하는, 소중한
design [dizáin] n.
의도, 목적, 속마음
in spite of:
~에도 불구하고

his immense area of plaited, ravelling shirt bosom, and the little black string tie with the bow always slipping on one side, both was smiled at and liked in Mrs. Vardeman's select boarding house. Some of the young department clerks would often "string him," as they called it, getting him started upon the subject dearest to him—the traditions and history of his **beloved** Southland. During his talks he would quote freely from the "Anecdotes and Reminiscences." But they were very careful not to let him see their **designs**, for **in spite of** his sixty-eight years, he could make the boldest of them uncomfortable under the steady regard of his piercing gray eyes.

plump [plʌmp] adj.
포동포동한
antebellum [æ̀ntibéləm] adj.
전전(戰前)의; 남북 전쟁 전의
contemptible [kəntémptəbəl] adj. 멸시할 만한, 경멸할 만한, 비열한
nuisance [njúːs-əns] n.
폐, 성가심, 불쾌한 존재

Miss Lydia was a **plump**, little old maid of thirty-five, with smoothly drawn, tightly twisted hair that made her look still older. Old fashioned, too, she was; but **ante-bellum** glory did not radiate from her as it did from the major. She possessed a thrifty common sense; and it was she who handled the finances of the family, and met all comers when there were bills to pay. The major regarded board bills and wash bills as **contemptible nuisances**. They kept coming in so persistently and so often. Why, the major wanted to know, could they not be filed and paid in a lump sum at some convenient period—say when the "Anecdotes and Reminiscences" had been published and paid for? Miss Lydia would calmly go on with her sewing and say, "We'll pay as we go as long as the money lasts, and then perhaps they'll have to lump it."

Most of Mrs. Vardeman's boarders were away during the day, being nearly all department clerks and business men; but there was one of them who was about the house a great deal from morning to night. This was a young man named Henry Hopkins Hargraves—every one in the house addressed him by his full name—who was engaged at one of the popular **vaudeville** theatres. Vaudeville has risen to such a respectable **plane** in the last few years, and Mr. Hargraves was such a modest and well-mannered person, that Mrs. Vardeman could find no objection to **enrolling** him upon her list of boarders.

At the theatre Hargraves was known as an **all-round dialect** comedian, having a large **repertoire** of German, Irish, Swede, and black-face specialties. But Mr. Hargraves was ambitious, and often spoke of his great desire to succeed in **legitimate** comedy.

This young man appeared to conceive a strong fancy for Major Talbot. Whenever that gentleman would begin his Southern reminiscences, or repeat some of the liveliest of the

attentive [əténtiv] adj.
주의 깊은, 경청하는

indubitable [indjú:bətəbəl] adj. 의심의 여지가 없는, 확실한
appreciation [əprì:ʃiéiʃən] n.
평가, 인정, 감상
win over:
동의 또는 호의를 얻다

chum [tʃʌm] n.
친구
set apart:
따로 떼어놓다
entrance [entræns, -trá:ns] v.
넋을 잃게 하다, 매혹하다

bale [beil] n.
꾸러미, 짐짝
on the contrary:
반대로
advance [ædvæns, -vá:ns, əd-]
v. 내놓다, 제출하다

anecdotes, Hargraves could always be found, the most **attentive** among his listeners.

For a time the major showed an inclination to discourage the advances of the "play actor," as he privately termed him; but soon the young man's agreeable manner and **indubitable appreciation** of the old gentleman's stories completely **won** him **over**.

It was not long before the two were like old **chums**. The major **set apart** each afternoon to read to him the manuscript of his book. During the anecdotes Hargraves never failed to laugh at exactly the right point. The major was moved to declare to Miss Lydia one day that young Hargraves possessed remarkable perception and a gratifying respect for the old regime. And when it came to talking of those old days—if Major Talbot liked to talk, Mr. Hargraves was **entranced** to listen.

Like almost all old people who talk of the past, the major loved to linger over details. In describing the splendid, almost royal, days of the old planters, he would hesitate until he had recalled the name of the Negro who held his horse, or the exact date of certain minor happenings, or the number of **bales** of cotton raised in such a year; but Hargraves never grew impatient or lost interest. **On the contrary**, he would **advance** questions on a variety of

extract [ikstrǽkt] v. 끌어내다, 끄집어 내다, 얻다	
ready [rédi] adj. 준비가 된, 즉석의	
hoedown [hóudàun] n. 스퀘어댄스	
jubilee [dʒúːbəlìː] n. 기념제, 축제	
banquet [bǽŋkwit] n. 연회, 향연	
feud [fjuːd] n. 불화, 반목	
gentry [dʒéntri] n. 신사 계급, 귀족	
quaint [kweint] adj. 예스러운, 고아한	
improvident [imprάvədənt / -próv-] adj. 선견지명이 없는, 앞일을 생각하지 않는	
beckon [békən] v. (손짓, 고갯짓, 몸짓으로) 신호하다, 부르다	
archly [άːrtʃli] adv. 짓궂게, 장난으로	
ceremonious [sèrəmóuniəs] adj. 예의바른, 격식을 차리는	
arduous [άːrdʒuəs / -dju-] adj. 힘드는, 곤란한	

subjects connected with the life of that time, and he never failed to **extract ready** replies.

The fox hunts, the 'possum suppers, the **hoe downs** and **jubilees** in the Negro quarters, the **banquets** in the plantation-house hall, when invitations went for fifty miles around; the occasional **feuds** with the neighbouring **gentry**; the major's duel with Rathbone Culbertson about Kitty Chalmers, who afterward married a Thwaite of South Carolina; and private yacht races for fabulous sums on Mobile Bay; the **quaint** beliefs, **improvident** habits, and loyal virtues of the old slaves—all these were subjects that held both the major and Hargraves absorbed for hours at a time.

Sometimes, at night, when the young man would be coming upstairs to his room after his turn at the theatre was over, the major would appear at the door of his study and **beckon archly** to him. Going in, Hargraves would find a little table set with a decanter, sugar bowl, fruit, and a big bunch of fresh green mint.

"It occurred to me," the major would begin—he was always **ceremonious**—"that perhaps you might have found your duties at the—at your place of occupation—sufficiently **arduous** to enable you, Mr. Hargraves, to appreciate what the poet might well have had in his mind when he wrote, 'tired Nature's sweet restorer,'—one

julep [dʒúːlip] n.
줄렙, 박하술
delicacy [délikəsi] n.
섬세함, 배려
bruise [bruːz] v.
찧다, 부수다, 으깨다
exquisite [ikskwízit, ékskwi-] adj. 절묘한, 세련된, 고상한
nicety [náis-əti] n.
정확함, 섬세함
ingredient [ingríːdiənt] n.
성분, 재료
solicitous [səlísətəs] adj.
열심인, 간절히 원하는

arrear [əríər] n.
늦음, 더딤, 밀림

attend [əténd] v.
보살피다, 돌보다

of our Southern **juleps**."

It was a fascination to Hargraves to watch him make it. He took rank among artists when he began, and he never varied the process. With what **delicacy** he **bruised** the mint; with what **exquisite nicety** he estimated the **ingredients**; with what **solicitous** care he capped the compound with the scarlet fruit glowing against the dark green fringe! And then the hospitality and grace with which he offered it, after the selected oat straws had been plunged into its tinkling depths!

After about four months in Washington, Miss Lydia discovered one morning that they were almost without money. The "Anecdotes and Reminiscences" was completed, but publishers had not jumped at the collected gems of Alabama sense and wit. The rental of a small house which they still owned in Mobile was two months in **arrears**. Their board money for the month would be due in three days. Miss Lydia called her father to a consultation.

"No money?" said he with a surprised look. "It is quite annoying to be called on so frequently for these petty sums. Really, I—"

The major searched his pockets. He found only a two-dollar bill, which he returned to his vest pocket.

"I must **attend** to this at once, Lydia," he said.

"Kindly get me my umbrella and I will go down town immediately. The congressman from our district, General Fulghum, assured me some days ago that he would use his influence to get my book published at an early date. I will go to his hotel at once and see what arrangement has been made."

With a sad little smile Miss Lydia watched him button his "Father Hubbard" and depart, pausing at the door, as he always did, to bow profoundly.

That evening, at dark, he returned. It seemed that Congressman Fulghum had seen the publisher who had the major's manuscript for reading. That person had said that if the anecdotes, etc., were carefully **pruned** down about one half, in order to **eliminate** the **sectional** and class **prejudice** with which the book was dyed from end to end, he might consider its publication.

The major was in a white heat of anger, but regained his **equanimity**, according to his **code** of manners, as soon as he was in Miss Lydia's presence.

"We must have money," said Miss Lydia, with a little wrinkle above her nose. "Give me the two dollars, and I will telegraph to Uncle Ralph for some to-night."

The major drew a small envelope from his

---

prune [pru:n] v.
잘라내다, 제거하다, 줄이다
eliminate [ilímənèit] v.
제거하다, 없애다
sectional [sékʃ-ən-əl] adj.
지방적인, 파벌적인
prejudice [prédʒudis] n.
편견, 선입관

equanimity [ì:kwəníməti, èk-]
n. 평정, 침착, 냉정
code [koud] n.
규약, 규칙, 예의범절

upper vest pocket and tossed it on the table.

"Perhaps it was **injudicious**," he said mildly, "but the sum was so merely **nominal** that I bought tickets to the theatre to-night. It's a new war drama, Lydia. I thought you would be pleased to witness its first production in Washington. I am told that the South has very fair treatment in the play. I confess I should like to see the performance myself."

Miss Lydia threw up her hands in silent despair.

Still, as the tickets were bought, they might as well be used. So that evening, as they sat in the theatre listening to the lively **overture**, even Miss Lydia was minded to **relegate** their troubles, for the hour, to second place. The major, in spotless linen, with his extraordinary coat showing only where it was closely buttoned, and his white hair smoothly roached, looked really fine and distinguished. The curtain went up on the first act of "A Magnolia Flower," revealing a typical Southern plantation scene. Major Talbot **betrayed** some interest.

"Oh, see!" exclaimed Miss Lydia, **nudging** his arm, and pointing to her programme.

The major put on his glasses and read the line in the cast of characters that her finger indicated.

Col. Webster Calhoun .. H. Hopkins Hargraves.

"It's our Mr. Hargraves," said Miss Lydia. "It must be his first appearance in what he calls 'the legitimate.' I'm so glad for him."

Not until the second act did Col. Webster Calhoun appear upon the stage. When he made his entry Major Talbot gave an audible **sniff**, glared at him, and seemed to freeze solid. Miss Lydia uttered a little, ambiguous squeak and crumpled her programme in her hand. For Colonel Calhoun was made up as nearly resembling Major Talbot as one pea does another. The long, thin white hair, curly at the ends, the aristocratic beak of a nose, the crumpled, wide, ravelling shirt front, the string tie, with the bow nearly under one ear, were almost exactly duplicated. And then, to **clinch** the imitation, he wore the twin to the major's supposed to be **unparalleled** coat. High-collared, baggy, empire-waisted, ample-skirted, hanging a foot lower in front than behind, the garment could have been designed from no other pattern. From then on, the major and Miss Lydia sat bewitched, and saw the **counterfeit** presentment of a **haughty** Talbot "dragged," as the major afterward expressed it, "through the **slanderous mire** of a corrupt stage."

Mr. Hargraves had used his opportunities

---

sniff [snif] n.
코웃음, 경멸
clinch [klintʃ] v.
매듭을 짓다, 결말을 내다
unparalleled [ʌnpǽrəlèld] adj.
비길 데 없는
counterfeit [káuntərfìt] adj.
모조의, 가짜의, 허위의
haughty [hɔ́:ti] adj.
도도한, 오만한, 불손한
slanderous [slǽnd-ərəs / slɑ́:n-] adj.
중상적인, 헐뜯는, 비방하는
mire [maiər] n.
늪

idiosyncrasy [ìdiəsíŋkrəsi] n.
(어느 개인의) 특이함, 성격, 경향
pompous [pámpəs / pɔ́m-] adj.
오만한, 뽐내는
courtliness [kɔ́:rtlinis] n.
예의바름, 정중함
pink [piŋk] n.
정화, 극치, 절정

culmination [kʌ̀lmənéiʃən] n.
최고점, 최고조
audacious [ɔ:déiʃəs] adj.
대담한, 과감한, 용감한

inimitable [inímitəbəl] adj.
비길 데 없는, 모방할 수 없는
rambling [rǽmbliŋ] adj.
산만한, 종작없는
character [kǽriktər] adj.
성격 배우의, 성격 연기의
monologue [mánəlɔ̀:g, -làg/ mɔ́nəlɔ̀g] n.
모놀로그, 독백
deftly [deftli] adv.
솜씨 좋게, 능숙하게

well. He had caught the major's little **idiosyncrasies** of speech, accent, and intonation and his **pompous courtliness** to perfection—exaggerating all to the purposes of the stage. When he performed that marvellous bow that the major fondly imagined to be the **pink** of all salutations, the audience sent forth a sudden round of hearty applause.

Miss Lydia sat immovable, not daring to glance toward her father. Sometimes her hand next to him would be laid against her cheek, as if to conceal the smile which, in spite of her disapproval, she could not entirely suppress.

The **culmination** of Hargraves's **audacious** imitation took place in the third act. The scene is where Colonel Calhoun entertains a few of the neighbouring planters in his "den."

Standing at a table in the centre of the stage, with his friends grouped about him, he delivers that **inimitable**, **rambling**, **character monologue** so famous in "A Magnolia Flower," at the same time that he **deftly** makes juleps for the party.

Major Talbot, sitting quietly, but white with indignation, heard his best stories retold, his pet theories and hobbies advanced and expanded, and the dream of the "Anecdotes and Reminiscences" served, exaggerated and garbled. His favourite narrative—that of his duel with Rathbone Culbertson—was not omitted, and it was delivered with more fire, egotism, and **gusto** than the major himself put into it.

The monologue concluded with a quaint, delicious, witty little lecture on the art of concocting a julep, illustrated by the act. Here Major Talbot's delicate but showy science was reproduced to **a hair's breadth**—from his dainty handling of the fragrant weed—"the one-thousandth part of a grain too much pressure, gentlemen, and you **extract** the bitterness, instead of the aroma, of this heaven-bestowed plant"—to his solicitous selection of the **oaten** straws.

At the close of the scene the audience raised a **tumultuous** roar of appreciation. The portrayal of the type was so exact, so sure and **thorough**, that the leading characters in the play were forgotten. After repeated calls, Hargraves came before the curtain and bowed, his rather boyish face bright and flushed with the knowledge of success.

At last Miss Lydia turned and looked at the major. His thin nostrils were working like the gills of a fish. He laid both shaking hands upon the arms of his chair to rise.

"We will go, Lydia," he said chokingly. "This is an **abominable—desecration**."

Before he could rise, she pulled him back

into his seat. "We will stay it out," she declared. "Do you want to advertise the copy by exhibiting the original coat?" So they remained to the end.

Hargraves's success must have kept him up late that night, for neither at the breakfast nor at the dinner table did he appear.

About three in the afternoon he tapped at the door of Major Talbot's study. The major opened it, and Hargraves walked in with his hands full of the morning papers—too full of his triumph to notice anything unusual in the major's **demeanour**.

"I put it all over 'em last night, major," he began **exultantly**. "I had my **inning**, and, I think, **scored**. Here's what the *Post* says:

His conception and portrayal of the old-time Southern colonel, with his absurd **grandiloquence**, his eccentric **garb**, his quaint idioms and phrases, his moth-eaten pride of family, and his really kind heart, **fastidious** sense of honour, and lovable simplicity, is the best **delineation** of a character role on the boards to-day. The coat worn by Colonel Calhoun is itself nothing less than an evolution of genius. Mr. Hargraves has captured his public.

"How does that sound, major, for a first

disconcerted [dìskənsə́:rtid] adj. 당혹한, 당황한, 혼란한
pointer [pɔ́intər] n. 조언, 충고, 시사, 암시

unpardonable [ʌnpá:rdənəbəl] adj. 용서할 수 없는
burlesque [bə:rlésk] v. 우습게 하다, 흉내내다, 익살 부리다
grossly [grousli] adv. 상스럽게, 파렴치하게
betray [bitréi] v. 누설하다, 폭로하다
confidence [kánfidəns / kɔ́n-] n. 속내 이야기, (남이 비밀을 지켜준다는) 신뢰
misuse [misjú:z] v. 오용하다, 악용하다

take offence: 화를 내다

nighter?"

"I had the honour"—the major's voice sounded ominously frigid—"of witnessing your very remarkable performance, sir, last night."

Hargraves looked **disconcerted**.

"You were there? I didn't know you ever—I didn't know you cared for the theatre. Oh, I say, Major Talbot," he exclaimed frankly, "don't you be offended. I admit I did get a lot of **pointers** from you that helped me out wonderfully in the part. But it's a type, you know—not individual. The way the audience caught on shows that. Half the patrons of that theatre are Southerners. They recognized it."

"Mr. Hargraves," said the major, who had remained standing, "you have put upon me an **unpardonable** insult. You have **burlesqued** my person, **grossly betrayed** my **confidence**, and **misused** my hospitality. If I thought you possessed the faintest conception of what is the sign manual of a gentleman, or what is due one, I would call you out, sir, old as I am. I will ask you to leave the room, sir."

The actor appeared to be slightly bewildered, and seemed hardly to take in the full meaning of the old gentleman's words.

"I am truly sorry you **took offence**," he said regretfully. "Up here we don't look at things just as you people do. I know men who would buy out half the house to have their personality put on the stage so the public would recognize it."

"They are not from Alabama, sir," said the major **haughtily**.

"Perhaps not. I have a pretty good memory, major; let me quote a few lines from your book. In response to a toast at a banquet given in—Milledgeville, I believe—you uttered, and intend to have printed, these words:

The Northern man is utterly without sentiment or warmth except in so far as the feelings may be turned to his own commercial profit. He will suffer without **resentment** any **imputation** cast upon the honour of himself or his loved ones that does not bear with it the consequence of **pecuniary** loss. In his charity, he gives with a liberal hand; but it must be **heralded** with the trumpet and **chronicled** in brass.

"Do you think that picture is fairer than the one you saw of Colonel Calhoun last night?"

"The description," said the major frowning, "is—not without grounds. Some exag—**latitude** must be allowed in public speaking."

"And in public acting," replied Hargraves.

"That is not the point," persisted the major, unrelenting. "It was a personal **caricature**. I

---

haughtily [hɔ́:tili] adv.
오만하게, 도도하게

resentment [rizéntmənt] n.
노함, 분개
imputation [ìmpjutéiʃən] n.
비난, 비방, 오명
pecuniary [pikjú:nièri / -njəri] adj. 금전의, 재정상의
herald [hérəld] v.
보도하다, 포고하다
chronicle [kránikl / krɔ́n-] v.
기록하다

latitude [lǽtətjù:d] n.
자유, 허용 정도, 여유

caricature [kǽrikətʃùər, -tʃər] n. (풍자) 만화, 풍자 예술

overlook [òuvərlúk] v.
관대히 봐주다, 눈감아주다
winning [wíniŋ] adj.
매력적인, 사람을 끄는
let it go at that:
그쯤 해두다, 더 이상 논하지 않다
pinch [pintʃ] n.
압박, 고통, 곤란, 위기

salve [sæ(ː)v, sɑːv / sælv] n.
연고, 고약, 위안
casual [kǽʒuəl] adj.
우연한, 우발적인, 즉석의
acquaintance [əkwéintəns] n.
아는 사람, 친분관계
as to ~:
~에 관하여
relative to:
~에 관하여, ~와 관련하여

positively decline to **overlook** it, sir."

"Major Talbot," said Hargraves, with a **winning** smile, "I wish you would understand me. I want you to know that I never dreamed of insulting you. In my profession, all life belongs to me. I take what I want, and what I can, and return it over the footlights. Now, if you will, let's **let it go at that**. I came in to see you about something else. We've been pretty good friends for some months, and I'm going to take the risk of offending you again. I know you are hard up for money—never mind how I found out; a boarding house is no place to keep such matters secret—and I want you to let me help you out of the **pinch**. I've been there often enough myself. I've been getting a fair salary all the season, and I've saved some money. You're welcome to a couple hundred—or even more—until you get—"

"Stop!" commanded the major, with his arm outstretched. "It seems that my book didn't lie, after all. You think your money **salve** will heal all the hurts of honour. Under no circumstances would I accept a loan from a **casual acquaintance**; and **as to** you, sir, I would starve before I would consider your insulting offer of a financial adjustment of the circumstances we have discussed. I beg to repeat my request **relative to** your quitting the apartment."

Hargraves took his departure without another word. He also left the house the same day, moving, as Mrs. Vardeman explained at the supper table, nearer the vicinity of the down-town theatre, where "A Magnolia Flower" was booked for a week's run.

Critical was the situation with Major Talbot and Miss Lydia. There was no one in Washington to whom the major's **scruples** allowed him to apply for a loan. Miss Lydia wrote a letter to Uncle Ralph, but it was doubtful whether that relative's constricted affairs would permit him to furnish help. The major was forced to make an apologetic address to Mrs. Vardeman regarding the delayed payment for board, referring to "delinquent rentals" and "delayed remittances" in a rather confused strain.

Deliverance came from an entirely unexpected source.

Late one afternoon the door maid came up and announced an old coloured man who wanted to see Major Talbot. The major asked that he be sent up to his study. Soon an old darkey appeared in the doorway, with his hat in hand, bowing, and scraping with one **clumsy** foot. He was quite decently dressed in a baggy suit of black. His big, coarse shoes shone with a metallic lustre suggestive of stove polish. His bushy wool was gray—almost white. After middle life, it is difficult to estimate the age of a Negro. This one might have seen as many years as had Major Talbot.

"**I be bound** you don't know me, Mars' Pendleton," were his first words.

The major rose and came forward at the old, familiar style of address. It was one of the old plantation darkeys without a doubt; but they had been widely scattered, and he could not **recall** the voice or face.

"I don't believe I do," he said kindly—"unless you will assist my memory."

"Don't you 'member Cindy's Mose, Mars' Pendleton, what 'migrated 'mediately after de war?"

"Wait a moment," said the major, rubbing his forehead with the tips of his fingers. He loved to recall everything connected with those beloved days. "Cindy's Mose," he reflected. "You worked among the horses—**breaking** the **colts**. Yes, I remember now. After the surrender, you took the name of—don't **prompt** me—Mitchell, and went to the West—to Nebraska."

"Yassir, yassir,"—the old man's face stretched with a delighted grin—"dat's him, dat's it. Newbraska. Dat's me—Mose Mitchell. Old Uncle Mose Mitchell, dey calls me now. Old mars', your pa, gimme a pah of dem **mule** colts when

---

I'll be bound:
정말 ~라고 생각하다, 확신하다
recall [rikɔ́:l] v.
생각해내다, 상기하다

break [breik] v.
(동물을) 길들이다
colt [koult] n.
망아지
prompt [prɑmpt / prɔmpt] v.
암시해 주다, 일러주다

mule [mju:l] n.
노새

The Duplicity of Hargraves   237

I lef' fur to staht me goin' with. You 'member dem colts, Mars' Pendleton?"

"I don't seem to recall the colts," said the major. "You know I was married the first year of the war and living at the old Follinsbee place. But sit down, sit down, Uncle Mose. I'm glad to see you. I hope you have prospered."

Uncle Mose took a chair and laid his hat carefully on the floor beside it.

"Yassir; of late I done mouty famous. When I first got to Newbraska, dey folks come all roun' me to see dem mule colts. Dey ain't see no mules like dem in Newbraska. I sold dem mules for three hundred dollars. Yassir—three hundred.

"Den I open a blacksmith shop, suh, and made some money and bought some lan'. Me and my old 'oman done raised up seb'm chillun, and all doin' well 'cept two of 'em what died. Fo' year ago a railroad come along and staht a town slam ag'inst my lan', and, suh, Mars' Pendleton, Uncle Mose am worth leb'm thousand dollars in money, property, and lan'."

"I'm glad to hear it," said the major heartily. "Glad to hear it."

"And dat little baby of yo'n, Mars' Pendleton— one what you name Miss Lyddy—I be bound dat little **tad** done growed up tell nobody wouldn't know her."

> "... Dey ain't see no mules like dem in Newbraska. I sold dem mules for three hundred dollars. Yassir— three hundred.

tad [tæd] n.
어린아이; (특히) 소년

The major stepped to the door and called: "Lydia, dear, will you come?"

Miss Lydia, looking quite grown up and a little worried, came in from her room.

"Dar, now! What'd I tell you? I knowed dat baby done be plum growed up. You don't 'member Uncle Mose, child?"

"This is Aunt Cindy's Mose, Lydia," explained the major. "He left Sunnymead for the West when you were two years old."

"Well," said Miss Lydia, "I can hardly be expected to remember you, Uncle Mose, at that age. And, as you say, I'm 'plum growed up,' and was a blessed long time ago. But I'm glad to see you, even if I can't remember you."

And she was. And so was the major. Something alive and **tangible** had come to link them with the happy past. The three sat and talked over the olden times, the major and Uncle Mose correcting or prompting each other as they reviewed the plantation scenes and days.

The major inquired what the old man was doing so far from his home.

"Uncle Mose am a delicate," he explained, "to de grand Baptis' convention in dis city. I never preached none, but bein' a residin' elder in de church, and able fur to pay my own expenses, dey sent me along."

---

tangible [tǽndʒəb-əl] adj. 만져서 알 수 있는, 실체적인, 확실한

"And how did you know we were in Washington?" inquired Miss Lydia.

"Dey's a cullud man works in de hotel whar I stops, what comes from Mobile. He told me he seen Mars' Pendleton comin' outen dish here house one mawnin'.

"What I come fur," continued Uncle Mose, reaching into his pocket—"besides de sight of home folks—was to pay Mars' Pendleton what I owes him."

"Owe me?" said the major, in surprise.

"Yassir—three hundred dollars." He handed the major a roll of bills. "When I lef' old mars' says: 'Take dem mule colts, Mose, and, if it be so you gits able, pay fur 'em'. Yassir—dem was his words. De war had done lef' old mars' po' hisself. Old mars' bein' 'long ago dead, de debt **descends** to Mars' Pendleton. Three hundred dollars. Uncle Mose is plenty able to pay now. When dat railroad buy my lan' I laid off to pay fur dem mules. Count de money, Mars' Pendleton. Dat's what I sold dem mules fur. Yassir."

Tears were in Major Talbot's eyes. He took Uncle Mose's hand and laid his other upon his shoulder.

"Dear, faithful, old **servitor**," he said in an unsteady voice, "I don't mind saying to you that 'Mars' Pendleton' spent his last dollar in

---

descend [disénd] v.
전해지다, 상속되다

servitor [sə́:rvətə:r] n.
하인, 종복

the world a week ago. We will accept this money, Uncle Mose, since, in a way, it is a sort of payment, as well as a token of the loyalty and devotion of the old regime. Lydia, my dear, take the money. You are better fitted than I to manage its expenditure."

"Take it, honey," said Uncle Mose. "Hit belongs to you. Hit's Talbot money."

After Uncle Mose had gone, Miss Lydia had a good cry—for joy; and the major turned his face to a corner, and smoked his clay pipe volcanically.

The succeeding days saw the Talbots restored to peace and ease. Miss Lydia's face lost its worried look. The major appeared in a new frock coat, in which he looked like a wax figure **personifying** the memory of his golden age. Another publisher who read the manuscript of the "Anecdotes and Reminiscences" thought that, with a little retouching and **toning down** of the high lights, he could make a really bright and **salable** volume of it. Altogether, the situation was comfortable, and not without the touch of hope that is often sweeter than arrived blessings.

One day, about a week after their piece of good luck, a maid brought a letter for Miss Lydia to her room. The postmark showed that it was from New York. Not knowing any one there, Miss Lydia, in a mild flutter of wonder, sat down by her table and opened the letter with her scissors. This was what she read:

Dear Miss Talbot:

I thought you might be glad to learn of my good fortune. I have received and accepted an offer of two hundred dollars per week by a New York stock company to play Colonel Calhoun in "A Magnolia Flower."

There is something else I wanted you to know. I guess you'd better not tell Major Talbot. I was anxious to **make** him some **amends** for the great help he was to me in studying the part, and for the bad **humour** he was in about it. He refused to let me, so I did it anyhow. I could easily **spare** the three hundred.

Sincerely yours,
H. Hopkins Hargraves,

P.S. How did I play Uncle Mose?

Major Talbot, passing through the hall, saw Miss Lydia's door open and stopped.

"Any mail for us this morning, Lydia, dear?" he asked.

Miss Lydia slid the letter beneath a fold of her dress.

"The *Mobile Chronicle* came," she said promptly. "It's on the table in your study."

---

make amends:
갚다, 보상하다, 벌충하다
humor [hjú:mər] n.
기분, 심정, 일시적인 마음의 상태
spare [spεə:r] v.
떼어 두다, 나누어 주다, 할애하다

One Dollar's Worth

The judge of the United States court of the district lying along the Rio Grande border found the following letter one morning in his mail:

JUDGE:

When you sent me up for four years you made a talk. Among other hard things, you called me a rattlesnake. Maybe I am one—anyhow, you hear me rattling now. One year after I got to the **pen**, my daughter died of—well, they said it was poverty and the disgrace together. You've got a daughter, Judge, and I'm going to make you know how it feels to lose one. And I'm going to bite that **district attorney** that

---

pen [pen] n.
교도소
district attorney:
지방 검사

spoke against me. I'm free now, and I guess I've turned to rattlesnake all right. I feel like one. I don't say much, but this is my rattle. Look out when I strike.

Yours respectfully,
RATTLESNAKE.

Judge Derwent threw the letter carelessly aside. It was nothing new to receive such **epistles** from desperate men whom he had been called upon to judge. He felt no alarm. Later on he showed the letter to Littlefield, the young district attorney, for Littlefield's name was included in the threat, and the judge was **punctilious** in matters between himself and his fellow men.

Littlefield honoured the rattle of the writer, as far as it concerned himself, with a smile of **contempt**; but he **frowned** a little over the **reference** to the Judge's daughter, for he and Nancy Derwent were to be married in the fall.

Littlefield went to the clerk of the court and looked over the records with him. They decided that the letter might have been sent by Mexico Sam, a half-breed border **desperado** who had been imprisoned for manslaughter four years before. Then official duties **crowded** the matter from his mind, and the rattle of the **revengeful** serpent was forgotten.

---

epistle [ipísl] n.
편지
punctilious [pʌŋktíliəs] adj.
예의 범절에 까다로운, 형식에 치우친

contempt [kəntémpt] n.
경멸, 멸시
frown [fraun] v.
눈살을 찌푸리다, 얼굴을 찡그리다
reference [réf-ərəns] n.
언급, 논급
desperado [dèspəréidou, -pərá:-] n.
무법자, 악한
crowd [kraud] v.
밀어내다
revengeful [rivéndʒfəl] adj.
복수심에 불타는, 앙심 깊은

session [séʃ-ən] n.
(법정이) 개정(開廷) 중임, (회의, 의회 등이) 개회 중임
counterfeit [káuntərfìt] adj.
모조의, 가짜의, 허위의
deviation [dìːviéiʃən] n.
벗어남, 탈선, 일탈
rectitude [réktətjùːd] n.
정직, 청렴, 올바름, 정확
courthouse [kɔ́ːrthàus] n.
법원
druggist [drʌ́gist] n.
약제사
docket [dákit / dɔ́k-] n.
소송사건 일람표, 사건 등록서, 소송인 명부

expert [ékspəːrt] n.
전문가, 숙련자
lump [lʌmp] n.
덩어리, 조각
putty [pʌ́ti] n.
퍼티 (창유리 등에 쓰이는 접합제)

Court was in **session** at Brownsville. Most of the cases to be tried were charges of smuggling, counterfeiting, post-office robberies, and violations of Federal laws along the border. One case was that of a young Mexican, Rafael Ortiz, who had been rounded up by a clever deputy marshal in the act of passing a **counterfeit** silver dollar. He had been suspected of many such **deviations** from **rectitude**, but this was the first time that anything provable had been fixed upon him. Ortiz languished cozily in jail, smoking brown cigarettes and waiting for trial. Kilpatrick, the deputy, brought the counterfeit dollar and handed it to the district attorney in his office in the **courthouse**. The deputy and a reputable **druggist** were prepared to swear that Ortiz paid for a bottle of medicine with it. The coin was a poor counterfeit, soft, dull-looking, and made principally of lead. It was the day before the morning on which the **docket** would reach the case of Ortiz, and the district attorney was preparing himself for trial.

"Not much need of having in high-priced **experts** to prove the coin's queer, is there, Kil?" smiled Littlefield, as he thumped the dollar down upon the table, where it fell with no more ring than would have come from a **lump** of **putty**.

greaser [grí:sər] n.
(속어) 멕시코 사람, 스페인계 미국인
behind the bars:
교도소에서, 옥중에
rascal [rǽskəl / rá:s-] n.
악당, 건달
jacal [həkáːl] n.
하칼 (멕시코와 미국 남서부의 토벽 초가집)

winsome [wínsəm] adj.
사람의 눈을 끄는, 매력 있는

adjourn [ədʒə́:rn] v.
휴회하다, 연기하다, 휴정하다

ruling [rúːliŋ] n.
판결

livery stable:
말(마차) 대여소, 말 보관소

One Dollar's Worth 245

"I guess the **Greaser**'s as good as **behind the bars**," said the deputy, easing up his holsters. "You've got him dead. If it had been just one time, these Mexicans can't tell good money from bad; but this little yaller **rascal** belongs to a gang of counterfeiters, I know. This is the first time I've been able to catch him doing the trick. He's got a girl down there in them Mexican **jacals** on the river bank. I seen her one day when I was watching him. She's as pretty as a red heifer in a flower bed."

Littlefield shoved the counterfeit dollar into his pocket, and slipped his memoranda of the case into an envelope. Just then a bright, **winsome** face, as frank and jolly as a boy's, appeared in the doorway, and in walked Nancy Derwent.

"Oh, Bob, didn't court **adjourn** at twelve to-day until to-morrow?" she asked of Littlefield.

"It did," said the district attorney, "and I'm very glad of it. I've got a lot of **rulings** to look up, and—"

"Now, that's just like you. I wonder you and father don't turn to law books or rulings or something! I want you to take me out plover-shooting this afternoon. Long Prairie is just alive with them. Don't say no, please! I want to try my new twelve-bore hammerless. I've sent to the **livery stable** to engage Fly and Bess

buckboard [bʌ́kbɔ̀:rd] n.
4륜 짐마차

glamour [glǽmər] n.
매력

plover [plʌ́vər, plóuvər] n.
물떼새

calfbound [kǽfbàund, kάːf-] adj. (책이) 송아지 가죽으로 장정된

voluble [váljəbəl / vɔ́l-] adj.
말 잘하는, 능변인, 유창한

mix up:
관련되다, 연루되다

for the **buckboard**; they stand fire so nicely. I was sure you would go."

They were to be married in the fall. The **glamour** was at its height. The **plovers** won the day—or, rather, the afternoon—over the **calf-bound** authorities. Littlefield began to put his papers away.

There was a knock at the door. Kilpatrick answered it. A beautiful, dark-eyed girl with a skin tinged with the faintest lemon colour walked into the room. A black shawl was thrown over her head and wound once around her neck.

She began to talk in Spanish, a **voluble**, mournful stream of melancholy music. Littlefield did not understand Spanish. The deputy did, and he translated her talk by portions, at intervals holding up his hand to check the flow of her words.

"She came to see you, Mr. Littlefield. Her name's Joya Treviñas. She wants to see you about—well, she's **mixed up** with that Rafael Ortiz. She's his—she's his girl. She says he's innocent. She says she made the money and got him to pass it. Don't you believe her, Mr. Littlefield. That's the way with these Mexican girls; they'll lie, steal, or kill for a fellow when they get stuck on him. Never trust a woman that's in love!"

One Dollar's Worth **247**

"Mr. Kilpatrick!"

Nancy Derwent's **indignant exclamation** caused the deputy to **flounder** for a moment in attempting to explain that he had **misquoted** his own sentiments, and then he went on with the translation:

"She says she's willing to **take his place** in the jail if you'll let him out. She says she was down sick with the fever, and the doctor said she'd die if she didn't have medicine. That's why he passed the lead dollar on the drug store. She says it saved her life. This Rafael seems to be her honey, all right; there's a lot of stuff in her talk about love and such things that you don't want to hear."

It was an old story to the district attorney.

"Tell her," said he, "that I can do nothing. The case comes up in the morning, and he will have to make his fight before the court."

Nancy Derwent was not so hardened. She was looking with sympathetic interest at Joya Treviñas and at Littlefield alternately. The deputy repeated the district attorney's words to the girl. She spoke a sentence or two in a low voice, pulled her shawl closely about her face, and left the room.

"What did she say then?" asked the district attorney.

"Nothing special," said the deputy. "She said:

---

indignant [indígnənt] adj.
성난, 화난
exclamation [èkskləméiʃən] n.
외침, 절규, 감탄
flounder [fláundər] v.
버둥거리다, 몸부림치다, 허둥대다
misquote [miskwóut] v.
그릇 인용하다
take (someone's or something's) place:
대신하다

"... She says she was down sick with the fever, and the doctor said she'd die if she didn't have medicine. That's why he passed the lead dollar on the drug store. She says it saved her life. ..."

'If the life of the one'—let's see how it went—'*Si la vida de ella á quien tu amas*—if the life of the girl you love is ever in danger, remember Rafael Ortiz.'"

Kilpatrick strolled out through the corridor in the direction of the marshal's office.

"Can't you do anything for them, Bob?" asked Nancy. "It's such a little thing—just one counterfeit dollar—to ruin the happiness of two lives! She was in danger of death, and he did it to save her. Doesn't the law know the feeling of pity?"

"It hasn't a place in **jurisprudence**, Nan," said Littlefield, "especially *in re* the district attorney's duty. I'll promise you that the **prosecution** will not be **vindictive**; but the man is as good as convicted when the case is called. Witnesses will swear to his passing the bad dollar which I have in my pocket at this moment as '**Exhibit** A.' There are no Mexicans on the jury, and it will vote Mr. Greaser guilty without leaving the box."

The plover-shooting was fine that afternoon, and in the excitement of the sport the case of Rafael and the grief of Joya Treviñas was forgotten. The district attorney and Nancy Derwent drove out from the town three miles along a smooth, grassy road, and then struck

rolling [róuliŋ] adj.
기복이 있는
prairie [préəri] n.
대평원
haunt [hɔːnt, hɑːnt] n.
서식지, 번식지
swarthy [swɔ́ːrði, -θi] adj.
거무스름한, 까무잡잡한

place [pleis] v.
확인하다,생각해내다,알아내다
shortcut [ʃɔ́ːrtkʌt] n.
지름길

trot [trɑt / trɔt] n.
(말 등의) 속보, (사람의) 빠른 걸음
timber [tímbəːr] n.
수목, 삼림, 삼림 지대

team [tiːm] n.
(수레에 맨) 한 떼의 동물
scabbard [skǽbəːrd] n.
검이나 라이플 등의 집

across a **rolling prairie** toward a heavy line of timber on Piedra Creek. Beyond this creek lay Long Prairie, the favourite **haunt** of the plover. As they were nearing the creek they heard the galloping of a horse to their right, and saw a man with black hair and a **swarthy** face riding toward the woods at a tangent, as if he had come up behind them.

"I've seen that fellow somewhere," said Littlefield, who had a memory for faces, "but I can't exactly **place** him. Some ranchman, I suppose, taking a **short cut** home."

They spent an hour on Long Prairie, shooting from the buckboard. Nancy Derwent, an active, outdoor Western girl, was pleased with her twelve-bore. She had bagged within two brace of her companion's score.

They started homeward at a gentle **trot**. When within a hundred yards of Piedra Creek a man rode out of the **timber** directly toward them.

"It looks like the man we saw coming over," remarked Miss Derwent.

As the distance between them lessened, the district attorney suddenly pulled up his **team** sharply, with his eyes fixed upon the advancing horseman. That individual had drawn a Winchester from its **scabbard** on his saddle and thrown it over his arm.

mutter [mʌ́tə:r] v.
낮게 중얼거리다
epistle [ipísl] n.
편지

superfluous [su:pə́:rfluəs] adj.
불필요한, 쓸데없는

ruffian [rʌ́fiən, -fjən] n.
불한당, 악한
get even:
되갚음하다, 복수하다

"Now I know you, Mexico Sam!" **muttered** Littlefield to himself. "It *was* you who shook your rattles in that gentle **epistle**."

Mexico Sam did not leave things long in doubt. He had a nice eye in all matters relating to firearms, so when he was within good rifle range, but outside of danger from No. 8 shot, he threw up his Winchester and opened fire upon the occupants of the buckboard.

The first shot cracked the back of the seat within the two-inch space between the shoulders of Littlefield and Miss Derwent. The next went through the dashboard and Littlefield's trouser leg.

The district attorney hustled Nancy out of the buck-board to the ground. She was a little pale, but asked no questions. She had the frontier instinct that accepts conditions in an emergency without **superfluous** argument. They kept their guns in hand, and Littlefield hastily gathered some handfuls of cartridges from the pasteboard box on the seat and crowded them into his pockets.

"Keep behind the horses, Nan," he commanded. "That fellow is a **ruffian** I sent to prison once. He's trying to **get even**. He knows our shot won't hurt him at that distance."

"All right, Bob," said Nancy steadily. "I'm not afraid. But you come close, too. Whoa, Bess;

stand still, now!"

She stroked Bess's mane. Littlefield stood with his gun ready, praying that the desperado would come within range.

But Mexico Sam was playing his **vendetta** along safe lines. He was a bird of different feather from the plover. His accurate eye drew an imaginary line of circumference around the area of danger from **bird-shot**, and upon this line he rode. His horse wheeled to the right, and as his victims rounded to the safe side of their **equine breastwork** he sent a ball through the district attorney's hat. Once he miscalculated in making a **détour**, and over-stepped his margin. Littlefield's gun flashed, and Mexico Sam ducked his head to the harmless patter of the shot. A few of them stung his horse, which pranced promptly back to the safety line.

The desperado fired again. A little cry came from Nancy Derwent. Littlefield whirled, with blazing eyes, and saw the blood trickling down her cheek.

"I'm not hurt, Bob—only a **splinter** struck me. I think he hit one of the wheel-spokes."

"Lord!" groaned Littlefield. "If I only had a charge of **buckshot**!"

The ruffian got his horse still, and took careful aim. Fly gave a snort and fell in the harness,

trace [treis] n. (수레에 매는) 봇줄	struck in the neck. Bess, now disabused of the idea that plover were being fired at, broke her **traces** and galloped wildly away. Mexican Sam sent a ball neatly through the fulness of Nancy Derwent's shooting jacket.
	"Lie down—lie down!" snapped Littlefield. "Close to the horse—flat on the ground—so."
recumbent [rikʌ́mbənt] adj. 누워 있는, 기대고 있는	He almost threw her upon the grass against the back of the **recumbent** Fly. Oddly enough, at that moment the words of the Mexican girl returned to his mind:
	"If the life of the girl you love is ever in danger, remember Rafael Ortiz."
	Littlefield uttered an exclamation.
"If the life of the girl you love is ever in danger, remember Rafael Ortiz."	"Open fire on him, Nan, across the horse's back. Fire as fast as you can! You can't hurt him, but keep him dodging shot for one minute while I try to work a little scheme."
	Nancy gave a quick glance at Littlefield, and saw him take out his pocket-knife and open it. Then she turned her face to obey orders, keeping up a rapid fire at the enemy.
innocuous [inʌ́kju:əs / inɔ́k-] adj. 무해한, 해롭지 않은 fusillade [fjú:səlèid,-là:d,-zə-] n. 일제 사격, 연속 사격 Stetson [stétsn] n. 카우보이 모자	Mexico Sam waited patiently until this **innocuous fusillade** ceased. He had plenty of time, and he did not care to risk the chance of a bird-shot in his eye when it could be avoided by a little caution. He pulled his heavy **Stetson** low down over his face until the shots ceased. Then he drew a little nearer, and fired with

careful aim at what he could see of his victims above the fallen horse.

Neither of them moved. He urged his horse a few steps nearer. He saw the district attorney rise to one knee and deliberately level his shotgun. He pulled his hat down and awaited the harmless rattle of the tiny **pellets**.

The shotgun blazed with a heavy report. Mexico Sam sighed, turned limp all over, and slowly fell from his horse—a dead rattlesnake.

At ten o'clock the next morning court opened, and the case of the United States *versus* Rafael Ortiz was called. The district attorney, with his arm in a **sling**, rose and addressed the court.

"May it please your honour," he said, "I desire to enter a ***nolle pros.*** in this case. Even though the **defendant** should be guilty, there is not sufficient evidence in the hands of the government to secure a conviction. The piece of counterfeit coin upon the identity of which the case was built is not now available as evidence. I ask, therefore, that the case be **stricken off**."

At the noon **recess** Kilpatrick strolled into the district attorney's office.

"I've just been down to take a **squint** at old Mexico Sam," said the deputy. "They've got him laid out. Old Mexico was a tough outfit, I reckon. The boys was wonderin' down there

slug [slʌg] n.
총탄, 산탄

what you shot him with. Some said it must have been nails. I never see a gun carry anything to make holes like he had."

"I shot him," said the district attorney, "with Exhibit A of your counterfeiting case. Lucky thing for me—and somebody else—that it was as bad money as it was! It sliced up into **slugs** very nicely. Say, Kil, can't you go down to the jacals and find where that Mexican girl lives? Miss Derwent wants to know."

While the Auto Waits

Promptly at the beginning of twilight, came again to that quiet corner of that quiet, small park the girl in gray. She sat upon a bench and read a book, for there was yet to come a half hour in which print could be accomplished.

To repeat: Her dress was gray, and plain enough to mask its **impeccancy** of style and fit. A large-meshed veil imprisoned her turban hat and a face that shone through it with a calm and unconscious beauty. She had come there at the same hour on the day previous, and on the day before that; and there was one who knew it.

The young man who knew it hovered near, relying upon burnt sacrifices to the great **joss**,

---

impeccancy [impékənsi] n.
결백, 죄없음

joss [dʒɑs, dʒɔːs / dʒɔs] n.
(중국인이 섬기는) 우상, 신상

piety [páiəti] n.
(종교적인) 경건, 신앙심

avidity [əvídəti] n.
갈망, 욕심
on the beat:
순찰 중에
inconsequent [inkánsikwènt, -kwənt / -kɔ́nsikwənt] adj.
사소한, 가치 없는

contralto [kəntrǽltou] n.
콘트랄토, 여성 최저 음역
(소프라노와 테너 사이)

vassal [vǽsəl] n.
봉신, 가신, 부하
complaisance [kəmpléisəns, -zəns, kámpləzæns] n.
친절, 정중, 공손
bowl over:
깊은 인상을 남기다, 놀라게 하다
lamp [læmp] n.
(속어) 눈(eyes)

Luck. His **piety** was rewarded, for, in turning a page, her book slipped from her fingers and bounded from the bench a full yard away.

The young man pounced upon it with instant **avidity**, returning it to its owner with that air that seems to flourish in parks and public places—a compound of gallantry and hope, tempered with respect for the policeman **on the beat**. In a pleasant voice, he risked an **inconsequent** remark upon the weather—that introductory topic responsible for so much of the world's unhappiness—and stood poised for a moment, awaiting his fate.

The girl looked him over leisurely; at his ordinary, neat dress and his features distinguished by nothing particular in the way of expression.

"You may sit down, if you like," she said, in a full, deliberate **contralto**. "Really, I would like to have you do so. The light is too bad for reading. I would prefer to talk."

The **vassal** of Luck slid upon the seat by her side with **complaisance**.

"Do you know," he said, speaking the formula with which park chairmen open their meetings, "that you are quite the stunningest girl I have seen in a long time? I had my eye on you yesterday. Didn't know somebody was **bowled over** by those pretty **lamps** of yours, did you,

circle [sə́:rkl] n.
(교제, 활동, 세력 등의) 범위, 영역
constitute [kánstətjù:t / kɔ́n-] v. 선정하다, 지명하다, 임명하다

penitence [pénətəns] n.
후회, 개전, 속죄
humility [hju:mílət̬i] n.
겸손, 겸양

coquetry [kóukitri] n.
아양, 교태
cue [kju:] n.
(연극의) 큐, 배우의 연기를 시작하기 위한 대사 또는 행동의 신호
postulate [pást∫əlèit / pɔ́s-] v.
가정하다

honeysuckle?"

"Whoever you are," said the girl, in icy tones, "you must remember that I am a lady. I will excuse the remark you have just made because the mistake was, doubtless, not an unnatural one—in your **circle**. I asked you to sit down; if the invitation must **constitute** me your honeysuckle, consider it withdrawn."

"I earnestly beg your pardon," pleaded the young man. His expression of satisfaction had changed to one of **penitence** and **humility**. "It was my fault, you know—I mean, there are girls in parks, you know—that is, of course, you don't know, but—"

"Abandon the subject, if you please. Of course I know. Now, tell me about these people passing and crowding, each way, along these paths. Where are they going? Why do they hurry so? Are they happy?"

The young man had promptly abandoned his air of **coquetry**. His **cue** was now for a waiting part; he could not guess the rôle he would be expected to play.

"It *is* interesting to watch them," he replied, **postulating** her mood. "It is the wonderful drama of life. Some are going to supper and some to—er—other places. One wonders what their histories are."

"I do not," said the girl; "I am not so

inquisitive. I come here to sit because here, only, can I be near the great, common, throbbing heart of humanity. My part in life is cast where its beats are never felt. Can you surmise why I spoke to you, Mr.—?"

"Parkenstacker," supplied the young man. Then he looked eager and hopeful.

"No," said the girl, holding up a slender finger, and smiling slightly. "You would recognize it immediately. It is impossible to keep one's name out of print. Or even one's portrait. This veil and this hat of my maid furnish me with an *incog*. You should have seen the chauffeur stare at it when he thought I did not see. Candidly, there are five or six names that belong in the **holy of holies**, and mine, by the accident of birth, is one of them. I spoke to you, Mr. Stackenpot—"

"Parkenstacker," corrected the young man, modestly.

"—Mr. Parkenstacker, because I wanted to talk, for once, with a natural man—one unspoiled by the **despicable** gloss of wealth and supposed social superiority. Oh! you do not know how **weary** I am of it—money, money, money! And of the men who surround me, dancing like little **marionettes** all cut by the same pattern. I am sick of pleasure, of jewels, of travel, of society, of luxuries of all kinds."

venture [véntʃər] v.
과감히 말하다

competence [kámpətəns / kɔ́m-] n.
충분한 재산, 소득
monotony [mənátəni / -nɔ́t-] n.
지루함, 단조로움
pall [pɔ:l] v.
시시해지다, 흥미를 잃다
superfluous [su:pə́:rfluəs] adj.
과잉의, 여분의

ingenuously [indʒénju:əsli] adv. 솔직하게, 꾸밈없이

folk [fouk] n.
사람들
snob [snɑb / snɔb] n.
속물

indulgent [indʌ́ldʒənt] adj.
관대한, 너그럽게 봐주는
fad [fæd] n.
일시적 유행, 변덕, 취미 a

"I always had an idea," **ventured** the young man, hesitatingly, "that money must be a pretty good thing."

"A **competence** is to be desired. But when you have so many millions that—!" She concluded the sentence with a gesture of despair. "It is the **monotony** of it," she continued, "that **palls**. Drives, dinners, theatres, balls, suppers, with the gilding of **superfluous** wealth over it all. Sometimes the very tinkle of the ice in my champagne glass nearly drives me mad."

Mr. Parkenstacker looked **ingenuously** interested.

"I have always liked," he said, "to read and hear about the ways of wealthy and fashionable **folks**. I suppose I am a bit of a **snob**. But I like to have my information accurate. Now, I had formed the opinion that champagne is cooled in the bottle and not by placing ice in the glass."

The girl gave a musical laugh of genuine amusement.

"You should know," she explained, in an **indulgent** tone, "that we of the non-useful class depend for our amusement upon departure from precedent. Just now it is a **fad** to put ice in champagne. The idea was originated by a visiting Prince of Tartary while dining at the Waldorf. It will soon give way to some other whim. Just as at a dinner party this week on

Madison Avenue a green kid glove was laid by the plate of each guest to be put on and used while eating olives."

"I see," admitted the young man, humbly. "These special **diversions** of the **inner circle** do not become familiar to the common public."

"Sometimes," continued the girl, acknowledging his confession of error by a slight bow, "I have thought that if I ever should love a man it would be one of **lowly station**. One who is a worker and not a **drone**. But, doubtless, the claims of **caste** and wealth will prove stronger than my inclination. Just now I am besieged by two. One is a Grand Duke of a German principality. I think he has, or has had, a wife, somewhere, driven mad by his **intemperance** and cruelty. The other is an English Marquis, so cold and **mercenary** that I even prefer the diabolism of the Duke. What is it that impels me to tell you these things, Mr. Packenstacker?

"Parkenstacker," breathed the young man. "Indeed, you cannot know how much I appreciate your confidences."

The girl **contemplated** him with the calm, impersonal regard that **befitted** the difference in their stations.

"What is your line of business, Mr. Parkenstacker?" she asked.

earnest [ə́:rnist] adj.
성실한, 진지한, 진정인

calling [kɔ́:liŋ] n.
직업

reticule [rétikjùːl] n.
(여성용) 손가방

"A very humble one. But I hope to rise in the world. Were you really in **earnest** when you said that you could love a man of lowly position?"

"Indeed I was. But I said 'might.' There is the Grand Duke and the Marquis, you know. Yes; no **calling** could be too humble were the man what I would wish him to be."

"I work," declared Mr. Parkenstacker, "in a restaurant."

The girl shrank slightly.

"Not as a waiter?" she said, a little imploringly. "Labor is noble, but personal attendance, you know—valets and—"

"I am not a waiter. I am cashier in"—on the street they faced that bounded the opposite side of the park was the brilliant electric sign "RESTAURANT"—"I am cashier in that restaurant you see there."

The girl consulted a tiny watch set in a bracelet of rich design upon her left wrist, and rose, hurriedly. She thrust her book into a glittering **reticule** suspended from her waist, for which, however, the book was too large.

"Why are you not at work?" she asked.

"I am on the night turn," said the young man; "it is yet an hour before my period begins. May I not hope to see you again?"

"I do not know. Perhaps—but the whim may

round [raund] n.
연속, 되풀이, 정해진 일상

not seize me again. I must go quickly now. There is a dinner, and a box at the play—and, oh! the same old **round**. Perhaps you noticed an automobile at the upper corner of the park as you came. One with a white body."

"And red running gear?" asked the young man, knitting his brows reflectively.

"Yes. I always come in that. Pierre waits for me there. He supposes me to be shopping in the department store across the square. Conceive of the bondage of the life wherein we must deceive even our chauffeurs. Good-night."

"But it is dark now," said Mr. Parkenstacker, "and the park is full of rude men. May I not walk—"

monogram [mánəgræ̀m/mɔ́n-] n.
모노그램(성명 첫 글자 등을 도안화하여 짜맞춘 글자)

"If you have the slightest regard for my wishes," said the girl, firmly, "you will remain at this bench for ten minutes after I have left. I do not mean to accuse you, but you are probably aware that autos generally bear the **monogram** of their owner. Again, good-night."

Swift and stately she moved away through the dusk. The young man watched her graceful form as she reached the pavement at the park's edge, and turned up along it toward the corner where stood the automobile. Then he treacherously and unhesitatingly began to dodge and skim among the park trees and shrubbery in a course parallel to her route, keeping her well in sight.

When she reached the corner she turned her head to glance at the motor car, and then passed it, continuing on across the street. Sheltered behind a convenient standing cab, the young man followed her movements closely with his eyes. Passing down the sidewalk of the street opposite the park, she entered the restaurant with the blazing sign. The place was one of those frankly glaring **establishments**, all white paint and glass, where one may dine cheaply and **conspicuously**. The girl penetrated the restaurant to some retreat at its rear, **whence** she quickly emerged without her hat and veil.

The cashier's desk was well to the front. A red-haired girl on the stool climbed down, glancing pointedly at the clock as she did so. The girl in gray mounted in her place.

The young man thrust his hands into his pockets and walked slowly back along the sidewalk. At the corner his foot struck a small, paper-covered volume lying there, sending it sliding to the edge of the **turf**. By its **picturesque** cover he recognized it as the book the girl had been reading. He picked it up carelessly, and saw that its title was "New Arabian Nights," the author being of the name of Stevenson. He dropped it again upon the grass,

establishment [istǽbliʃmənt] n. 시설, 건물
conspicuously [kənspíkjuəsli] adv. 눈에 띄게, 현저히
whence [hwens] adv. 어디에서, 어디로부터

turf [təːrf] n. 잔디, 잔디밭
picturesque [pìktʃərésk] adj. 그림같은, 아름다운

irresolute [irézəlù:t] adj.
망설이는, 우유부단한
recline [rikláin] v.
기대다, 눕다

and lounged, **irresolute**, for a minute. Then he stepped into the automobile, **reclined** upon the cushions, and said two words to the chauffeur:

"Club, Henri."

Squaring the Circle

At the hazard of wearying you this tale of **vehement** emotions must be **prefaced** by a **discourse** on geometry.

Nature moves in circles; Art in straight lines. The natural is rounded; the artificial is made up of angles. A man lost in the snow wanders, in spite of himself, in perfect circles; the city man's feet, denaturalized by rectangular streets and floors, carry him ever away from himself.

The round eyes of childhood **typify** innocence; the narrowed line of the flirt's optic proves the invasion of art. The horizontal mouth is the mark of determined cunning; who has not read Nature's most **spontaneous** lyric in lips rounded for the candid kiss?

behold [bihóuld] interj.
(명령형) 보라, 주목하라

deflect [diflékt] v.
빗나가다, 굴절하다, 비뚤어지다

defiance [difáiəns] n.
도전, 저항, 반항

Beauty is Nature in perfection; circularity is its chief attribute. **Behold** the full moon, the enchanting gold ball, the domes of splendid temples, the huckleberry pie, the wedding ring, the circus ring, the ring for the waiter, and the "round" of drinks.

On the other hand, straight lines show that Nature has been **deflected**. Imagine Venus's girdle transformed into a "straight front"!

When we begin to move in straight lines and turn sharp corners our natures begin to change. The consequence is that Nature, being more adaptive than Art, tries to conform to its sterner regulations. The result is often a rather curious product—for instance: A prize chrysanthemum, wood alcohol whiskey, a Republican Missouri, cauliflower *au gratin*, and a New Yorker.

Nature is lost quickest in a big city. The cause is geometrical, not moral. The straight lines of its streets and architecture, the rectangularity of its laws and social customs, the undeviating pavements, the hard, severe, depressing, uncompromising rules of all its ways—even of its recreation and sports—coldly exhibit a sneering **defiance** of the curved line of Nature.

Wherefore, it may be said that the big city has demonstrated the problem of squaring the circle. And it may be added that this mathematical introduction **precedes** an account of the fate of a Kentucky **feud** that was imported to the city that has a habit of making its importations conform to its angles.

The feud began in the Cumberland Mountains between the Folwell and the Harkness families. The first victim of the homespun vendetta was a 'possum dog belonging to Bill Harkness. The Harkness family evened up this dire loss by laying out the chief of the Folwell clan. The Folwells were prompt at **repartee**. They oiled up their squirrel rifles and made it feasible for Bill Harkness to follow his dog to a land where the 'possums come down when treed without the stroke of an ax.

The feud flourished for forty years. Harknesses were shot at the plough, through their lamp-lit cabin windows, coming from camp-meeting, asleep, in **duello**, sober and otherwise, singly and in family groups, prepared and unprepared. Folwells had the branches of their **family tree lopped** off in similar ways, as the traditions of their country prescribed and authorized.

By and by the pruning left but a single member of each family. And then Cal Harkness, probably reasoning that further **pursuance** of the controversy would give a too decided personal flavour to the feud, suddenly disappeared from the relieved Cumberlands, baulking the avenging hand of Sam, the ultimate opposing Folwell.

A year afterward Sam Folwell learned that his **hereditary**, unsuppressed enemy was living in New York City. Sam turned over the big iron wash-pot in the yard, scraped off some of the soot, which he mixed with lard and shined his boots with the compound. He put on his store clothes of butternut dyed black, a white shirt and collar, and packed a carpet-sack with Spartan *lingerie*. He took his squirrel rifle from its hooks, but put it back again with a sigh. However **ethical** and **plausible** the habit might be in the Cumberlands, perhaps New York would not swallow his pose of hunting squirrels among the **skyscrapers** along Broadway. An ancient but reliable Colt's revolver that he resurrected from a bureau drawer seemed to **proclaim** itself the **pink** of weapons for **metropolitan** adventure and vengeance. This and a hunting-knife in a leather sheath, Sam packed in the carpet-sack. As he started, muleback, for the lowland railroad station the last Folwell turned in his saddle and looked grimly at the little **cluster** of white-pine **slabs** in the **clump** of cedars that marked the Folwell burying-ground.

---

hereditary [hirédətèri / -təri] adj. 세습의, 부모한테 물려받은
ethical [éθikəl] adj. 도덕상의, 윤리적인
plausible [plɔ́:zəbəl] adj. 그럴듯한, 믿을만한
skyscraper [skáiskrèipə:r] n. 초고층 빌딩, 마천루
proclaim [proukléim, prə-] v. 선언하다, 공포하다
pink [piŋk] n. 정화, 극치, 절정
metropolitan [mètrəpálitən / -pɔ́l-] adj. 수도의, 대도시의
cluster [klʌ́stər] n. 떼, 집단, 무리
slab [slæb] n. 넓은 후판
clump [klʌmp] n. 숲, 덤불, 풀숲

Sam Folwell arrived in New York in the night. Still moving and living in the free circles of nature, he did not **perceive** the formidable, pitiless, restless, fierce angles of the great city waiting in the dark to close about the **rotundity** of his heart and brain and mould him to the form of its millions of reshaped victims. A cabby picked him out of the whirl, as Sam himself had often picked a nut from a bed of wind-tossed autumn leaves, and whisked him away to a hotel **commensurate** to his boots and carpet-sack.

On the next morning the last of the Folwells made his **sortie** into the city that sheltered the last Harkness. The Colt was thrust beneath his coat and secured by a narrow leather belt; the hunting-knife hung between his shoulder-blades, with the haft an inch below his coat collar. He knew this much—that Cal Harkness drove an express wagon somewhere in that town, and that he, Sam Folwell, had come to kill him. And as he stepped upon the sidewalk the red came into his eye and the feud-hate into his heart.

The **clamor** of the central avenues drew him **thitherward**. He had half expected to see Cal coming down the street in his shirt-sleeves, with a jug and a whip in his hand, just as he would have seen him in Frankfort or Laurel City. But an hour went by and Cal did not

ambush [ǽmbuʃ] n.
매복, 복병

spirit level:
기포 수준기
rote [rout] n.
기계적 방법, 반복적인 암기,
지루한 되풀이
din [din] n.
소음, 시끄러운 소리
stupefy [stjú:pəfài] v.
마비시키다, 망연하게 하다,
대경 실색케 하다

spirit [spírit] n.
유령
smite [smait] v.
엄습하다, 괴롭히다, 사로잡다

tumult [tjú:mʌlt, -məlt] n.
법석, 소동, 떠들썩함

appear. Perhaps he was waiting in **ambush**, to shoot him from a door or a window. Sam kept a sharp eye on doors and windows for a while.

About noon the city tired of playing with its mouse and suddenly squeezed him with its straight lines.

Sam Folwell stood where two great, rectangular arteries of the city cross. He looked four ways, and saw the world hurled from its orbit and reduced by **spirit level** and tape to an edged and cornered plane. All life moved on tracks, in grooves, according to system, within boundaries, by **rote**. The root of life was the cube root; the measure of existence was square measure. People streamed by in straight rows; the horrible **din** and crash **stupefied** him.

Sam leaned against the sharp corner of a stone building. Those faces passed him by thousands, and none of them were turned toward him. A sudden foolish fear that he had died and was a **spirit**, and that they could not see him, seized him. And then the city **smote** him with loneliness.

A fat man dropped out of the stream and stood a few feet distant, waiting for his car. Sam crept to his side and shouted above the **tumult** into his ear:

"The Rankinses' hogs weighed more'n ourn

a whole passel, but the mast in thar neighborhood was a fine chance better than what it was down—"

The fat man moved away **unostentatiously**, and bought roasted chestnuts to cover his alarm.

Sam felt the need of a drop of **mountain dew**. Across the street men passed in and out through swinging doors. Brief glimpses could be had of a glistening bar and its bedeckings. The **feudist** crossed and **essayed** to enter. Again had Art eliminated the familiar circle. Sam's hand found no door-knob—it slid, in vain, over a rectangular brass plate and polished oak with nothing even so large as a pin's head upon which his fingers might close.

Abashed, reddened, heartbroken, he walked away from the **bootless** door and sat upon a step. A locust club tickled him in the ribs.

"Take a walk for yourself," said the policeman. "You've been **loafing** around here long enough."

At the next corner a shrill whistle sounded in Sam's ear. He wheeled around and saw a black-browed **villain scowling** at him over peanuts heaped on a steaming machine. He started across the street. An immense engine, running without mules, with the voice of a bull and the smell of a smoky lamp, whizzed past, grazing his knee. A cab-driver bumped him

clang [klæŋ] v.
쨍하고 울리다
newsy [njúːzi] n.
신문 판매원
pelt [pelt] v.
내던지다
rind [raind] n.
껍질, 껍데기

cheek [tʃiːk] n.
뻔뻔스러움, 건방진 말이나 행동
implacable [implǽkəbəl, -pléik-] adj.
달랠 수 없는, 무자비한
foe [fou] n.
적, 원수, 적대자
kith and kin [kiθ -] n.
일가친척
waver [wéivəːr] v.
흔들리다, 망설이다, 주저하다

with a hub and explained to him that kind words were invented to be used on other occasions. A motorman **clanged** his bell wildly and, for once in his life, corroborated a cab-driver. A large lady in a changeable silk waist dug an elbow into his back, and a **newsy** pensively **pelted** him with banana **rinds**, murmuring, "I hates to do it—but if anybody seen me let it pass!"

Cal Harkness, his day's work over and his express wagon stabled, turned the sharp edge of the building that, by the **cheek** of architects, is modelled upon a safety razor. Out of the mass of hurrying people his eye picked up, three yards away, the surviving bloody and **implacable foe** of his **kith and kin**.

He stopped short and **wavered** for a moment, being unarmed and sharply surprised. But the keen mountaineer's eye of Sam Folwell had picked him out.

There was a sudden spring, a ripple in the stream of passers-by and the sound of Sam's voice crying:

"Howdy, Cal! I'm durned glad to see ye."

And in the angles of Broadway, Fifth Avenue and Twenty-third Street the Cumberland feudists shook hands.

The Princess and the Puma

six-shooter [-ˈʃúːtəːr] n.
6연발 권총
spur [spəːr] n.
박차
rattler [rǽtləːr] n.
방울뱀
prairie [prέəri] n.
대평원
prickly pear:
선인장의 일종

There had to be a king and queen, of course. The king was a terrible old man who wore **six-shooters** and **spurs**, and shouted in such a tremendous voice that the **rattlers** on the **prairie** would run into their holes under the **prickly pear**. Before there was a royal family they called the man "Whispering Ben." When he came to own 50,000 acres of land and more cattle than he could count, they called him O'Donnell "the Cattle King."

The queen had been a Mexican girl from Laredo. She made a good, mild, Colorado-claro wife, and even succeeded in teaching Ben to modify his voice sufficiently while in the house to keep the dishes from being broken. When Ben got to be king she would sit on the gallery of Espinosa Ranch and weave rush mats. When wealth became so irresistible and oppressive that upholstered chairs and a centre table were brought down from San Antone in the wagons, she bowed her smooth, dark head, and shared the fate of the Danaë.

To avoid **lèse-majesté** you have been presented first to the king and queen. They do not enter the story, which might be called "The Chronicle of the Princess, the Happy Thought, and the Lion that Bungled his Job."

Josefa O'Donnell was the surviving daughter, the princess. From her mother she inherited warmth of nature and a dusky, semi-tropic beauty. From Ben O'Donnell the royal she acquired a store of **intrepidity**, common sense, and the faculty of ruling. The combination was one worth going miles to see. Josefa while riding her pony at a **gallop** could put five out of six bullets through a tomato-can swinging at the end of a string. She could play for hours with a white kitten she owned, dressing it in all manner of absurd clothes. **Scorning** a pencil, she could tell you out of her head what 1545 two-year-olds would bring **on the hoof**, at $8.50 per head. Roughly speaking, the Espinosa Ranch

---

lese-majeste:
군주에 대한 모독

intrepidity [ìntrəpídəti] n.
두려움을 모름, 용맹, 대담
gallop [gǽləp] n.
말 등의 가장 빠른 발놀림, 질주
scorn [skɔ:rn] v.
경멸하다, 가볍게 여기다
on the hoof:
살아있는

Josefa while riding her pony at a gallop could put five out of six bullets through a tomato-can swinging at the end of a string.

The Princess and the Puma

cowpuncher [kaupʌnʃər] n. 카우보이	
range [reindʒ] n. 방목장	
vassal [væsəl] n. 봉신, 가신, 부하	
matrimonial[mætrəmóuniəl] adj. 결혼의, 부부의	
presumptuous [prizʌmptʃuəs] adj. 주제넘은, 뻔뻔한, 건방진	
presuppose [prìːsəpóuz] v. 미리 가정하다, 전제로 하다	
blood royal: 왕족	
yearling [jíəːrliŋ / jɔ́ːr-] n. (동물의) 1년생	
water hole: 물웅덩이, 못	

is forty miles long and thirty broad—but mostly leased land. Josefa, on her pony, had prospected over every mile of it. Every **cow-puncher** on the **range** knew her by sight and was a loyal **vassal**. Ripley Givens, foreman of one of the Espinosa outfits, saw her one day, and made up his mind to form a royal **matrimonial** alliance. **Presumptuous**? No. In those days in the Nueces country a man was a man. And, after all, the title of cattle king does not **presuppose blood royal**. Often it only signifies that its owner wears the crown in token of his magnificent qualities in the art of cattle stealing.

One day Ripley Givens rode over to the Double Elm Ranch to inquire about a bunch of strayed **yearlings**. He was late in setting out on his return trip, and it was sundown when he struck the White Horse Crossing of the Nueces. From there to his own camp it was sixteen miles. To the Espinosa ranch it was twelve. Givens was tired. He decided to pass the night at the Crossing.

There was a fine **water hole** in the river-bed. The banks were thickly covered with great trees, undergrown with brush. Back from the water hole fifty yards was a stretch of curly mesquite grass—supper for his horse and bed for himself. Givens staked his horse, and spread out

timber [tímbə:r] n.
수목, 삼림, 삼림 지대
wail [weil] n.
울부짖음

arroyo [ərɔ́iou] n.
(미국남서부) 물이 마른 수로;
협곡
burden [bə́:rdn] n.
취지, 요지
carnivorous [kɑ:rnívərəs] adj.
육식의

sojourner [sóudʒə:rnər] n.
머무는 사람, 거류자
ranchero [ræntʃɛ́-ərou] n.
목장주, 목동

his saddle blankets to dry. He sat down with his back against a tree and rolled a cigarette. From somewhere in the dense **timber** along the river came a sudden, rageful, shivering **wail**. The pony danced at the end of his rope and blew a whistling snort of comprehending fear. Givens puffed at his cigarette, but he reached leisurely for his pistol-belt, which lay on the grass, and twirled the cylinder of his weapon tentatively. A great gar plunged with a loud splash into the water hole. A little brown rabbit skipped around a bunch of catclaw and sat twitching his whiskers and looking humorously at Givens. The pony went on eating grass.

It is well to be reasonably watchful when a Mexican lion sings soprano along the **arroyos** at sundown. The **burden** of his song may be that young calves and fat lambs are scarce, and that he has a **carnivorous** desire for your acquaintance.

In the grass lay an empty fruit can, cast there by some former **sojourner**. Givens caught sight of it with a grunt of satisfaction. In his coat pocket tied behind his saddle was a handful or two of ground coffee. Black coffee and cigarettes! What **ranchero** could desire more?

In two minutes he had a little fire going clearly. He started, with his can, for the water hole. When within fifteen yards of its edge he

crop [krɑp / krɔp] v. (풀 등을) 뜯어먹다 clump [klʌmp] n. 숲, 덤불, 풀숲 amber [ǽmbər] adj. 호박색의, 황갈색의 glare [glɛər] v. 번쩍이다, 노려보다 preliminary [prilímənèri / -nəri] adj. 예비의, 준비의	saw, between the bushes, a side-saddled pony with down-dropped reins **cropping** grass a little distance to his left. Just rising from her hands and knees on the brink of the water hole was Josefa O'Donnell. She had been drinking water, and she brushed the sand from the palms of her hands. Ten yards away, to her right, half concealed by a **clump** of sacuista, Givens saw the crouching form of the Mexican lion. His **amber** eyeballs **glared** hungrily; six feet from them was the tip of the tail stretched straight, like a pointer's. His hind-quarters rocked with the motion of the cat tribe **preliminary** to leaping.
	Givens did what he could. His six-shooter was thirty-five yards away lying on the grass. He gave a loud yell, and dashed between the lion and the princess.
ruckus [rʌ́kəs] n. 법석, 소동, 논쟁 streak [stri:k] n. 줄, 선, 줄무늬 crack [kræk] n. 사격음, 총성 plump [plʌmp] v. 털썩 떨어지다 jar [dʒɑ:r] n. 충격 lump [lʌmp] n. 혹	The "**rucus**," as Givens called it afterward, was brief and somewhat confused. When he arrived on the line of attack he saw a dim **streak** in the air, and heard a couple of faint **cracks**. Then a hundred pounds of Mexican lion **plumped** down upon his head and flattened him, with a heavy **jar**, to the ground. He remembered calling out: "Let up, now—no fair gouging!" and then he crawled from under the lion like a worm, with his mouth full of grass and dirt, and a big **lump** on the back of his head where

fiasco [fiǽskou] n.
큰 실패
Momus [móuməs] n.
(그리스 신화) 모모스. 비난과 조소의 신
satyr [séitəːr, sǽt-] n.
(그리스신화) 사티로스 (술의 신 Bacchus를 따르는 숲의 신)
hilarious [hiléəriəs, hai-] adj.
유쾌한, 즐거운, 법석대는
knockabout [nákəbàut / nɔ́k-] adj.
소란스러운, 법석 떠는
stuffed [stʌft] adj.
속을 채운

saccharine [sǽkəràin, -rin] adj.
달콤한, 매우 정중한
contralto [kəntrǽltou] n.
콘트랄토, 여성 최저 음역 (소프라노와 테너 사이)
ignominiously [ìgnəmíniəsli] adv. 수치스럽게, 불명예스럽게

it had struck the root of a water-elm. The lion lay motionless. Givens, feeling aggrieved, and suspicious of fouls, shook his fist at the lion, and shouted: "I'll rastle you again for twenty—" and then he got back to himself.

Josefa was standing in her tracks, quietly reloading her silver-mounted .38. It had not been a difficult shot. The lion's head made an easier mark than a tomato-can swinging at the end of a string. There was a provoking, teasing, maddening smile upon her mouth and in her dark eyes. The would-be-rescuing knight felt the fire of his **fiasco** burn down to his soul. Here had been his chance, the chance that he had dreamed of; and **Momus**, and not Cupid, had presided over it. The **satyrs** in the wood were, no doubt, holding their sides in **hilarious**, silent laughter. There had been something like vaudeville—say Signor Givens and his funny **knockabout** act with the **stuffed** lion.

"Is that you, Mr. Givens?" said Josefa, in her deliberate, **saccharine contralto**. "You nearly spoilt my shot when you yelled. Did you hurt your head when you fell?"

"Oh, no," said Givens, quietly; "that didn't hurt." He stooped **ignominiously** and dragged his best Stetson hat from under the beast. It was crushed and wrinkled to a fine comedy effect. Then he knelt down and softly stroked the fierce, open-jawed head of the dead lion.

"Poor old Bill!" he exclaimed mournfully.

"What's that?" asked Josefa, sharply.

"Of course you didn't know, Miss Josefa," said Givens, with an air of one allowing **magnanimity** to triumph over grief. "Nobody can blame you. I tried to save him, but I couldn't let you know **in time**."

"Save who?"

"Why, Bill. I've been looking for him all day. You see, he's been our camp pet for two years. Poor old fellow, he wouldn't have hurt a cottontail rabbit. It'll break the boys all up when they hear about it. But you couldn't tell, of course, that Bill was just trying to play with you."

Josefa's black eyes burned steadily upon him. Ripley Givens met the test successfully. He stood **rumpling** the yellow-brown curls on his head pensively. In his eye was regret, not unmingled with a gentle **reproach**. His smooth features were set to a pattern of **indisputable** sorrow. Josefa **wavered**.

"What was your pet doing here?" she asked, making a **last stand**. "There's no camp near the White Horse Crossing."

"The old rascal ran away from camp yesterday," answered Givens readily. "It's a wonder the coyotes didn't scare him to death. You see,

wrangler [rǽŋg-ələ:r] n.
말지기, 카우보이
reckon [rék-ən] v.
생각하다, 간주하다

bring down:
쏘아 넘어뜨리다, 쓰러뜨리다
ignoble [ignóubəl] adj.
비천한, 열등한
quarry [kwɔ́:ri / kwɑ́ri] n.
사냥감, 공격의 대상
mockery [mɑ́kəri, mɔ́(:)k-] n.
비웃음, 조소

Josefa's black eyes burned steadily upon him. Ripley Givens met the test successfully. He stood rumpling the yellow-brown curls on his head pensively.

Jim Webster, our horse **wrangler**, brought a little terrier pup into camp last week. The pup made life miserable for Bill—he used to chase him around and chew his hind legs for hours at a time. Every night when bedtime came Bill would sneak under one of the boy's blankets and sleep to keep the pup from finding him. I **reckon** he must have been worried pretty desperate or he wouldn't have run away. He was always afraid to get out of sight of camp."

Josefa looked at the body of the fierce animal. Givens gently patted one of the formidable paws that could have killed a yearling calf with one blow. Slowly a red flush widened upon the dark olive face of the girl. Was it the signal of shame of the true sportsman who has **brought down ignoble quarry**? Her eyes grew softer, and the lowered lids drove away all their bright **mockery**.

"I'm very sorry," she said humbly; "but he looked so big, and jumped so high that—"

"Poor old Bill was hungry," interrupted Givens, in quick defence of the deceased. "We always made him jump for his supper in camp. He would lie down and roll over for a piece of meat. When he saw you he thought he was going to get something to eat from you."

Suddenly Josefa's eyes opened wide.

"I might have shot you!" she exclaimed. "You

ran right in between. You risked your life to save your pet! That was fine, Mr. Givens. I like a man who is kind to animals."

Yes; there was even admiration in her gaze now. After all, there was a hero rising out of the ruins of the **anti-climax**. The look on Givens's face would have secured him a high position in the **S.P.C.A.**

"I always loved 'em," said he; "horses, dogs, Mexican lions, cows, alligators—"

"I hate alligators," instantly **demurred** Josefa; "**crawly**, muddy things!"

"Did I say alligators?" said Givens. "I meant antelopes, of course."

Josefa's conscience drove her to make further amends. She held out her hand **penitently**. There was a bright, unshed drop in each of her eyes.

"Please forgive me, Mr. Givens, won't you? I'm only a girl, you know, and I was frightened at first. I'm very, very sorry I shot Bill. You don't know how ashamed I feel. I wouldn't have done it for anything."

Givens took the proffered hand. He held it for a time while he allowed the generosity of his nature to overcome his grief at the loss of Bill. At last it was clear that he had forgiven her.

"Please don't speak of it any more, Miss Josefa. 'Twas enough to frighten any young lady the way Bill looked. I'll explain it all right to the boys."

"Are you really sure you don't hate me?" Josefa came closer to him impulsively. Her eyes were sweet—oh, sweet and pleading with gracious penitence. "I would hate anyone who would kill my kitten. And how daring and kind of you to risk being shot when you tried to save him! How very few men would have done that!" Victory **wrested** from defeat! **Vaudeville** turned into drama! **Bravo**, Ripley Givens!

It was now twilight. Of course Miss Josefa could not be allowed to ride on to the ranch-house alone. Givens **resaddled** his pony **in spite of** that animal's **reproachful** glances, and rode with her. Side by side they galloped across the smooth grass, the princess and the man who was kind to animals. The prairie odours of fruitful earth and delicate bloom were thick and sweet around them. Coyotes **yelping** over there on the hill! No fear. And yet—

Josefa rode closer. A little hand seemed to grope. Givens found it with his own. The ponies kept an even gait. The hands lingered together, and the owner of one explained:

"I never was frightened before, but just think! How terrible it would be to meet a really wild lion! Poor Bill! I'm so glad you came with me!"

O'Donnell was sitting on the ranch gallery.

obliged [əbláidʒd] adj.
감사한, 고마운

push on:
계속 나아가다
steer [stiə:r] n.
수송아지, 수소

range [reindʒ] n.
방목장
settle one's hash:
처치하다, 해치우다
machete [məʃéti, -tʃé-] n.
마체테; 중남미에서 쓰는 벌채용 칼

bully [búli] int.
멋지다, 잘했다

"Hello, Rip!" he shouted—"that you?"

"He rode in with me," said Josefa. "I lost my way and was late."

"Much **obliged**," called the cattle king. "Stop over, Rip, and ride to camp in the morning."

But Givens would not. He would **push on** to camp. There was a bunch of **steers** to start off on the trail at daybreak. He said good-night, and trotted away.

An hour later, when the lights were out, Josefa, in her night-robe, came to her door and called to the king in his own room across the brick-paved hallway:

"Say, pop, you know that old Mexican lion they call the 'Gotch-eared Devil'—the one that killed Gonzales, Mr. Martin's sheep herder, and about fifty calves on the Salado **range**? Well, I **settled his hash** this afternoon over at the White Horse Crossing. Put two balls in his head with my .38 while he was on the jump. I knew him by the slice gone from his left ear that old Gonzales cut off with his **machete**. You couldn't have made a better shot yourself, daddy."

"**Bully** for you!" thundered Whispering Ben from the darkness of the royal chamber.

A Cosmopolite in a Café

venal [ví:nl] adj.
돈으로 얻을 수 있는, 돈으로 좌우되는
influx [ínflʌks] n.
유입, 도래, 쇄도
patron [péitrən] n
고객, 손님
cosmopolite [kɑzmɑ́pəlàit / kɔzmɔ́p-] n.
국제인, 세계주의자

invoke [invóuk] v.
호소하다, 청하다

At midnight the café was crowded. By some chance the little table at which I sat had escaped the eye of incomers, and two vacant chairs at it extended their arms with **venal** hospitality to the **influx** of **patrons**.

And then a **cosmopolite** sat in one of them, and I was glad, for I held a theory that since Adam no true citizen of the world has existed. We hear of them, and we see foreign labels on much luggage, but we find travellers instead of cosmopolites.

I **invoke** your consideration of the scene— the marble-topped tables, the range of

gay [gei] adj.
명랑한, 즐거운, 쾌활한
opulence [ápjələns / ɔ́p-] n.
풍부, 부유
sedulous [sédʒuləs] adj.
근면한, 부지런한, 공들인
garcon [gɑːrsɔ́ː] n.
사환, 급사
melange [meilɑ́ːnʒ, -lɑ́ːndʒ] n.
혼합, 뒤범벅

kingly [kíŋli] adj.
왕의, 당당한, 위엄 있는
diversion [divə́ːrʒən, -ʃən, dai-] n.
기분 전환, 오락, 유희
table d'hôte [tɑ́ːb-əldóut, tǽb-] n. (호텔 등의) 공동식탁
equator [ikwéitər] n.
적도
zone [zoun] n.
(한대·열대 따위의) 대(帶)
high seas:
공해(公海)

leather-upholstered wall seats, the **gay** company, the ladies dressed in demi-state toilets, speaking in an exquisite visible chorus of taste, economy, **opulence** or art; the **sedulous** and largess-loving *garçons*, the music wisely catering to all with its raids upon the composers; the *mélange* of talk and laughter—and, if you will, the Würzburger in the tall glass cones that bend to your lips as a ripe cherry sways on its branch to the beak of a robber jay. I was told by a sculptor from Mauch Chunk that the scene was truly Parisian.

My cosmopolite was named E. Rushmore Coglan, and he will be heard from next summer at Coney Island. He is to establish a new "attraction" there, he informed me, offering **kingly diversion**. And then his conversation rang along parallels of latitude and longitude. He took the great, round world in his hand, so to speak, familiarly, contemptuously, and it seemed no larger than the seed of a Maraschino cherry in a *table d'hôte* grape fruit. He spoke disrespectfully of the **equator**, he skipped from continent to continent, he derided the **zones**, he mopped up the **high seas** with his napkin. With a wave of his hand he would speak of a certain bazaar in Hyderabad. Whiff! He would have you on skis in Lapland. Zip! Now you rode the breakers with the Kanakas at

presto [préstou] int.
급히, 빨리
archduke [á:rtʃdú:k, -djú:k] n.
대공; (옛 오스트리아의) 왕자
anon [ənán / ənɔ́n] adv.
이윽고, 곧

discourse [dískɔ:rs] n.
강연, 설교, 담화
lest [lest] conj.
~하지 않을까(라는)
impartial [impá:rʃəl] adj.
공정한, 치우치지 않은, 편견이 없는

prattle [prǽtl] v.
재잘재잘 지껄이다, 떠듬떠듬 말하다
glee [gli:] n.
기쁨, 즐거움
rivalry [ráiv-əlri] n.
경쟁, 대항, 맞겨룸

Kealaikahiki. **Presto**! He dragged you through an Arkansas post-oak swamp, let you dry for a moment on the alkali plains of his Idaho ranch, then whirled you into the society of Viennese **archdukes**. **Anon** he would be telling you of a cold he acquired in a Chicago lake breeze and how old Escamila cured it in Buenos Ayres with a hot infusion of the *chuchula* weed. You would have addressed a letter to "E. Rushmore Coglan, Esq., the Earth, Solar System, the Universe," and mailed it, feeling confident that it would be delivered to him.

I was sure that I had found at last the one true cosmopolite since Adam, and I listened to his worldwide **discourse** fearful **lest** I should discover in it the local note of the mere globe-trotter. But his opinions never fluttered or drooped; he was as **impartial** to cities, countries and continents as the winds or gravitation.

And as E. Rushmore Coglan **prattled** of this little planet I thought with **glee** of a great almost-cosmopolite who wrote for the whole world and dedicated himself to Bombay. In a poem he has to say that there is pride and **rivalry** between the cities of the earth, and that "the men that breed from them, they traffic up and down, but cling to their cities' hem as a child to the mother's gown." And whenever they walk "by roaring streets unknown" they remember their native city "most faithful, foolish, fond; making her mere-breathed name their bond upon their bond." And my glee was roused because I had **caught Mr. Kipling napping**. Here I had found a man not made from dust; one who had no narrow **boasts** of birthplace or country, one who, if he **bragged** at all, would brag of his whole round globe against the Martians and the inhabitants of the Moon.

Expression on these subjects was precipitated from E. Rushmore Coglan by the third corner to our table. While Coglan was describing to me the **topography** along the Siberian Railway the orchestra glided into a medley. The concluding **air** was "Dixie," and as the exhilarating notes tumbled forth they were almost overpowered by a great clapping of hands from almost every table.

It is worth a paragraph to say that this remarkable scene can be witnessed every evening in numerous cafés in the City of New York. Tons of brew have been consumed over theories to account for it. Some have **conjectured** hastily that all Southerners in town **hie** themselves to cafés at nightfall. This applause of the "rebel" air in a Northern city does puzzle a little; but it is not **insolvable**. The war with Spain, many years' generous mint and watermelon crops, a few long-shot winners at the New Orleans racetrack, and the brilliant banquets given by the Indiana and Kansas citizens who compose the North Carolina Society have made the South rather a "fad" in Manhattan. Your manicure will lisp softly that your left forefinger reminds her so much of a gentleman's in Richmond, Va. Oh, certainly; but many a lady has to work now—the war, you know.

When "Dixie" was being played a dark-haired young man sprang up from somewhere with a Mosby guerrilla yell and waved frantically his soft-brimmed hat. Then he strayed through the smoke, dropped into the vacant chair at our table and pulled out cigarettes.

The evening was at the period when **reserve** is thawed. One of us mentioned three Würzburgers to the waiter; the dark-haired young man acknowledged his inclusion in the order by a smile and a nod. I hastened to ask him a question because I wanted to try out a theory I had.

"Would you mind telling me," I began, "whether you are from—"

The fist of E. Rushmore Coglan banged the table and I was jarred into silence.

"Excuse me," said he, "but that's a question I never like to hear asked. What does it matter where a man is from? Is it fair to judge a man

---

reserve [rizə́:rv] n.
삼감, 자제

by his post-office address? Why, I've seen Kentuckians who hated whiskey, Virginians who weren't descended from Pocahontas, Indianians who hadn't written a novel, Mexicans who didn't wear velvet trousers with silver dollars sewed along the seams, funny Englishmen, **spendthrift** Yankees, cold-blooded Southerners, **narrow-minded** Westerners, and New Yorkers who were too busy to stop for an hour on the street to watch a one-armed grocer's clerk do up cranberries in paper bags. Let a man be a man and don't **handicap** him with the label of any section."

"Pardon me," I said, "but my curiosity was not altogether an **idle** one. I know the South, and when the band plays 'Dixie' I like to observe. I have formed the belief that the man who applauds that air with special violence and **ostensible sectional** loyalty is invariably a native of either Secaucus, N.J., or the district between Murray Hill Lyceum and the Harlem River, this city. I was about to put my opinion to the test by inquiring of this gentleman when you interrupted with your own—larger theory, I must confess."

And now the dark-haired young man spoke to me, and it became evident that his mind also moved along its own set of grooves.

"I should like to be a periwinkle," said he,

mighty [máiti] adv.
대단히, 몹시, 아주

genuine [ʤénjuin] adj.
진짜의, 진정한 거짓없는
decry [dikrái] v.
비난하다, 헐뜯다, 비방하다
patriotism [péitriətìzəm / pǽt-] n.
애국심
relic [rélik] n.
유적, 유물
warmly [wɔ́:rmli] adv.
흥분하여, 격하게

mysteriously, "on the top of a valley, and sing tooralloo-ralloo."

This was clearly too obscure, so I turned again to Coglan.

"I've been around the world twelve times," said he. "I know an Esquimau in Upernavik who sends to Cincinnati for his neckties, and I saw a goatherder in Uruguay who won a prize in a Battle Creek breakfast food puzzle competition. I pay rent on a room in Cairo, Egypt, and another in Yokohama all the year around. I've got slippers waiting for me in a tea-house in Shanghai, and I don't have to tell 'em how to cook my eggs in Rio de Janeiro or Seattle. It's a **mighty** little old world. What's the use of bragging about being from the North, or the South, or the old manor house in the dale, or Euclid avenue, Cleveland, or Pike's Peak, or Fairfax County, Va., or Hooligan's Flats or any place? It'll be a better world when we quit being fools about some mildewed town or ten acres of swampland just because we happened to be born there."

"You seem to be a **genuine** cosmopolite," I said admiringly. "But it also seems that you would **decry patriotism**."

"A **relic** of the stone age," declared Coglan, **warmly**. "We are all brothers—Chinamen, Englishmen, Zulus, Patagonians and the people

petty [péti] adj.
옹졸한, 속 좁은
wipe out:
없애다, 파괴하다

revert [rivə́ːrt] v.
되돌아가다, 다시 ~하기 시작하다

nary [nέəri] adj.
조금도 없는, 하나도 없는
terrestrial [təréstriəl] adj.
지구의, 지상의
globular [glábjələr / glɔ́b-] adj.
공 모양의, 세계적인
planetary [plǽnətèri / -təri] adj. 행성의, 지구의
hunk [hʌŋk] n.
두꺼운 조각, 큰 덩어리
abode [əbóud] n.
주거, 거처
drainage [dréinidʒ] n.
배수, 배수 체계
canal [kənǽl] n.
운하, 수로
not bat an eye(eyelid):
조금도 흔들리지 않다, 놀라거나 동요하지 않다
bandit [bǽndit] n.
산적, 강도

in the bend of the Kaw River. Some day all this **petty** pride in one's city or State or section or country will be **wiped out**, and we'll all be citizens of the world, as we ought to be."

"But while you are wandering in foreign lands," I persisted, "do not your thoughts **revert** to some spot—some dear and—"

"**Nary** a spot," interrupted E. R. Coglan, flippantly. "The **terrestrial, globular, planetary hunk** of matter, slightly flattened at the poles, and known as the Earth, is my **abode**. I've met a good many object-bound citizens of this country abroad. I've seen men from Chicago sit in a gondola in Venice on a moonlight night and brag about their **drainage canal**. I've seen a Southerner on being introduced to the King of England hand that monarch, **without batting his eyes**, the information that his grand-aunt on his mother's side was related by marriage to the Perkinses, of Charleston. I knew a New Yorker who was kidnapped for ransom by some Afghanistan **bandits**. His people sent over the money and he came back to Kabul with the agent. 'Afghanistan?' the natives said to him through an interpreter. 'Well, not so slow, do you think?' 'Oh, I don't know,' says he, and he begins to tell them about a cab driver at Sixth avenue and Broadway. Those ideas don't suit me. I'm not tied down to anything that isn't

8,000 miles in diameter. Just put me down as E. Rushmore Coglan, citizen of the terrestrial sphere."

My cosmopolite made a large **adieu** and left me, for he thought he saw some one through the chatter and smoke whom he knew. So I was left with the **would-be** periwinkle, who was reduced to Würzburger without further ability to voice his **aspirations** to perch, melodious, upon the summit of a valley.

I sat reflecting upon my evident cosmopolite and wondering how the poet had managed to miss him. He was my discovery and I believed in him. How was it? "The men that breed from them they traffic up and down, but cling to their cities' hem as a child to the mother's gown."

Not so E. Rushmore Coglan. With the whole world for his—

My meditations were interrupted by a tremendous noise and conflict in another part of the café. I saw above the heads of the seated patrons E. Rushmore Coglan and a stranger to me engaged in terrific battle. They fought between the tables like Titans, and glasses crashed, and men caught their hats up and were knocked down, and a brunette screamed, and a blonde began to sing "Teasing."

My cosmopolite was sustaining the pride and reputation of the Earth when the waiters

---

adieu [ədjúː] n.
작별, 고별, 하직
would-be [wúdbìː] adj.
~이 되려고 하는, ~할 작정인
aspiration [æ̀spəréiʃən] n.
강렬한 소망, 동경

combatant [kəmbǽtənt, kǽmbət-, kʌ́m-] n.
싸우는 사람, 전투원
flying wedge:
(선수나 경찰관들의) V자형 대형

on account of:
~ 때문에
bum [bʌm] adj.
싸구려의, 보잘것없는, 하찮은

stand [stænd] v.
참다, 견디다
knock [nɑk / nɔk] v.
험담하다, 흠잡다

closed in on both **combatants** with their famous **flying wedge** formation and bore them outside, still resisting.

I called McCarthy, one of the French *garçons*, and asked him the cause of the conflict.

"The man with the red tie" (that was my cosmopolite), said he, "got hot **on account of** things said about the **bum** sidewalks and water supply of the place he come from by the other guy."

"Why," said I, bewildered, "that man is a citizen of the world—a cosmopolite. He—"

"Originally from Mattawamkeag, Maine, he said," continued McCarthy, "and he wouldn't **stand** for no **knockin**' the place."

Witches' Loaves

Miss Martha Meacham kept the little bakery on the corner (the one where you go up three steps, and the bell tinkles when you open the door).

Miss Martha was forty, her bank-book showed a credit of two thousand dollars, and she possessed two false teeth and a sympathetic heart. Many people have married whose chances to do so were much inferior to Miss Martha's.

Two or three times a week a customer came in in whom she began to take an interest. He was a middle-aged man, wearing spectacles and a brown beard trimmed to a careful point.

He spoke English with a strong German

accent. His clothes were worn and darned in places, and wrinkled and baggy in others. But he looked neat, and had very good manners.

He always bought two loaves of **stale** bread. Fresh bread was five cents a loaf. Stale ones were two for five. Never did he call for anything but stale bread.

Once Miss Martha saw a red and brown stain on his fingers. She was sure then that he was an artist and very poor. No doubt he lived in a **garret**, where he painted pictures and ate stale bread and thought of the good things to eat in Miss Martha's bakery.

Often when Miss Martha sat down to her chops and light rolls and jam and tea she would sigh, and wish that the gentle-mannered artist might share her tasty meal instead of eating his dry crust in that draughty attic. Miss Martha's heart, as you have been told, was a sympathetic one.

In order to test her theory as to his occupation, she brought from her room one day a painting that she had bought at a sale, and set it against the shelves behind the bread counter.

It was a Venetian scene. A splendid marble **palazzio** (so it said on the picture) stood in the **foreground**—or rather forewater. For the rest there were gondolas (with the lady trailing her hand in the water), clouds, sky, and

chiaroscuro [kiɑ̀:rəskjú:rou] n.
명암의 배합

revel [rév-əl] v.
한껏 즐기다, 매우 기뻐하다

live on:
주로 무엇을 먹고 지내다

chiaro-oscuro in plenty. No artist could fail to notice it.

Two days afterward the customer came in. "Two loafs of stale bread, if you blease.

"You haf here a fine bicture, madame," he said while she was wrapping up the bread.

"Yes?" says Miss Martha, **revelling** in her own cunning. "I do so admire art and" (no, it would not do to say "artists" thus early) "and paintings," she substituted. "You think it is a good picture?"

"Der balace," said the customer, "is not in good drawing. Der bairspective of it is not true. Goot morning, madame."

He took his bread, bowed, and hurried out.

Yes, he must be an artist. Miss Martha took the picture back to her room.

How gentle and kindly his eyes shone behind his spectacles! What a broad brow he had! To be able to judge perspective at a glance—and to **live on** stale bread! But genius often has to struggle before it is recognized.

What a thing it would be for art and perspective if genius were backed by two thousand dollars in bank, a bakery, and a sympathetic heart to— But these were day-dreams, Miss Martha.

Often now when he came he would chat for a while across the showcase. He seemed to crave Miss Martha's cheerful words.

He kept on buying stale bread. Never a cake, never a pie, never one of her delicious Sally Lunns.

She thought he began to look thinner and discouraged. Her heart ached to add something good to eat to his **meagre** purchase, but her courage failed at the act. She did not dare **affront** him. She knew the pride of artists.

Miss Martha took to wearing her blue-dotted silk waist behind the counter. In the back room she cooked a mysterious compound of **quince** seeds and **borax**. Ever so many people use it for the complexion.

One day the customer came in as usual, laid his nickel on the showcase, and called for his stale loaves. While Miss Martha was reaching for them there was a great tooting and clanging, and a fire-engine came **lumbering** past.

The customer hurried to the door to look, as any one will. Suddenly inspired, Miss Martha seized the opportunity.

On the bottom shelf behind the counter was a pound of fresh butter that the dairyman had left ten minutes before. With a bread knife Miss Martha made a deep slash in each of the stale loaves, inserted a generous quantity of butter, and pressed the loaves tight again.

When the customer turned once more she

---

meager [míːgəːr] adj.
빈약한, 불충분한
affront [əfrʌ́nt] v.
모욕하다, 욕보이다

quince [kwins] n.
마르멜로, 마르멜로 열매
borax [bóurəks, bɔ́ː-] n.
붕사

lumber [lʌ́mbər] v.
무겁게 움직이다, 소란스럽게 움직이다

was tying the paper around them.

When he had gone, after an unusually pleasant little chat, Miss Martha smiled to herself, but not without a slight fluttering of the heart.

Had she been too bold? Would he take offense? But surely not. There was no language of **edibles**. Butter was no **emblem** of unmaidenly **forwardness**.

For a long time that day her mind dwelt on the subject. She imagined the scene when he should discover her little deception.

He would lay down his brushes and palette. There would stand his easel with the picture he was painting in which the perspective was beyond criticism.

He would prepare for his **luncheon** of dry bread and water. He would slice into a loaf—ah!

Miss Martha blushed. Would he think of the hand that placed it there as he ate? Would he—

The front door bell **jangled** viciously. Somebody was coming in, making a great deal of noise.

Miss Martha hurried to the front. Two men were there. One was a young man smoking a pipe—a man she had never seen before. The other was her artist.

His face was very red, his hat was on the

---

edible [édəbəl] n.
식품, 음식
emblem [émbləm] n.
상징, 표상
forwardness [fɔ́:rwə:rdnis] n.
주제넘음, 건방짐

luncheon [lʌ́ntʃən] n.
점심, 오찬

jangle [dʒǽŋgəl] v.
딸랑딸랑 울리다

back of his head, his hair was wildly rumpled. He clinched his two fists and shook them ferociously at Miss Martha. *At Miss Martha.*

"***Dummkopf!***" he shouted with extreme loudness; and then "*Tausendonfer!*" or something like it in German.

The young man tried to draw him away.

"I vill not go," he said angrily, "else I shall told her."

He made a bass drum of Miss Martha's counter.

"You haf shpoilt me," he cried, his blue eyes blazing behind his spectacles. "I vill tell you. You vas von *meddingsome old cat!*"

Miss Martha leaned weakly against the shelves and laid one hand on her blue-dotted silk waist. The young man took the other by the collar.

"Come on," he said, "you've said enough." He dragged the angry one out at the door to the sidewalk, and then came back.

"Guess you ought to be told, ma'am," he said, "what the row is about. That's Blumberger. He's an **architectural draftsman**. I work in the same office with him.

"He's been working hard for three months drawing a **plan** for a new city hall. It was a prize competition. He finished inking the lines yesterday. You know, a draftsman always makes

---

dummkopf:
(독일어) 바보, 어리석은 사람

architectural [à:rkətéktʃərəl] adj. 건축학의, 건축의
draftsman [dræftsmən, drá:fts-] n.
도안공, 제도가
plan [plæn] n.
도면, 설계도

crumb [krʌm] n. 작은 조각, 빵부스러기	his drawing in pencil first. When it's done he rubs out the pencil lines with handfuls of stale bread **crumbs**. That's better than India rubber.

"Blumberger's been buying the bread here. Well, to-day—well, you know, ma'am, that butter isn't—well, Blumberger's plan isn't good for anything now except to cut up into railroad sandwiches."

serge [sə:rdʒ] n. 서지; 옷감 등으로 쓰는 능직물	Miss Martha went into the back room. She took off the blue-dotted silk waist and put on the old brown **serge** she used to wear. Then she poured the quince seed and borax mixture out of the window into the ash can.

Hearts and Hands

influx [ínflʌks] n.
유입, 도래, 쇄도
coach [koutʃ] n.
객차
eastbound [i:stbaund] adj.
동쪽으로 가는
newcomer [njú:kʌmə:r] n.
새로 온 사람
countenance [káuntənəns] n.
얼굴 표정, 안색

At Denver there was an **influx** of passengers into the **coaches** on the **eastbound** B. & M. express. In one coach there sat a very pretty young woman dressed in elegant taste and surrounded by all the luxurious comforts of an experienced traveller. Among the **newcomers** were two young men, one of handsome presence with a bold, frank **countenance** and manner; the other a ruffled, glum-faced person, heavily built and roughly dressed. The two were handcuffed together.

As they passed down the aisle of the coach the only vacant seat offered was a reversed one facing the attractive young woman. Here the linked couple seated themselves. The young woman's glance fell upon them with a distant, swift **disinterest**; then with a lovely smile brightening her countenance and a tender pink tingeing her rounded cheeks, she held out a little gray-gloved hand. When she spoke her voice, full, sweet, and deliberate, proclaimed that its owner was accustomed to speak and be heard.

"Well, Mr. Easton, if you *will* make me speak first, I suppose I must. Don't you ever recognize old friends when you meet them in the West?"

The younger man roused himself sharply at the sound of her voice, seemed to struggle with a slight **embarrassment** which he **threw off** instantly, and then clasped her fingers with his left hand.

"It's Miss Fairchild," he said, with a smile. "I'll ask you to excuse the other hand; it's otherwise engaged just at present."

He slightly raised his right hand, bound at the wrist by the shining "bracelet" to the left one of his companion. The glad look in the girl's eyes slowly changed to a bewildered horror. The glow faded from her cheeks. Her lips parted in a vague, relaxing distress. Easton, with a little laugh, as if amused, was about to speak again when the other **forestalled** him. The glum-faced man had been watching the

veiled [veild] adj.
베일에 싸인, 숨겨진, 드러나지 않은
marshal [mά:rʃ-əl] n.
연방 보안관, 연방 집행관
pen [pen] n.
교도소

crowd [kraud] n.
그룹, 동료, 패거리

dashing [dǽʃiŋ] adj.
용감한, 기운찬, 멋있는, 화려한

girl's countenance with **veiled** glances from his keen, shrewd eyes.

"You'll excuse me for speaking, miss, but, I see you're acquainted with the **marshal** here. If you'll ask him to speak a word for me when we get to the **pen** he'll do it, and it'll make things easier for me there. He's taking me to Leavenworth prison. It's seven years for counterfeiting."

"Oh!" said the girl, with a deep breath and returning color. "So that is what you are doing out here? A marshal!"

"My dear Miss Fairchild," said Easton, calmly, "I had to do something. Money has a way of taking wings unto itself, and you know it takes money to keep step with our **crowd** in Washington. I saw this opening in the West, and—well, a marshalship isn't quite as high a position as that of ambassador, but—"

"The ambassador," said the girl, warmly, "doesn't call any more. He needn't ever have done so. You ought to know that. And so now you are one of these **dashing** Western heroes, and you ride and shoot and go into all kinds of dangers. That's different from the Washington life. You have been missed from the old crowd."

The girl's eyes, fascinated, went back, widening a little, to rest upon the glittering handcuffs.

"Don't you worry about them, miss," said the

other man. "All marshals handcuff themselves to their prisoners to keep them from getting away. Mr. Easton knows his business."

"Will we see you again soon in Washington?" asked the girl.

"Not soon, I think," said Easton. "My butterfly days are over, I fear."

"I love the West," said the girl **irrelevantly**. Her eyes were shining softly. She looked away out the car window. She began to speak truly and simply without the **gloss** of style and manner: "Mamma and I spent the summer in Denver. She went home a week ago because father was slightly ill. I could live and be happy in the West. I think the air here agrees with me. Money isn't everything. But people always misunderstand things and remain stupid—"

"Say, Mr. Marshal," **growled** the glum-faced man. "This isn't quite fair. I'm needing a drink, and haven't had a smoke all day. Haven't you talked long enough? Take me in the **smoker** now, won't you? I'm half dead for a pipe."

The bound travellers rose to their feet, Easton with the same slow smile on his face.

"I can't deny a **petition** for tobacco," he said, lightly. "It's the one friend of the unfortunate. Good-bye, Miss Fairchild. Duty calls, you know." He held out his hand for a farewell.

"It's too bad you are not going East," she said,

reclothe [ri:klóuð] v.
다시 입다

chap [tʃæp] n.
사내, 친구

catch on:
이해하다, 알아차리다

"... Say—did you ever know an officer to handcuff a prisoner to his *right* hand?"

reclothing herself with manner and style. "But you must go on to Leavenworth, I suppose?"

"Yes," said Easton, "I must go on to Leavenworth."

The two men sidled down the aisle into the smoker.

The two passengers in a seat near by had heard most of the conversation. Said one of them: "That marshal's a good sort of **chap**. Some of these Western fellows are all right."

"Pretty young to hold an office like that, isn't he?" asked the other.

"Young!" exclaimed the first speaker, "why—Oh! didn't you **catch on**? Say—did you ever know an officer to handcuff a prisoner to his *right* hand?"

Mammon and the Archer

proprietor [prəpráiətər] n.
소유자, 경영자
aristocratic [ərìstəkrǽtik, æ̀rəs-] adj.
귀족의, 귀족적인
contumelious [kɑ̀ntjumíːljəs / kɔ̀n-] adj.
오만 불손한, 무례한

stuck-up [stʌ́kʌ́p] adj.
거만한, 건방진
statuette [stæ̀tʃuét] n.
작은 조상(彫像)

Old Anthony Rockwall, retired manufacturer and **proprietor** of Rockwall's Eureka Soap, looked out the library window of his Fifth Avenue mansion and grinned. His neighbour to the right—the **aristocratic** clubman, G. Van Schuylight Suffolk-Jones—came out to his waiting motor-car, wrinkling a **contumelious** nostril, as usual, at the Italian renaissance sculpture of the soap palace's front elevation.

"**Stuck-up** old **statuette** of nothing doing!" commented the ex-Soap King. "The Eden Musee'll get that old frozen Nesselrode yet if he don't watch out. I'll have this house painted red, white, and blue next summer and see if that'll make his Dutch nose turn up any higher."

And then Anthony Rockwall, who never cared for bells, went to the door of his library and shouted "Mike!" in the same voice that had once chipped off pieces of the **welkin** on the Kansas **prairies**.

"Tell my son," said Anthony to the answering **menial**, "to come in here before he leaves the house."

When young Rockwall entered the library the old man laid aside his newspaper, looked at him with a kindly grimness on his big, smooth, ruddy countenance, **rumpled** his mop of white hair with one hand and rattled the keys in his pocket with the other.

"Richard," said Anthony Rockwall, "what do you pay for the soap that you use?"

Richard, only six months home from college, was startled a little. He had not yet **taken the measure** of this **sire** of his, who was as full of unexpectednesses as a girl at her first party.

"Six dollars a dozen, I think, dad."

"And your clothes?"

"I suppose about sixty dollars, as a rule."

"You're a gentleman," said Anthony, decidedly. "I've heard of these **young bloods** spending $24 a dozen for soap, and going over the hundred mark for clothes. You've got as much money to waste as any of 'em, and yet you stick to what's **decent** and **moderate**. Now I use the old Eureka—not only for sentiment, but it's the purest soap made. Whenever you pay more than 10 cents a cake for soap you buy bad perfumes and labels. But 50 cents is doing very well for a young man in your generation, position and condition. As I said, you're a gentleman. They say it takes three generations to make one. They're off. Money'll do it as **slick** as soap grease. It's made you one. By hokey! It's almost made one of me. I'm nearly as impolite and disagreeable and ill-mannered as these two old **Knickerbocker gents** on each side of me that can't sleep of nights because I bought in between 'em."

"There are some things that money can't accomplish," remarked young Rockwall, rather gloomily.

"Now, don't say that," said old Anthony, shocked. "I bet my money on money every time. I've been through the encyclopaedia down to Y looking for something you can't buy with it; and I expect to have to take up the appendix next week. I'm for money against the field. Tell me something money won't buy."

"For one thing," answered Richard, **rankling** a little, "it won't buy one into the **exclusive** circles of society."

"Oho! won't it?" thundered the champion of **the root of evil**. "You tell me where your exclusive circles would be if the first Astor hadn't had the money to pay for his **steerage passage** over?"

Richard sighed.

"And that's what I was coming to," said the old man, less **boisterously**. "That's why I asked you to come in. There's something going wrong with you, boy. I've been noticing it for two weeks. **Out with it**. I guess I could lay my hands on eleven millions within twenty-four hours, besides the real estate. If it's your liver, there's the *Rambler* down in the bay, coaled, and ready to steam down to the Bahamas in two days."

"Not a bad guess, dad; you haven't missed it far."

"Ah," said Anthony, keenly; "what's her name?"

Richard began to walk up and down the library floor. There was enough comradeship and sympathy in this crude old father of his to draw his confidence.

"Why don't you ask her?" demanded old Anthony. "She'll jump at you. You've got the money and the looks, and you're a decent boy. Your hands are clean. You've got no Eureka soap on 'em. You've been to college, but she'll overlook that."

"I haven't had a chance," said Richard.

"Make one," said Anthony. "Take her for a walk in the park, or a straw ride, or walk home with her from church. Chance! **Pshaw**!"

"You don't know the social mill, dad. She's part of the stream that turns it. Every hour and minute of her time is arranged for days in advance. I must have that girl, dad, or this town is a blackjack swamp forevermore. And I can't write it—I can't do that."

"Tut!" said the old man. "Do you mean to tell me that with all the money I've got you can't get an hour or two of a girl's time for yourself?"

"I've **put** it **off** too late. She's going to sail for Europe at noon day after to-morrow for a two years' stay. I'm to see her alone to-morrow evening for a few minutes. She's at Larchmont now at her aunt's. I can't go there. But I'm allowed to meet her with a cab at the Grand Central Station to-morrow evening at the 8.30 train. We drive down Broadway to Wallack's at a gallop, where her mother and a box party will be waiting for us in the lobby. Do you think she would listen to a declaration from me during that six or eight minutes under those circumstances? No. And what chance would

tangle [tǽŋg-əl] n.
얽힘, 혼란
unravel [ʌnrǽvəl] v.
풀다, 해결하다

punk [pʌŋk] n.
(막대기 모양의) 불쏘시개
joss [dʒɑs, dʒɔːs / dʒɔs] n.
(중국인이 섬기는) 우상, 신상
mazuma [məzúːmə] n.
(미국속어) 금전, 돈
from time to time:
때때로, 가끔
eternity [itə́ːrnəti] n.
영원, 무궁, 불멸

woe [wou] n.
비애, 비통, 고뇌

knock [nɑk / nɔk] v.
험담하다, 흠잡다

I have in the theatre or afterward? None. No, dad, this is one **tangle** that your money can't **unravel**. We can't buy one minute of time with cash; if we could, rich people would live longer. There's no hope of getting a talk with Miss Lantry before she sails."

"All right, Richard, my boy," said old Anthony, cheerfully. "You may run along down to your club now. I'm glad it ain't your liver. But don't forget to burn a few **punk** sticks in the **joss** house to the great god **Mazuma from time to time**. You say money won't buy time? Well, of course, you can't order **eternity** wrapped up and delivered at your residence for a price, but I've seen Father Time get pretty bad stone bruises on his heels when he walked through the gold diggings."

That night came Aunt Ellen, gentle, sentimental, wrinkled, sighing, oppressed by wealth, in to Brother Anthony at his evening paper, and began discourse on the subject of lovers' **woes**.

"He told me all about it," said brother Anthony, yawning. "I told him my bank account was at his service. And then he began to **knock** money. Said money couldn't help. Said the rules of society couldn't be bucked for a yard by a team of ten-millionaires."

"Oh, Anthony," sighed Aunt Ellen, "I wish

all-powerful [ɔ́:lpáuərfəl] adj.
전능한, 만능의

quaint [kweint] adj.
예스러운, 고아한

you would not think so much of money. Wealth is nothing where a true affection is concerned. Love is **all-powerful**. If he only had spoken earlier! She could not have refused our Richard. But now I fear it is too late. He will have no opportunity to address her. All your gold cannot bring happiness to your son."

At eight o'clock the next evening Aunt Ellen took a **quaint** old gold ring from a moth-eaten case and gave it to Richard.

"Wear it to-night, nephew," she begged. "Your mother gave it to me. Good luck in love she said it brought. She asked me to give it to you when you had found the one you loved."

Young Rockwall took the ring reverently and tried it on his smallest finger. It slipped as far as the second joint and stopped. He took it off and stuffed it into his vest pocket, after the manner of man. And then he 'phoned for his cab.

At the station he captured Miss Lantry out of the gadding mob at eight thirty-two.

"We mustn't keep mamma and the others waiting," said she.

"To Wallack's Theatre as fast as you can drive!" said Richard loyally.

They whirled up Forty-second to Broadway, and then down the white-starred lane that leads from the soft meadows of sunset to the rocky hills of morning.

At Thirty-fourth Street young Richard quickly thrust up the trap and ordered the cabman to stop.

"I've dropped a ring," he apologised, as he climbed out. "It was my mother's, and I'd hate to lose it. I won't detain you a minute—I saw where it fell."

In less than a minute he was back in the cab with the ring.

But within that minute a **crosstown** car had stopped directly in front of the cab. The cabman tried to pass to the left, but a heavy express wagon cut him off. He tried the right, and had to back away from a furniture van that had no business to be there. He tried to back out, but dropped his reins and swore dutifully. He was **blockaded** in a tangled **mess** of vehicles and horses.

One of those street blockades had occurred that sometimes tie up commerce and movement quite suddenly in the big city.

"Why don't you drive on?" said Miss Lantry, impatiently. "We'll be late."

Richard stood up in the cab and looked around. He saw a congested flood of wagons, trucks, cabs, vans and street cars filling the vast space where Broadway, Sixth Avenue and Thirty-fourth street cross one another as a

---

crosstown [krɔːstaun/ krɔstaun] adj.
도시를 가로지르는
blockade [blɑkéid / blɔk-] v.
봉쇄하다, 가로막다
mess [mes] n.
엉망인 상태, 혼란

imprecation [imprikeiʃən] n. (사람 등에게 재앙이 내리라고) 빌기, 저주하기
clamor [klǽmər] n. 함성, 와글거림

jumble [dʒʌ́mbl] n. 혼잡, 뒤범벅

piratical [paiərǽtikəl] adj. 해적의

twenty-six inch maiden fills her twenty-two inch girdle. And still from all the cross streets they were hurrying and rattling toward the converging point at full speed, and hurling themselves into the struggling mass, locking wheels and adding their drivers' **imprecations** to the **clamour**. The entire traffic of Manhattan seemed to have jammed itself around them. The oldest New Yorker among the thousands of spectators that lined the sidewalks had not witnessed a street blockade of the proportions of this one.

"I'm very sorry," said Richard, as he resumed his seat, "but it looks as if we are stuck. They won't get this **jumble** loosened up in an hour. It was my fault. If I hadn't dropped the ring we—"

"Let me see the ring," said Miss Lantry. "Now that it can't be helped, I don't care. I think theatres are stupid, anyway."

At 11 o'clock that night somebody tapped lightly on Anthony Rockwall's door.

"Come in," shouted Anthony, who was in a red dressing-gown, reading a book of **piratical** adventures.

Somebody was Aunt Ellen, looking like a grey-haired angel that had been left on earth by mistake.

"They're engaged, Anthony," she said, softly.

"She has promised to marry our Richard. On their way to the theatre there was a street blockade, and it was two hours before their cab could get out of it.

"And oh, brother Anthony, don't ever boast of the power of money again. A little **emblem** of true love—a little ring that symbolised **unending** and **unmercenary** affection—was the cause of our Richard finding his happiness. He dropped it in the street, and got out to recover it. And before they could continue the blockade occurred. He spoke to his love and won her there while the cab was hemmed in. Money is **dross** compared with true love, Anthony."

"All right," said old Anthony. "I'm glad the boy has got what he wanted. I told him I wouldn't spare any expense in the matter if—"

"But, brother Anthony, what good could your money have done?"

"Sister," said Anthony Rockwall. "I've got my pirate in a devil of a **scrape**. His ship has just been **scuttled**, and he's too good a judge of the value of money to let drown. I wish you would let me go on with this chapter."

The story should end here. I wish it would as heartily as you who read it wish it did. But we must go to the bottom of the well for truth.

The next day a person with red hands and a blue polka-dot necktie, who called himself

Kelly, called at Anthony Rockwall's house, and was at once received in the library.

"Well," said Anthony, reaching for his chequebook, "it was a good bilin' of soap. Let's see—you had $5,000 in cash."

"I paid out $300 more of my own," said Kelly. "I had to go a little above the estimate. I got the express wagons and cabs mostly for $5; but the trucks and two-horse teams mostly raised me to $10. The motormen wanted $10, and some of the loaded teams $20. The cops struck me hardest—$50 I paid two, and the rest $20 and $25. But didn't it work beautiful, Mr. Rockwall? I'm glad William A. Brady wasn't onto that little outdoor vehicle mob scene. I wouldn't want William to break his heart with jealousy. And never a **rehearsal**, either! The boys was **on time** to the fraction of a second. It was two hours before a snake could get below Greeley's statue."

"Thirteen hundred—there you are, Kelly," said Anthony, tearing off a check. "Your thousand, and the $300 you were out. You don't **despise** money, do you, Kelly?"

"Me?" said Kelly. "I can **lick** the man that invented poverty."

Anthony called Kelly when he was at the door.

"You didn't notice," said he, "anywhere in

tie-up [táiʌp] n.
정체, 막힘

pinch [pintʃ] v.
체포하다

the **tie-up**, a kind of a fat boy without any clothes on shooting arrows around with a bow, did you?"

"Why, no," said Kelly, mystified. "I didn't. If he was like you say, maybe the cops **pinched** him before I got there."

"I thought the little rascal wouldn't be on hand," chuckled Anthony. "Good-by, Kelly."